DATE DUE

P9-BJT-910

Guide to Tourist Railroads and Railroad Museums

COMPILED BY GEORGE H. DRURY

Editor: Bob Hayden
Editorial Secretary: Monica Borowicki
Art Director: Lawrence Luser

Researcher and Copy Editor: Marcia Stern
Research Assistant: Carmen Persson
Art and Layout: Philip Kirchmeier

On the cover: Norfolk & Western No. 1218, a class A 2-6-6-4, leads the *Independence Limited* across the Bluestone River at Cooper, West Virginia, on June 10, 1988. Photo by Robert W. Lyndall, StackTalk Graphic Image, P. O. Box 670243, Windy Hill Station, Marietta, GA 30067-0005.

KALMBACH BOOKS

INTRODUCTION

Tourist railroads and railroad museums don't have a long history — most are creations of the past three decades. Until about 1950 you didn't need tourist railroads: If you wanted to ride a train, you went down to the station; if you wanted to see old locomotives and passenger cars, you just looked around. There was plenty to see, thanks to the Depression, when the railroads couldn't afford new rolling stock, and World War Two, when the railroads needed every car and locomotive they could find.

Then diesels replaced steam locomotives. Passenger trains were discontinued. Lines were abandoned. As it became more and more difficult to see or ride trains, more and more people said, "They were interesting" and "They were fun to ride."

And that, quite simply, is what railroad museums and tourist railroads are about. They preserve some of the most fascinating machinery mankind has ever devised, and they re-create an enjoyable aspect of the past — and if fascination and enjoyment aren't enough, no other industry is so intimately tied to the history and development of North America.

What is a tourist railroad?

A tourist railroad is one whose passengers have as their main reason for riding the train the enjoyment of the ride itself rather than the serious business of getting somewhere. Amtrak's chief business is moving people, and for the purposes of this book it's not a tourist railroad, despite the increasing number of riders who choose the train because it is more enjoyable than flying or driving.

Metro-North Commuter Railroad has leaflets advertising package tours to points along its lines, and its line along the east bank of the Hudson River is one of the most scenic in North America — but Metro-North's primary mission is to take people to and from work in New York City.

The distinction between a freight railroad and a tourist railroad is often a matter of the day of the week. Many freight-hauling short lines run excursion trains on the weekends. Some mainline railroads run excursion trains, usually in conjunction with a museum or club that provides passenger cars.

Steam rides again

Today, steam locomotives are as fascinating as ever. When diesels replaced steam locomotives in the 1950s, many railroads offered steam locomotives to cities and towns for display in parks. Three and four decades later those stuffed-and-mounted locomotives are being restored to operation. The process begins with moving a chunk of rusting machinery that has sat outdoors in one place for a long time and may weigh upwards of 150 tons!

Next, every piece of the locomotive has to be made able to slide or turn or hold water or withstand air or steam pressure. Many parts have to be produced from scratch; the companies that built the locomotives and furnished spare parts are long gone. There is probably not a steam locomotive on display in North America that hasn't been evaluated for the possibility of operation. It is an amazing testimony to the people who do the work that so many steamers have been restored to working condition.

Metro-North Commuter Railroad's route includes vistas that make it look, at times, like a tourist railroad. Perhaps it depends on the state of mind of the rider.

Recently factories in China shipped *new* steam locomotives to three U. S. tourist railroads: the Boone & Scenic Valley Railroad, Boone, Iowa; the Knox, Kane & Kinzua Railroad, Marienville, Pennsylvania; and the Valley Railroad, Essex, Connecticut.

Mainline steam excursions

The principal operator of mainline steam excursion trains in North America is the Norfolk Southern Corporation, which has continued the program begun by the Southern Railway in 1966. NS plans to operate more than two dozen trips throughout its system between March and November 1990, using Norfolk & Western 1218, a 2-6-6-4 (pictured on the cover), and 611, a streamlined 4-8-4. NS's trips are sponsored by various museums, railroad clubs, and chapters of the National Railway Historical Society. Tickets for the excursions must be purchased from those organizations, not from the railroad. For a copy of Norfolk Southern's steam excursion schedule, which lists the sponsors, send a stamped, self-addressed envelope to:

Carl S. Jensen, Manager — Steam Operations
Norfolk Southern Corporation
8 North Jefferson Street
Roanoke, VA 24042-0002

Several other railroads operate steam-powered excursion trains from time to time. For news of such trips, watch the "Running Extra" column of TRAINS Magazine, published monthly by Kalmbach Publishing Co., P. O. Box 1612, Waukesha, WI 53187.

Dinner trains

The fastest-growing facet of the tourist-railroad industry in the past couple of years has been dinner trains — trains that are rolling restaurants. They generally offer elegant dining, rather than hamburgers and hot dogs, and more luxurious decor and ambience than has been seen on U. S. railroads since World War Two. The attraction seems to be the experience of eating on a train rather than the view out the windows — the dinner trips usually start about sundown, though several dinner trains now carry floodlights to illuminate the scenery. The trips take 3 to 4 hours, but they don't cover much mileage (net mileage is zero) because speeds are kept low so the soup won't splash.

For years railfans took advantage of nearby trains at mealtime: "Let's ride the *Abraham Lincoln* down to Bloomington for dinner, then come back to Chicago on the *Prairie State*," or "Want to ride the *California Zephyr* up to Sacramento for breakfast? They serve a breakfast steak which is really their standard dinner sirloin." The first dinner train to operate on a regular schedule was the *Star Clipper Dinner Train*, which runs on the Cedar Valley Railroad out of Waterloo, Iowa. Then the breed proliferated. Some didn't last long — such an operation needs to draw on a major metropolitan area, since the prices usually make riding a dinner train a special event rather than a weekly affair. For a fuller documentation of the dinner train phenomenon, see the article by Steven Glischinski in the June 1990 issue of TRAINS Magazine.

The story is typical: Pennsylvania Railroad K4 No. 1361 was placed on display at Horseshoe Curve near Altoona, Pennsylvania, in 1957. In September 1985 it was moved to Conrail's shops at Altoona for restoration, and on April 11, 1987, moved under its own power again.

Visiting a tourist railroad or museum

Visiting a railroad museum or a tourist line is an enjoyable way to spend an afternoon. You'll have a better time if you are prepared for the conditions you'll encounter. Most museums are out in the open. Visitors (and the exhibits) have little protection from the weather. Further, summer is the prime season for most railroad museums. It will be hot and sunny. When riding a train in the mountains, though, you'll want to be ready for cool weather and maybe rain.

Walking surfaces at the museums are more often dirt roads and paths and gravel track areas than they are pavement. Choose your footwear with that in mind. Conditions are usually less than ideal for wheelchairs and strollers and for those who have difficulty walking. Safety rule: Always step over the rails, not on them.

A visit to a railroad museum is an excellent family activity. Remember that operating museums are working railroads, which means "Any time is train time." Keep an eye on your children, and consider the attention spans of your children and of adults who may not share your depth of enthusiasm. Rather than start by riding the train or streetcar and then browse through the exhibits until everyone is tired, plan to look at some exhibits, take the ride (you'll welcome the chance to sit down, particularly if you've had to carry or lift small children), then look at more exhibits.

A break for refreshments is another good way to perk up sagging youngsters and ward off your own "museum feet." Many museums offer refreshment facilities, which can range from a soft-drink machine to a small restaurant. Some have picnic areas, too. If you plan a cookout, ask in advance. Since much historic railroad rolling stock is wood, museums may be reluctant to allow fires nearby.

Riding a train is another good family experience, and another place to make sure children aren't hanging out the windows or jumping from car to car (the same goes for adults). Children who have known only the automobile may be amazed that something the size of a train can move and that there can be room on board to walk around, get a drink of water, or even go to the bathroom. (It's

A picnic can be a welcome break in a visit to a railroad museum. Many museums provide picnic tables; this scene at the Western Railway Museum in California is typical.

at the end of the car, and it's a good idea to ask if it's usable — some tourist railroads consider toilet facilities unnecessary for a 30-minute ride.)

Ironically most railroad museums are accessible only by car. Few railroad museums and tourist railroads are fortunate enough to have Amtrak or even a city bus stop at their door. The California State Railroad Museum at Sacramento and the Baltimore Streetcar Museum, which are within easy walking distance of Amtrak stations, are exceptions to the rule. Most museums and tourist railroads offer free parking.

Most museums welcome groups and offer guided tours. Some can even accommodate midweek visits by groups of students or retired persons. Advance notice is necessary for groups.

If you are planning a long trip to visit a museum or see and ride specific equipment, call or write to confirm the schedules. In the latter case as a courtesy enclose a stamped, self-addressed envelope (an international reply coupon if your letter is crossing a border).

Cass Scenic Railroad 7 and 5 illustrate the workings of the Shay locomotive. Three vertically mounted cylinders drive a lengthwise drive shaft, which in turn drives the axles through bevel gears.

Most of the railroad museums in this book are nonprofit organizations staffed by volunteers who give time to the museum, and they are financed through admission charges, fares, profits from refreshment and souvenir sales, and donations from visitors and from those same volunteers who keep the museum running.

Drive it yourself

What's the ultimate railfan fantasy occupation? Engineer, of course. For several years it has been possible to hire a locomotive and run it yourself on several European railways. The first American museum to advertise that offering is the Portola Railroad Museum in Portola, California, which will put you in the engineer's seat with an instructor at your side for $60 an hour — not a bad price for something you've wanted to do since you were five years old!

Glossary

Railroading has a jargon of its own. Defined below are a few of the terms used frequently in this book.

Track gauge: the distance between the rails. In North America the usual or standard gauge is 4'8½". Anything less is called "narrow gauge." The most common narrow gauge is 3'.

Shay: An ordinary steam locomotive has rods connecting the steam pistons directly to the wheels; it's called a "rod locomotive." Logging railroads needed locomotives that could handle steep grades and roughly built track. In the late 1870s and 1880s Ephraim Shay developed a locomotive with vertical cylinders turning a lengthwise drive shaft geared to the wheels. Shays look (and are) lopsided, carrying their cylinders along the right side of the boiler, which is off-center to compensate for the weight of the cylinders and the drive shaft, and they sound like they are going faster than they are because they're geared down, like your car when it's in first gear.

Climax: a geared locomotive like the Shay, with cylinders arranged more or less conventionally (though inclined) turning a crosswise crankshaft under the middle of the locomotive. Two sets of bevel gears transmit power through a lengthwise drive shaft to the axles.

Heisler: a geared locomotive like the Shay, with two cylinders arranged in a V driving a lengthwise drive shaft along the center line of the locomotive.

Streetcar: an electrically powered railcar of lighter construction and smaller dimensions than traditional "steam railroad" equipment, drawing power from a wire suspended over the tracks. It is intended for urban transportation rather than intercity service, and the tracks are usually laid along streets rather than on a private right of way.

Interurban: an electrically powered railcar, like a streetcar but intended for service between cities and towns with more comfortable accommodations and running on a private right of way between towns. Interurbans often shared tracks with streetcars within cities and towns. Interurban railways flourished in the U. S. and Canada between 1900 and 1930; most were abandoned by 1950.

Trolley: The word "trolley" used to mean a streetcar. Nowadays

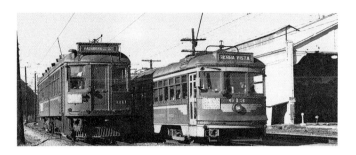

The difference between a streetcar and an interurban car is illustrated by Pacific Electric cars 1111 and 613 passing the Macy Street carbarn in February 1950.

streetcars have become Light Rail Vehicles and "trolley" often means a bus or truck with a body that is supposed to look like an old streetcar — it's not always electric and it may not run on rails.

Holidays

Most museums make a point of being open on holidays; for others it's just the opposite. Here are the 1990 and 1991 dates of the holidays mentioned in the schedules throughout the book.

	1990	1991
New Year's Day	January 1	January 1
Easter	April 15	March 31
Memorial Day	May 28	May 27
Independence Day	July 4	July 4
Labor Day	September 3	September 2
Columbus Day	October 8	October 14
Thanksgiving (Canada)	October 8	October 14
Thanksgiving (U. S.)	November 22	November 28
Christmas Eve	December 24	December 24
Christmas	December 25	December 25

Tourist railroads and railroad museums abroad

In Europe you can find major railroad museums in York, England; Belfast, Northern Ireland; Utrecht, Netherlands; Mulhouse France (a few minutes from Basel, Switzerland); Lucerne, Switzerland; Nuremberg, West Germany; Odense, Denmark; Gävle, Sweden; Hyvinkää, Finland; and Hamar, Norway.

The *Thomas Cook European Timetable* carries references to many tourist railroads (plus schedules of all the through-train service in Europe). You can buy a copy from Forsyth Travel Library, P. O. Box 2975, Shawnee Mission, KS 66201. Other useful books are:

Railways Restored, the Yearbook of the Association of Railway Preservation Societies, published by Ian Allan Ltd., Coombelands House, Addlestone, Weybridge, Surrey KR15 1HY, England

Railways For Pleasure, by Kenneth Westcott Jones, a guide to the steam and scenic lines in Britain and Ireland, available from Merrimack Book Service, 99 Main Street, Salem, NH 03079

Nostalgie auf Schienen: Europa-Kursbuch für Eisenbahnfreunde [Nostalgia on Rails: European Timetable for Railfans], available from Verlag Schweers & Wall, Postfach 1586, D-5100 Aachen, West Germany

Guide des Petits Trains Touristiques en France, Belgique, Luxembourg, Pays-Bas, et Suisse [Guide to Little Tourist Trains in France, Belgium, Luxembourg, Netherlands, and Switzerland], by Victor R Belot, available from La Vie du Rail, 11 rue de Milan, 75440 Paris Cedex 09, France

The tourist railroads and railroad museums of Australia are documented in the *Directory of Australian Tourist Railways and Museums*, published by the Light Railway Research Society of Australia, P. O. Box 21, Surrey Hills, Victoria 3127, Australia.

About this book

This book is considerably larger than its first two editions Tourist railroads and railroad museums are flourishing, and new ones are being established almost daily. See the last few pages of the book for those that came into being while the book was being prepared.

This guide was compiled in early 1990 with the best information available. Schedules and equipment are subject to change, and before you make a long drive specifically to visit a museum or ride a train, consider a letter or phone call to verify that the gate will be open or the train will be running. While most of these museums and railroads welcome groups, advance arrangements are mandatory for groups.

Schedules and prices usually remain much the same from one year to the next. Dates for 1990 will serves as guidelines for 1991 and 1992; telephone or write the museum or railroad for confirmation if the date is near the beginning or the end of the season. In a few cases where we could not obtain updated information by press time we have published information from the previous edition and noted it as such.

The entries in this book are arranged alphabetically by state, with Canada's provinces following the U. S., then Mexico. Within states and provinces the attractions are listed alphabetically by town and city. The index at the back of the book lists the museums and railroads alphabetically by name and type.

The entry for each railroad and museum includes a brief description and a row of symbols indicates whether it offers:

℗ Parking (usually free of charge)

♿ Facilities accessible to the handicapped

🎪 Picnic area

🎁 Gift, souvenir, or book shop

🍴 Soda or snacks available at the museum or on the train

🍽 Restaurant, cafeteria, or dining car serving full meals

$ Discount coupon at the back of this book

Each entry also includes a quick-look table showing:

Locomotives	Quantity and types of locomotives operating on the railroad. "Steam outline" means it looks like a steam locomotive but is powered by a diesel or gasoline engine.
Cars	Types of cars that carry passengers
Displays	Non-operating equipment on display
Dates open	Seasons, days, and times the museum is open to visitors
Schedule	Seasons, days, and times the trains operate
Admission	Price to enter the museum
Fares	Price to ride the train
Memberships	Price to become a member of the sponsoring organization
Radio frequency	Radio frequency used by the railroad in its operation
Special events	Annual events at the museum or on the railroad
Nearby attractions	Other attractions nearby you and your family might enjoy

Special thanks go to Marcia Stern, Carmen Persson, and Monica Borowicki for gathering the information for this book. Without their efforts this guide could not have been compiled.

GEORGE H. DRURY

Waukesha, Wisconsin
March 1990

Dates open	Summer, Tuesday-Sunday, 11 a.m.-5 p.m.; winter, Wednesday-Sunday, 11-4. Closed during January.
Admission	Adults $2.50, children 4-12 $1.50, age 65 and over $1.50. Checks accepted. Group discounts available.
Special events	Spring Fest (third weekend in April), Harvest Festival (third weekend in October)
Nearby attractions	Alabama Space and Rocket Center, Constitution Hall Village
Mailing address	320 Church Street, Huntsville, AL 35801
Phone	(205) 539-1860

HUNTSVILLE DEPOT

The station built at Huntsville, Alabama, in 1860 by the Memphis & Charleston Railroad is now a museum, with emphasis on the relationship of the railroad to the commerce, industry, and development of the surrounding area. The museum exhibits include a 20-minute multimedia presentation and a ticket office brought to life through robotics. Huntsville is in the northern part of the state, only a few miles south of the Tennessee border, on U. S. Routes 72, 231, and 431. Food and lodging can be found within a mile of the museum.

Locomotives	Diesel, usually GP40-2s and GP38s
Cars	Anchorage-Fairbanks: reclining-seat coaches, dome coaches, diners, snack bar/lounge cars; Anchorage-Seward: RDCs (Rail Diesel Cars)
Displays	On display in parking lot at Anchorage depot is the 1915 steam locomotive used to construct the railroad.
Schedule	May 19-September 20, 1990: Anchorage-Denali Park-Fairbanks, daily: leave Anchorage and Fairbanks 8:30 a.m., arrive Fairbanks and Anchorage 8 p.m. Anchorage-Seward, leave Anchorage 7 a.m. daily, arrive Seward 11 a.m.; leave Seward 6 p.m., arrive Anchorage at 10 p.m. Additional local services are offered. September-May, Anchorage-Fairbanks only on weekends.
Fares	Vary with trip. Anchorage-Fairbanks, $98 one way. Anchorage-Seward, $60 round trip. Children 2-11 half fare; under 2 free. Age 65 and up 50 percent discount mid-September through mid-May. Credit cards and checks accepted. Group discounts and charters available. Tickets and reservations are available

through travel agents. In addition, several tour operators offer deluxe service.

Mailing address	Passenger Services Department, P. O. Box 107500, Anchorage, AK 99510
Phone	(800) 554-0552, (907) 265-2494

ALASKA RAILROAD CORPORATION

The Alaska Railroad, owned by the state of Alaska, was completed in 1923. It is a full-size, common-carrier railroad offering freight and passenger service. It is included in this book because most of its passenger service is aimed at the tourist. The line stretches 470 miles from Seward through Anchorage and past Mount McKinley to Fairbanks, and there is a 12-mile branch from Portage to Whittier. It is a mountainous line, traveling through some of the most rugged and remote scenery in North America, including Mount McKinley.

The Seward line passes glaciers, hangs at one point on top of a canyon wall, and uses four tunnels within one mile to get up the mountain.

Reservations are mandatory for the Anchorage-Fairbanks trains and Anchorage-Seward excursions. The Anchorage and Fairbanks offices have staff on hand year-round. The Anchorage-Fairbanks train carries a dining car; the Anchorage-Seward train offers sandwich service.

Displays	Alaska Railroad RS-1 and F7 diesels, more than 30 pieces of rolling stock
Dates open	Tuesday-Saturday 8 a.m.-4 p.m.
Admission	Adults $3, children 6-12 $1.50, family $7. Checks accepted. Group discount available.
Memberships	Write for information.
Special events	Alaska State Fair (end of August to beginning of September) — free admission to museum with fair admission
Nearby attractions	Musk-ox farm, reindeer farm, abandoned gold mine, salmon stream, hiking trails
Mailing address	P. O. Box 909, Palmer, AK 99645
Phone	(907) 745-4493

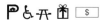

MUSEUM OF ALASKA TRANSPORTATION & INDUSTRY

The Museum of Alaska Transportation & Industry was founded in Anchorage as part of the Alaska Purchase Centennial of 1967. It was known as the Air Progress Museum. A fire in 1973 destroyed much of the museum; it was re-established in 1976 at its present location as a museum of broader scope with aircraft, tractors, firefighting equipment, and trains. The museum grounds are grass with gravel walkways. The buildings are accessible to handicapped persons and to persons with baby strollers. Palmer is on Alaska Route 1, Glenn Highway, about 40 miles northeast of Anchorage. Food and lodging are available in Palmer, half a mile from the museum.

Cars	Coaches, parlor cars				
Schedule	May 21-September 21: Summit excursion, leave Skagway 9 a.m. and 1:30 p.m., returning at 11:45 and 4:20; to Fraser, B. C., leave Skagway 7:45 a.m. and 1 p.m., arrive Fraser 9:25 and 2:35; leave Fraser 10:25 a.m. and 2:55 p.m., arrive Skagway 12:10 and 4:39; to Whitehorse (bus north of Fraser), leave Skagway 1 p.m., arrive Whitehorse 6:30 p.m., leave Whitehorse 8:30 a.m., arrive Skagway 12:10 p.m.				

LOCOMOTIVES

Number	Type	Former owner	Builder	Date
STEAM				
73	2-8-2	WP&Y	Baldwin	1947
DIESEL				
90-100	boxcab	WP&Y	GE	1954-1966

Fares	Round trip to Summit, adults $69, children 12 and under $34.50; Whitehorse, adults $89 one way, children $44.50 one way
Radio frequencies	160.170, 160.305
Nearby attractions	Klondike Gold Rush National Historical Park, sightseeing by helicopter and airplane
Mailing address	P. O. Box 435, Skagway, AK 99840
Phone	(907) 983-2217, (800) 343-7373; in British Columbia, Northwest Territories, and Yukon, (800) 478-7373

WHITE PASS & YUKON ROUTE

The White Pass & Yukon was opened in 1900 between Skagway, Alaska, and Whitehorse, Yukon Territory, a product of the Yukon gold rush of 1898. The 3'-gauge line settled into an existence of carrying supplies into the Yukon and silver, lead, and zinc out. During World War Two the railroad carried much of the equipment used to build the Alaska Highway, and after the war it developed a tourist excursion business in connection with cruise ships calling at Skag-way. The mines on which the railroad depended for business shut down in 1983 and the railroad with them, but excursion trains resumed operating in 1988. Trains make round trips from Skagway to the summit of White Pass and also from Skagway to Fraser, British Columbia, where buses connect to and from Whitehorse. Skagway is a tourist attraction in itself, and restaurants and lodging can be found near the station.

Skagway **ALASKA-11**

Cars	5/12 scale gondola and cattle cars and caboose
Displays	Magma Arizona 2-6-0, baggage car, Pullman car, railroad antiques, 2 railroad stations, 3 model railroads, live-steam club
Schedule	Monday-Friday every 30 minutes 10 a.m. to dusk. Weekends continuous 11 a.m. to dusk.
Fares	Age 3 and up 50 cents (under 3 free). In-state checks accepted. Group discounts available.
Memberships	Write for information.
Special events	Railfair (October)
Nearby attractions	Rawhide, Carefree, Old Scottsdale 5th Avenue shops
Mailing address	7301 East Indian Bend Road, Scottsdale, AZ 85253
Phone	(602) 994-2312

15"-GAUGE LOCOMOTIVES

Number	Type	Builder	Date
STEAM			
10	4-6-0	Bill Daney	1980
11	2-8-2	Bill Daney	1956
12	2-6-2	Texas & Pacific Railway Shops, Big Spring, Texas	1943
DIESEL OUTLINE			
207	SW8	Guy Stillman	
208	GP7	Chuck Schlosser	1960

P &. 木 ⛪ ▣

MCCORMICK RAILROAD PARK

McCormick Railroad Park is a 30-acre, railroad-theme park at the southeast corner of Scottsdale and Indian Bend Road in Scottsdale, Arizona. It has been operated by the city of Scottsdale Recreation Division since 1975.

The Paradise & Pacific features a 1-mile, 8-minute ride through the park on 15"-gauge track aboard a 5/12 scale gondola or cattle car. All rolling stock is modeled after Rio Grande Southern or Denver & Rio Grande Western equipment.

Model railroad clubs have O, HO, and N scale layouts for public viewing, and a live-steam club provides free rides Sundays on its ¾", 1", and 1½" scale equipment. Full-size equipment on display includes a 1907 2-6-0 Baldwin steam engine; 1914 Santa Fe baggage car; and the luxury Pullman car *Roald Amundsen*, built in 1928 and used by U. S. presidents and visiting dignitaries. Two railroad stations — the Peoria, built in 1894, and the Aguila, built in 1907 — house railroad memorabilia shops.

A special birthday party package is available at the park; make reservations well in advance. Seven picnic pavilions, available with reservations, will accommodate groups; other picnic areas are on a first-come, first-served basis. The park also has a volleyball court, playgrounds, and grass playing fields. The grounds and the train are accessible to handicapped or people with baby strollers.

Cars	Ex-Southern Pacific commuter coaches
Schedule	March 1-December 31, 1990, leave Williams 10 a.m., arrive Grand Canyon 12:45 p.m., leave Grand Canyon 4:30, arrive Williams 7:15. Additional train April 1-September 30, 1990, leave Williams 9 a.m., arrive Grand Canyon 11:45, leave Grand Canyon 3:30 p.m., arrive Williams 6:15.
Fares	Adults $47, children 12 and under $23. Reservations required. Credit cards accepted; checks are accepted for advance payments. Tickets are also available from travel agents.
Nearby attractions	Skiing, golf, national forests
Mailing address	518 East Bill Williams Avenue, Williams, AZ 86046-2704
Phone	(602) 635-4000, (800) THE-TRAIN (843-8724)

LOCOMOTIVES

Number	Type	Former owner	Builder	Date
STEAM				
18	2-8-0	Lake Superior & Ishpeming	Pittsburgh	1910
29	2-8-0	Lake Superior & Ishpeming	Pittsburgh	1906
DIESEL				
2072	GP7	Atchison, Topeka & Santa Fe	EMD	1953
2134	GP7	Atchison, Topeka & Santa Fe	EMD	1953

GRAND CANYON RAILWAY

The Atchison, Topeka & Santa Fe began operating trains between Williams and the south rim of the Grand Canyon, 64 miles, in 1901, and for many years operated sleeping cars between Chicago and Los Angeles that made a detour to Grand Canyon. Passenger service on the branch ceased in 1968; freight service ended in 1974. The Grand Canyon Railway purchased the line and resumed passenger service on September 17, 1989. Trains operate between Williams, about 30 miles west of Flagstaff on I-40, and a log-cabin-style station (built in 1910) at the south rim of the canyon. The railway owns four ex-Lake Superior & Ishpeming 2-8-0s and ex-Burlington 2-8-2 No. 4960. Two 2-8-0s are already in service, and the other steam locomotives are being restored to operating condition. Food and lodging are available within half a mile of the station in Williams and also at Grand Canyon. Call the railway for information on access for the handicapped.

Cars	Coaches	
Schedule	Weekends in April, then daily, May-October, hourly from 10 a.m. to 4 p.m. The dining car operates on trains at 11, 1, 5, and 8 p.m. Charter trips available.	
Fares	Adults $6, children 5-12 $3 (under 5 free). Group discount available. Credit cards accepted.	
Radio frequency	160.275	
Nearby attractions	Passion Play, country music shows	
Mailing address	P. O. Box 310, Eureka Springs, AR 72632	
Phone	(501) 253-9623; 253-6774 year-round	

LOCOMOTIVES

Number	Type	Former owner	Builder	Date
STEAM				
1	2-6-0	W. T. Carter Co.	Baldwin	1906
201	2-6-0	Isthmian Canal Commission	Alco	1906
226	2-8-2	Dierks Lumber	Baldwin	1927
DIESEL				
6000	SW1	Chicago & Eastern Illinois	EMD	1942

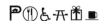

EUREKA SPRINGS & NORTH ARKANSAS RAILWAY

Established in 1980, the Eureka Springs & North Arkansas operates from a stone depot at 299 North Main Street (Highway 23 North at the Eureka Springs city limits). The train travels 2 miles north from the depot to the old mainline junction, then returns, a 45-minute round trip through the Ozark Mountain countryside in northern Arkansas. The line, formerly part of the Missouri & North Arkansas, was originally built in 1883. The *Eurekan*, a fully restored vintage dining car, serves lunch on the 11 a.m. and 1 p.m. trains, and dinner on the 5 and 8 p.m. trains. Reservations are required for trips in the diner. Visitors may park at the depot, ride the steam train, then ride the trolley through historic downtown Eureka Springs. The trolley stops at the depot approximately every 30 minutes. The ES&NA grounds are accessible to handicapped or people with baby strollers, and there are two acres of level recreational vehicle parking. Staff is on the premises year-round, and restaurants and lodging are available in Eureka Springs.

Cars	2 streetcars
Displays	3 cabooses, railroad memorabilia
Dates open	Saturdays 8 a.m.-4 p.m., Tuesdays 6-10 p.m.
Admission	Free

Special events	Open house, July 15, 1990
Nearby attractions	Fort Smith National Historic Site, Old Fort Museum, Belle Grove Historic District
Mailing address	2121 Wolfe Lane, Fort Smith, AR 72901
Phone	(501) 783-0205; 783-1237 year-round

FORT SMITH TROLLEY MUSEUM

The Fort Smith Streetcar Restoration Association, established in 1979, is restoring two streetcars that ran in Fort Smith, No. 205, built by Cincinnati Car Co. in 1919, and No. 224, built by St. Louis Car Co. in 1926. Work is carried on at the carbarn at 100 South 4th Street. The association has several other pieces of rolling stock — three cabooses, a Missouri-Kansas-Texas chair car, and a troop sleeper — and various artifacts and memorabilia. Fort Smith is on the western edge of Arkansas on I-40 and U. S. Routes 64 and 71. Motels and restaurants can be found within a few blocks of the carbarn.

Cars	Baggage, chair, and lounge cars
Displays	Cabooses, snow plow
Dates open	Monday-Saturday, 8:30 a.m.-3 p.m.
Admission	Free
Memberships	Cotton Belt Rail Historical Society, $10 per year
Nearby attractions	Arkansas River dam and lock
Mailing address	P. O. Box 2044, Pine Bluff, AR 71613
Phone	(501) 541-1819

ARKANSAS RAILROAD MUSEUM

The Cotton Belt Rail Historical Society, which operates the Arkansas Railroad Museum, was formed in 1983 to preserve and restore a steam locomotive, St. Louis Southwestern ("Cotton Belt") 819, a 4-8-4 built in 1942 by the Cotton Belt in its shops at Pine Bluff. The locomotive was donated to the city of Pine Bluff and placed on display in 1955; it returned to operation in 1986 and has appeared at numerous festivals and celebrations up and down the Cotton Belt.

The museum is located in the former Cotton Belt shops at the foot of East Second Street in Pine Bluff. Restaurants and motels can be found in Pine Bluff, which is about 45 miles southeast of Little Rock.

Locomotives	2 steam
Cars	Wood and steel coaches
Displays	Freight and passenger cars
Schedule	Memorial Day-Labor Day weekend, Saturday at 11 a.m. and 2 p.m.; Sunday at 2
Fares	Adults $6, children 4-11 $3.60 (under 4 free). Credit cards accepted. Discounts for groups of 15 or more reserving one week in advance. Charters available for a minimum of 70 adults.
Special events	Night trains; holiday events include Civil War reenactments and train robberies.
Nearby attractions	Crater of Diamonds State Park, White Oak Lake State Park, Old Washington Historic State Park, Hot Springs National Park
Mailing address	Reader Industries, Inc., P. O. Box 9, Malvern, AR 72104
Phone	(501) 337-9591 (office), 685-2692 (depot, weekends May-October)

READER RAILROAD

This historic logging line, founded in 1889 by A. S. Johnson, is the oldest all-steam, standard gauge, common carrier railroad in North America. The wood-burning locomotive and its train depart from the depot on Highway 368 in the old mill town of Reader, just off Highway 24 between Camden and Prescott, Arkansas. It travels 3 miles from the depot to the logging camp at Camp DeWoody, then returns, a 1 hour and 20 minute round trip through hilly woodlands. The 40-acre grounds are accessible to handicapped or people with baby strollers. Guided tours are offered by reservation, and staff is in the office at Malvern year-round. Restaurants and lodging are available in nearby Camden and Prescott. Special night trains, originating at Camp DeWoody, feature dinner at Adams Crossing and live bluegrass and country music. Write for a brochure and reservation form.

Cars	Open excursion cars			
Dates open	Monday-Friday 10 a.m.-6 p.m., Saturdays and Sundays 9 a.m.-midnight; 8 a.m.-1 a.m. during summer; other extended hours during holiday periods			
Admission	One day, adults $25.50, children 3-11 $20 (under 3 free), age 60 and over $20.50 (except Saturdays and except July and August). Discount for 2-day and 3-day tickets. Parking $4 (RVs and trailers, $5). Checks and credit cards accepted. Group discounts available. Admission includes all rides.			
Nearby attractions	Knott's Berry Farm, Universal Studios, Hollywood, Spruce Goose, Queen Mary, Sea World, Anaheim Stadium			
Mailing address	1313 Harbor Boulevard, Anaheim, CA 92803			
Phone	(714) 999-4000; 999-4565 for information			

STEAM LOCOMOTIVES

Number	Type	Former owner	Builder	Date
1	4-4-0	New	Disney-Dickson	1954
2	4-4-0	New	Disney-Dickson	1954
3	2-4-4T	Godchaux Co.	Baldwin	1894
4	2-4-0	Raritan River Sand Co.	Baldwin	1925

DISNEYLAND RAILROAD

The Disneyland Railroad circles Disneyland with more than a mile of 36"-gauge track. A complete trip takes about 22 minutes. The train stops and passengers may board or leave the train at Main Street, New Orleans Square, and Tomorrowland. The view from the train includes Bear Country, Big Thunder Ranch, Fantasyland, and Tomorrowland.

In Fantasyland is the Casey Jr. Circus Train. Seeing Disneyland calls for a lot of walking. Wheelchairs and strollers can be rented at the entrance, and an information guide for the handicapped is available. Restaurants and snack bars can be found all through Disneyland, and motels and hotels are plentiful nearby.

Displays	Southern Pacific 4-6-0; 7 cars; 1883 depot, turntable
Dates open	Daily, weather permitting, 10 a.m. to 4 p.m. March 15-November 15, all buildings open; some buildings closed during winter
Admission	Free; donations appreciated
Memberships	Bishop Museum & Historical Society, $7 per year
Nearby attractions	Hunting, fishing, camping, and skiing in High Sierras
Mailing address	P. O. Box 363, Bishop, CA 93514
Phone	(619) 873-5950

P & 🎁

LAWS RAILROAD MUSEUM & HISTORICAL SITE

From 1943 to 1960 Laws, California, was the northern terminal of Southern Pacific's narrow gauge line through the Owens Valley, the remnant of a 299-mile line that once reached north to Mound House, Nevada, near Carson City. The museum is located 4 miles northeast of Bishop, California, on Silver Canyon Road east of the junction of Highway 6 in what is left of the old town of Laws. The museum opened April 1, 1966, 83 years from the day the first scheduled train arrived at Laws from the north; it is operated by the Bishop Museum & Historical Society. Items of interest include Southern Pacific steam locomotive No. 9, nicknamed Slim Princess; freight and passenger cars; the original depot built in 1883; and numerous railroad artifacts and pioneer exhibits.

The 11-acre site is accessible to the handicapped and people with baby strollers, and about half the grounds are paved. Guided tours are offered for groups by reservation. Staff is on the premises year-round, and restaurants and lodging are available in Bishop.

	[1988 information]
Locomotives	2 steam, 1 motor car
Cars	Wood passenger and freight cars
Dates open	Daily except Christmas Day
Admission	Adults $16.95, children under 12 $11.95, age 60 and over $11.95. Includes all rides and attractions. Checks and credit cards accepted. Group discounts available. There is a charge for parking.
Nearby attractions	Disneyland, Movieland Wax Museum, Medieval Times
Mailing address	8039 Beach Boulevard, Buena Park, CA 90620
Phone	(714) 220-5200

GHOST TOWN & CALICO RAILROAD

   The Ghost Town & Calico Railroad was established in 1952 at Knott's Berry Farm, which even then was a good-sized theme park with a western motif. The 3'-gauge train offers a 7-minute, ¾-mile ride around the 150-acre park. Usual motive power is one of a pair of Denver & Rio Grande 2-8-0s. Also on the roster is Rio Grande Southern "Galloping Goose" motor car No. 3. Buena Park is about 30 minutes southeast of downtown Los Angeles near Anaheim and Fullerton. Knott's is on Beach Boulevard, State Route 39, south of the Santa Ana and Riverside freeways.

Locomotives	3 diesel
Cars	Open-window coaches, cafe-observation car on special occasions
Displays	Steam and diesel locomotives, freight and passenger cars
Dates open	Campo: weekends and holidays except Thanksgiving and Christmas, 9 a.m.-5 p.m.; La Mesa: weekends 1-4 p.m.
Schedule	Weekends and holidays except Thanksgiving and Christmas, leave Campo noon and 2:30 p.m. Charter trips available.
Admission	Free
Fares	Adults $7.00. Children 5-12 $3.50 (under 5 free). Credit cards and checks accepted. Reservations are recommended. Group discounts available.
Memberships	Write for information.
Nearby attractions	Laguna Mountain recreational area, Cuyamaca Lake, Morena Lake, Stone Store museum in Campo
Mailing address	4695 Railroad Avenue, La Mesa, CA 92041
Phone	Information (619) 697-7762; reservations (619) 466-6500

SAN DIEGO RAILROAD MUSEUM and SAN DIEGO & ARIZONA RAILWAY

The Pacific Southwest Railway Museum Association operates the San Diego Railroad Museum at two locations near San Diego. At 4695 Nebo Drive (Railroad Avenue) in La Mesa, visitors can see the original 1894 La Mesa depot, restored by volunteers, and an exhibit featuring a steam engine and freight and passenger cars.

The main collection is at the museum in Campo, off Highway 94; road signs will direct you to the museum. Here you can see restoration work in progress, visit the museum store, and ride on the association's San Diego & Arizona Railway. The 15-mile round trip from Campo to Miller Creek and back takes about 1½ hours. Scenery includes lush meadows, rock cuts and fills, and valleys with live oak groves. Children under 12 riding the train must be accompanied by an adult. The 8½-acre grounds at Campo are not paved, but are accessible to the handicapped or people with baby strollers. The best time to visit is in early to mid-spring, as temperatures in summer can climb to more than 100 degrees. Restaurants are located in Campo, and lodging is available in Pine Valley and Alpine.

Locomotives	5 steam
Cars	Open excursion cars, observation cars, caboose
Schedule	Daily, rain or shine, except Christmas Day, with one to five departures depending upon the season
Fares	Adults $10.75, children 3-15 $7.75. Discounts for groups of 25 or more (reservations required). Credit cards and checks accepted.
Special events	Moonlight Steam Train Party
Nearby attractions	Henry Cowell Redwoods State Park
Mailing address	P. O. Box G-1, Felton, CA 95018
Phone	(408) 335-4484

ROARING CAMP & BIG TREES NARROW-GAUGE RAILROAD

The Roaring Camp & Big Trees has been in operation since 1963. Roaring Camp is a re-creation of an early California logging camp with an 1880s depot, a general store, and a steam sawmill. Vehicles are banned at Roaring Camp, so visitors walk across a covered bridge and down a country lane to board the train. The train travels through a redwood forest and up an 8 percent grade to the top of Bear Mountain. The 6½-mile round trip lasts 1¼ hours. Along the way the conductor relates the history of the area.

A chuckwagon barbecue is served at Roaring Camp weekends, May through October. The general store sells gifts, candy, and dry goods, while the Red Caboose Saloon serves hamburgers, hot dogs, soft drinks, and ice cream. A Moonlight Steam Train Party runs certain Saturday nights from May through October, and features entertainment, dancing, and a barbecue; reservations are required.

The grounds are not paved, but assistance is available aboard the train for the handicapped. Roaring Camp is on Graham Hill Road in Felton, 80 miles south of San Francisco and 6 miles inland from Santa Cruz. Lodging and restaurants are available in Santa Cruz and Felton.

Locomotives	2 diesel
Cars	Coaches, combine, open cars
Schedule	Daily in summer; weekends in spring and fall. Departures at 11:30 a.m. and 2:30 p.m. Reduced winter schedule. Adults $12.50. Children 3-15 $8.50 (under 3 free). Group discounts available. Credit cards and checks accepted.
Nearby attractions	Henry Cowell Redwoods State Park, Santa Cruz beach and boardwalk
Mailing address	P. O. Box G-1, Felton, CA 95018
Phone	(408) 335-4484

P & ⚘ 🎁 ☕

SANTA CRUZ, BIG TREES & PACIFIC RAILWAY

This historic railroad line dates back to 1875, when the first narrow gauge locomotive of the Santa Cruz & Felton arrived at the Felton depot. A few years later the South Pacific Coast Railway assumed ownership of the line. Southern Pacific operated it from 1887 to 1985, when the line was purchased by F. Norman Clark, president and founder of the Roaring Camp & Big Trees Narrow-Gauge Railroad. Today standard gauge excursion trains run between Roaring Camp in Felton and the Pacific Ocean at Santa Cruz. This 14-mile round trip takes approximately 2½ hours. Along the way passengers will see redwood forests, the San Lorenzo River gorge, secluded fishing and swimming holes, and, in Santa Cruz, streets lined with Victorian homes. Passengers may board at either Roaring Camp or Santa Cruz. The grounds are not paved, but assistance is available aboard the train for the handicapped. Restaurants and lodging are plentiful in Felton and Santa Cruz.

Locomotives	2 steam (Shay), 1 diesel, 4 railcars
Cars	Open cars with sectioned logs for seats, coaches converted from flat cars
Displays	Freight cars, logging equipment
Schedule	Railcars operate daily April-October except when steam trains run. Steam trains run weekends June-Labor Day at 10:30 a.m., 12, 1:30, and 3:30 p.m.; weekdays from the beginning of July to Labor Day at 11 and 12:30; and weekends in May, September, and October at 11 and 12:30. Moonlight Special (steak barbecue, entertainment, and train ride) Saturday evenings June-September (reservations required). Charter trips available.
Fares	Adults $8, children 3-12 $4. Age 65 and over, 10 percent discount. Credit cards and in-state checks accepted. Group discounts available.
Special events	Hobo Stew Cookoff, Westside Railfan Day, melodrama presentation
Nearby attractions	Yosemite National Park, Bass Lake
Mailing address	56001 Highway 41, Fish Camp, CA 93623
Phone	(209) 683-7273

LOCOMOTIVES

Number	Type	Former owner	Builder	Date
STEAM				
10	Shay	Westside Lumber	Lima	1928
15	Shay	Hobart Mills	Lima	1913
DIESEL				
5			Vulcan	1935

YOSEMITE MOUNTAIN-SUGAR PINE RAILROAD

   The Yosemite Mountain Sugar Pine railroad is a reconstruction of part of the narrow gauge logging railroad of the Madera Sugar Pine Co., which was abandoned in 1931. Trains pulled by Shay-type steam locomotives or operated with railcars derived from Ford Model As provide a 45-minute round trip ride over 2 miles of sharply curving, steep-graded track. Fish Camp is on State Route 41 four miles south of Yosemite National Park and about 60 miles north of Fresno; the elevation is about 5000 feet. Food and lodging are available adjacent to the railroad area.

Fish Camp

Locomotives	2 steam
Cars	Gondolas and cattle cars
Displays	Farm implements, zoo
Dates open	Weekends and holidays January 15-November 15, noon-5 p.m. only in good weather
Fares	60 cents (children under 1 free). Checks accepted. Group discounts available.
Special events	Double-headers run last day of season
Nearby attractions	Old Folsom, California State Railroad Museum, Sacramento Valley Live Steamers Club, Folsom Lake State Recreation Area
Mailing address	P. O. Box 261, El Dorado, CA 95623
Phone	(916) 621-0039

FOLSOM VALLEY RAILWAY

The Folsom Valley Railway is a 12"-gauge railway at 50 Natoma Street, next to the zoo in the Folsom city park. It has been in operation since 1952. Three coal-burning 4-4-0s built in 1947 and 1950 pull trains on a 2/3-mile loop of track. The ride takes about 7 minutes. Food and lodging are available in Folsom, which is about 20 miles northeast of Sacramento between U. S. 50 and I-80.

Cars	Coaches, open observation car, 2 diesel cars
Schedule	Super Skunk service daily, third Saturday in June through second Saturday in September. Leave Fort Bragg 9:20 a.m. and 1:35 p.m.; leave Willits 8:50 a.m. and 1:45 p.m. Diesel car service daily, second Sunday in September through third Friday in June, leave Fort Bragg 9:20 a.m., arrive Willits 11:30; leave Willits 1:20 p.m., arrive Fort Bragg 3:30. Additional Fort Bragg-Northspur round trips operate most Saturdays and holiday weekends, plus Sundays in April and October, plus daily on the Super Skunk schedule during May, early June, and late September. Reservations advisable. Charter trips available.

Fares	(1989 fares — a 15 percent increase was pending at press time) Adults $20.00 all-day round trip, $16.00 half-day or one-way trip. Children 5-11 half fare (under 5 free if not occupying a seat). Discounts for groups of 35 or more. Credit cards and checks accepted.
Special events	Steam train specials between Fort Bragg and Northspur most Saturday from late March to mid-October and Fridays during the summer
Nearby attractions	Redwoods, botanical gardens, deep-sea fishing, North Coast Daylight
Mailing address	P. O. Box 907, Fort Bragg, CA 95437
Phone	(707) 964-6371

LOCOMOTIVES

Number	Type	Former owner	Builder	Date
STEAM				
45	2-8-2	Brownlee-Olds Lumber Co.	Baldwin	1924
DIESEL				
56	RS-12	McCloud River RR	Baldwin	1955
62, 63	RS-11	Southern Pacific	Alco	1955
64	GP9	Southern Pacific	EMD	1957

CALIFORNIA WESTERN RAILROAD

The California Western Railroad began in 1885 as a logging line. Steam passenger service started in 1904, was extended to Willits in 1911, and was replaced in 1925 by a Mack railbus nicknamed "Skunk." The nickname came from the smell of the exhaust of the rail car's gasoline engine.

"Super Skunk" passenger trains powered by diesel locomotives make two round trips from Fort Bragg and Willits to Northspur daily during the summer. Diesel car service is provided daily the rest of the year, except for Thanksgiving, Christmas, and New Year's Day. Food and beverages are available at Northspur, the halfway point, where passengers may change trains to continue their ride to the other terminal or return to their origin. The 80-mile round trip through the redwoods takes 7 hours; the one-way trip and the round trip to Northspur take 3 to 4 hours. The train makes frequent stops to deliver mail and groceries and crosses many bridges and trestles.

Restaurants and lodging are available in Fort Bragg and Willits. The Fort Bragg station is at the foot of Laurel Street; the Willits station is three blocks east of U. S. 101.

Displays	Southern Pacific station, caboose, model railroad
Dates open	Wednesday-Sunday, 1-4 p.m.
Schedule	Trains operate the second Saturday of each month, and the fourth Saturday of summer months, also July 4 and Depot Day. Standard gauge handcar rides are available the third Saturday of each month.
Admission	Free
Fares	$1 per person
Memberships	Write for information.
Special events	Depot Day (third Sunday of October)
Nearby attractions	Stow House, Santa Barbara Mission
Mailing address	P. O. Box 2125, Goleta, CA 93118
Phone	(805) 964-3540

P ♿ ⛲ 🎁 $

GOLETA DEPOT RAILROAD MUSEUM

The Institute for American Research has established a railroad museum in the former Southern Pacific station building at Goleta, California, 7 miles west of Santa Barbara. The building was moved to a new location in Lake Los Carneros Park. The exhibits include a Southern Pacific bay-window caboose, a model railroad depicting Santa Barbara in the 1930s, operating signal and communication equipment, and several period rooms in the station: freight office, waiting room, and agent's apartment. A 7½"-gauge miniature railroad runs on the museum grounds. To reach the museum, take the Los Carneros Road exit from U. S. 101; the museum is at 300 North Los Carneros Road. There are restaurants and motels in Goleta.

Cars	Coaches, open observation cars
Displays	Steam locomotives, freight and passenger cars, shop and roundhouse facilities
Dates open	Year round, 9 a.m.-4 p.m.; mid-May to mid-September, till 5. Roundhouse tours, daily May-September, weekends year round.
Schedule	*Cannon Ball*: April 7-November 24, 1990, Saturdays, Sundays, and holidays: leave Jamestown 10:30 a.m., noon, 1:30, and 3 p.m. *Keystone Special*, Saturdays April 7-June 23, September 8, 15, 22, October 6, 13, and 20, 1990, leave Jamestown 5 p.m. *Twi-Light Limited*, Saturday June 30-September 1 plus July 4 and September 2, 1990, leave Jamestown 5 p.m.
Admission	No charge for admission to grounds. Roundhouse tour: adults $2, children 3-12 $1.25
Fares	*Cannon Ball*, Adults $8, children 3-12 $4.

Keystone Special, $16/$10. *Twi-Light Limited* (includes Bar-B-Que dinner upon return), $32.50/$18.50. Family fares and group discounts available. Credit cards and checks accepted.

Special events	Press Day (March 28), Western Film Festival and Bar-B-Que (September 29), New Year's Eve party train
Nearby attractions	Columbia State Historic Park, Yosemite National Park
Mailing address	P. O. Box 1250, Jamestown, CA 95327
Phone	(209) 984-3953

STEAM LOCOMOTIVES

Number	Type	Former owner	Builder	Date
2	3-truck Shay	Feather River Rwy	Lima	1922
3	4-6-0	Sierra Railroad	Rogers	1891
28	2-8-0	Sierra Railroad	Baldwin	1922
32	2-8-2	Sierra Railroad	Baldwin	1925

P &. 유 🎁 ☕

RAILTOWN 1897 STATE HISTORIC PARK

The Sierra Railroad is possibly one of the world's best-known railroads because of the movies, television shows, and commercials filmed along its line and aboard its trains. The road's Jamestown, Calif., roundhouse, shop, and station facilities were purchased by the state of California in 1982 and now constitute the Railtown 1897 State Historic Park. The 26-acre park site is located at 5th Avenue and Reservoir Road in Jamestown. The grounds are accessible to handicapped or people with baby strollers. Restaurants and lodging are available in Jamestown.

In addition to viewing the museum displays, visitors can ride excursion trains through rolling Mother Lode foothills and oak woodlands. The *Cannon Ball* makes a 1-hour, 7-mile round trip; the *Keystone Special* and the *Twi-Light Limited* take 2½ hours for a 22-mile round trip. Snacks and beverages can be purchased on board the *Keystone Special* and *Twi-Light Limited*. Reservations are recommended for the *Keystone Specia*l, the *Twi-Light Limited*, and other special events.

Jamestown

Displays	Wood caboose, steam locomotive, wood box car, tank car
Dates open	Wednesday through Sunday, 10 a.m. to 5 p.m. Closed Monday, Tuesday, and Christmas Day. Guided tours available by reservation.
Admission	50 cents (infants free)
Nearby attractions	Banning Museum, Coast Botanical Gardens, Marineland, Cabrillo Museum, Maritime Museum, Port of Calls
Mailing address	2135-37 250th Street West, Lomita, CA 90717
Phone	(213) 326-6255

LOMITA RAILROAD MUSEUM

Established in 1966, this city-owned museum reproduces the era of the steam locomotive. It is located on the corner of Woodward Avenue and 250th Street West in Lomita, California. The building, a replica of Boston & Maine's Greenwood station in Wakefield, Massachusetts, includes an authentically furnished ticket office.

On display are Union Pacific caboose No. 25730; Southern Pacific locomotive No. 1765, a 2-6-0, and tender No. 7334; handcar; and railroad memorabilia such as whistles, marker lights, semaphore signals, number plates, builder's plates, photographs, and drawings.

The grounds also include a park that is ideal for picnics, and a "shower of rainbow" fountain. The museum is accessible to the handicapped. Restaurants and lodging are available in Lomita.

Displays	Locomotives, 8 passenger cars, 8 freight cars, 5 cabooses, work equipment, streetcars
Dates open	Daily 10 a.m.-4 p.m. (until 5 during the summer and on weekends) except Christmas and days of extremely heavy rain
Admission	Free
Memberships	Southern California Scenic Railway Association — write for information
Nearby attractions	Los Angeles Zoo, Griffith Observatory, Griffith Park & Southern Railroad, Universal Studios, Gene Autry Western Heritage Museum, Hollywood
Mailing address	3900 West Chevy Chase, Los Angeles, CA 90039
Phone	(213) 662-5874

LOCOMOTIVES ON DISPLAY

Railroad	Number	Type	Builder	Date
STEAM				
Consolidated Rock Products	1	0-6-0T	Alco (Cooke)	1925
Los Angeles Harbor	31	0-4-0T	Davenport	1921
Los Angeles Harbor	32	0-4-0T	Alco (Rogers)	1914
Oahu Railway & Land	85	4-6-0	Alco (Cooke)	1910
Oahu Sugar	5	0-6-2T	Baldwin	1908
Pickering Lumber	2	3-truck	Heisler	1918
Atchison, Topeka & Santa Fe	664	2-8-0	Baldwin	1899
Santa Maria Valley	1000	2-8-2	Alco (Schenectady)	1920
Sharp & Fellows	7	2-6-2	Alco (Dickson)	1902
Southern Pacific	1273	0-6-0	SP	1921
Southern Pacific	20	0-4-0T	Baldwin	1880
Southern Pacific	3025	4-4-2	Alco (Schenectady)	1904
Stockton Terminal & Eastern	1	4-4-0	Norris	1864
Union Pacific	4439	0-6-0	Baldwin	1918
Western Pacific	26	2-8-0	Alco (Schenectady)	1909
DIESEL, GASOLINE, AND ELECTRIC				
Atchison, Topeka & Santa Fe	M.177	Gas-electric	Pullman-EMD	1929
McDonnell-Douglas		Model 40	EMD	
Pacific Electric	1544	B-B	North Shore RR	1902

Ⓟ⑪&🚻🎁

TRAVEL TOWN MUSEUM

Travel Town began in 1952 with the donation of Southern Pacific locomotive 3025, a 4-4-2 built in 1904. By the time it was placed on display, it had been joined by freight cars, streetcars, and a station, plus other transportation equipment. Travel Town grew to include the largest collection of steam locomotives in the West. After a bright start, the collection was neglected for a while, but in recent years a plan for Travel Town has been developed by the Department of Recreation and Parks of the city of Los Angeles, and a number of the displays have already been refurbished.

The locomotive collection consists primarily of smaller locomotives — a Santa Maria Valley 2-8-2 built in 1920 is the largest engine and one of the newest. It includes an EMD Model 40 switcher which operates occasionally. Circling around the display is the Travel Town Railroad (see next entry).

In the main museum building is the N scale model railroad of the East Valley Lines, open Saturday and Sunday 11 a.m.-4 p.m. (no admission charge). About ¼ mile east of Travel Town are the facilities of the Los Angeles Live Steamers, who operate on 4¾"- and 7½"-gauge track. They are open to the public on Sunday and some holidays.

Travel Town is at 5200 Zoo Drive in the northwest corner of Griffith Park. The park is accessible from nearby freeways: State Route 134, U. S. 101, and I-5.

	GRIFFITH PARK & SOUTHERN
Locomotives	2 gasoline-powered (1 steam outline, 1 diesel outline)
Cars	10 open-air Pullman type, 4 wood gondolas, 1 caboose
	TRAVEL TOWN RAILROAD
Locomotives	2 gasoline-powered diesel outline
Cars	6 miniature Pullman cars
	BOTH
Schedule	Daily, 10 a.m.-4:30 p.m. Charter trips available.
Fares	Adults $1.50. Children 18 months-13 years $1.25 (under 18 months free). Senior citizens age 65 and up $1.00. Group discounts available. Checks accepted.
Nearby attractions	Travel Town, Griffith Park, East Valley Lines, Los Angeles Live Steamers, Griffith Park Zoo, Gene Autry Western Heritage Museum
Mailing address	GP Recreations, 115 South Victory Boulevard, Burbank, CA 91502
Phone	(213) 664-6788, 849-1352

P & ⚐ 🎁 ◼

GRIFFITH PARK & SOUTHERN RAILROAD and TRAVEL TOWN RAILROAD

The Griffith Park & Southern Railroad is located just inside the main entrance to Griffith Park, 4400 Crystal Springs Drive, Los Angeles, California. Griffith Park, 4300 acres, is the largest city-owned park in the world; it is at the intersection of Interstate Highways 5 (Golden State Freeway) and 134 (Ventura Freeway).

The 1/3 scale 18½"-gauge trains journey past pony corrals, through an 80-foot-long tunnel, across Lizzard Creek trestle, and back through the old Western town of Griffith Gulch to the depot, a reproduction of a nineteenth-century Midwestern station house. The 1¼-mile ride takes about 10 minutes.

Circling Travel Town (see the previous entry), which is at the northwest corner of Griffith Park, near the Forest Lawn entrance, is the 16"-gauge Travel Town Railroad, which takes visitors past the transportation museum and railroad yard. The 1-mile ride lasts about 10 minutes.

The grounds of both miniature railroads are paved and are accessible to handicapped or people with baby strollers. Discounted hotel accommodations in the Burbank area can be arranged with advance notice.

	Cars	Rebuilt heavyweight coaches, diners, and lounges

Cars Rebuilt heavyweight coaches, diners, and lounges

Schedule Brunch train leaves Napa Saturdays, Sundays, and holidays, 9 a.m. Lunch train, Monday-Friday, 11:30 a.m.; Saturdays, Sundays, and holidays, 12:20 p.m. Dinner train, Tuesday-Saturday, 6:30 p.m.; Sundays and holidays, 6 p.m. Boarding, 30 minutes before departure; trip takes 3½ hours

Fares Fare does not include meal. $25 Monday-Friday; $29 Saturday and Sunday. Dinner train for parties of two or more, $12.50 per person weekdays, $14.50 weekends. Children 13 and under, $7.50 on Saturday brunch train. Age 60 and over, 10 percent discount. Credit cards accepted. Group discount available. Meals: brunch or lunch, $20; dinner, $45.

Nearby attractions Wineries

Mailing address 1275 McKinstry Street, Napa, CA 94559

Phone (800) 522-4142 or (707) 253-2111 for reservations; offices (707) 253-2160

DIESEL LOCOMOTIVES

Number	Type	Former owner	Builder	Date
50	44 ton	Camino, Placerville & Lake Tahoe	General Electric	1941
		(No. 50 not used in passenger service)		
70-73	FPA4	Canadian National, VIA Rail Canada	Montreal	1958-1959

NAPA VALLEY WINE TRAIN

The Napa Valley Wine Train began operation September 16, 1989. It offers passengers an elegant meal and a leisurely ride through the vineyards of the Napa Valley. The heavyweight passenger cars were once on the rosters of Northern Pacific, Southern, and Penn Central; the locomotives are Montreal-built FPA4s purchased from VIA Rail Canada. The train runs from Napa to St. Helena, 18 miles, over a former Southern Pacific branch, then returns to Napa. The station in Napa is at 1275 McKinstry Street, near the intersection of First and Soscol — follow California Route 121 from the west; 221 from the east. Napa is about 50 miles north-northeast of San Francisco and about 60 miles southwest of Sacramento. Lodging is available in Napa.

Displays	Freight and passenger cars awaiting restoration
Dates open	Most weekends, weather permitting
Nearby attractions	Nevada City, Grass Valley, Northstar Mining Museum, Firehouse Museum, Empire Mine
Mailing address	P. O. Box 1300, Nevada City, CA 95959
Phone	(916) 265-3668, 265-5824

LOCOMOTIVES

Number	Type	Former owner	Builder	Date
STEAM				
5	2-6-2	Argent Lumber Co	Lima	1910
5	2-6-0	Nevada County Narrow Gauge	Baldwin	1875
GASOLINE				
10	6 ton	Nevada County Narrow Gauge	Plymouth	

NEVADA COUNTY HISTORICAL SOCIETY TRANSPORTATION MUSEUM

The Nevada County Narrow Gauge Railroad was opened in 1876 from Colfax to Grass Valley and Nevada City, 21 miles. Even though it had been profitable in the late 1930s, it was abandoned in 1942 when its scrap value overtook its transportation value. The Transportation Museum Division of the Nevada County Historical Society was founded in 1983 to acquire, preserve, and operate Nevada County transportation memorabilia. It has acquired several cars and locomotives, chief among them NCNG No. 5, on loan from Universal Studios. So far the group has no formal museum display, but a half mile of track is being laid near Gold Flat Road in Nevada City, and engine No. 5 can be viewed at the Nevada City Corporation Yard, 707 Zion Street, on Saturday mornings when restoration work is in progress. Nevada City is about 40 miles east of Marysville and 30 miles north of Auburn. Food and lodging can be found in Nevada City and Grass Valley.

Locomotives	1 steam, several diesel and electric
Cars	Streetcars and interurbans
Displays	150 trolleys, interurbans, passenger, freight, and maintenance of way cars, a Ventura County 2-6-2 steam locomotive, and several diesels
Dates open	Daily 9 a.m.-5 p.m. Closed Thanksgiving and Christmas.
Schedule	Cars operate every 20-30 minutes weekends and major holidays,11 a.m.-5 p.m.; daily, December 26-January 1 and the week between Palm Sunday and Easter. Charter trips available.
Admission	Free for grounds and parking except during special events. All-day pass (unlimited rides) adults $5; children 6-11 $3 (under 6 free). Group discounts available (apply in advance). Checks accepted. Memberships available.
Special events	Rail Festival last weekend in April, Fall Festival last weekend in October, railroadiana swap meet (October 6, 1990), Winter Rail Faire (December 23, 1990)
Nearby attractions	March Air Force Base museum, Perris Valley Museum, Temecula Wineries, Riverside Live Steamers, skydiving and hot air balloons
Mailing address	P. O. Box 548, Perris, CA 92370-0548
Phone	(714) 943-3020, (714) 657-2605 for recorded information

ORANGE EMPIRE RAILWAY MUSEUM

Organized in 1956 by electric rail enthusiasts interested in preserving the remnants of the trolley era, the museum occupies a 53-acre site at 2201 South A Street, about 1 mile south of the center of Perris, California. The 2-mile round trip trolley ride includes a main line that was part of the original Santa Fe route to San Diego, and a loop line through the center of the museum's grounds. The museum's collection includes approximately 150 streetcars, interurbans, passenger, freight, and maintenance of way cars, a Ventura County Railway 2-6-2 steam locomotive, and several diesels. The museum has both standard gauge and 3'6"-gauge track, the latter for Los Angeles streetcars.

Restaurants are located in Perris, and lodging is available in Sun City (5 miles) and Riverside (20 miles).

Displays	Steam locomotives, diesel locomotive, cars
Dates open	First Sunday of each month, 9 a.m.- 3 p.m.; other times by appointment; also during Los Angeles County Fair
Admission	Free, except during Los Angeles County Fair
Memberships	Write for information.
Nearby attractions	Disneyland, Knott's Berry Farm, Orange Empire Railway Museum
Mailing address	1021 Meeker Avenue, La Puente, CA 91746
Phone	(818) 917-8454

LOCOMOTIVES ON DISPLAY

Railroad and number	Type	Builder	Date
STEAM			
Atchison, Topeka & Santa Fe 3450	4-6-4	Baldwin	1927
Fruit Growers Supply Co. 3	3-truck	Climax	1909
Outer Harbor Terminal 2	0-6-0	Schenectady	1887
Southern Pacific 5021	4-10-2	Alco	1926
Union Pacific 4014	4-8-8-4	Alco	1941
Union Pacific 9000	4-12-2	Alco	1926
U. S. Potash Co. 3	2-8-0	Baldwin	1903
DIESEL			
Union Pacific 6915	DDA40X	EMD	1969

P ♿ 🎁

SOUTHERN CALIFORNIA CHAPTER, RAILWAY & LOCOMOTIVE HISTORICAL SOCIETY

The Southern California Chapter of the Railway & Locomotive Historical Society maintains a museum at the Los Angeles County Fairgrounds. In addition to the locomotives noted in the roster, the display includes a caboose, a business car, and a horse express car, plus the Santa Fe station from nearby Arcadia, which houses a collection of artifacts and memorabilia. The fairgrounds are north of I-10 and east of I-210; the R&LHS display is in the western part of the fairgrounds.

Locomotives	1 steam, 26 diesel
Cars	Caboose and flatcars with benches
Displays	Locomotives, freight, passenger cars
Dates open	10 a.m.-5 p.m. daily, from Memorial Day to the last weekend of September; weekends the rest of the year.
Schedule	Train operates weekends May-September, 11 a.m.-4 p.m.; steam power is used the second weekend of each month. Charter trips available.
Admission	Free
Fares	$2.00 per person, $5.00 for family ticket; good all day. Checks and credit cards accepted. Memberships available.
Special events	Feather River Railroad Days (August 25-26, 1990), Railfan's Day (September 15, 1990)
Nearby attractions	Fishing, golfing, boating; Reno, Nevada
Mailing address	P. O. Box 8, Portola, CA 96122
Phone	(916) 832-4131

PORTOLA RAILROAD MUSEUM

The Portola Railroad Museum, operated by the Feather River Rail Society, is housed in the former Western Pacific diesel shop in Portola, approximately 50 miles northwest of Reno, Nevada. A 1-mile train ride around a turning track through the High Sierra pine forest is offered. For $60 per hour, you can rent a locomotive and be instructed how to operate it. The museum's collection includes numerous locomotives, 50 freight cars, and 3 passenger cars. The 37-acre grounds are accessible to handicapped or people with baby strollers. Restaurants and lodging are available in Portola.

Locomotives	4 steam, 4 diesel, 4 electric
Cars	Many streetcars and interurbans
Dates open	Weekends year-round, plus July 4 and Labor Day, 11 a.m.-5 p.m. Closed New Year's Day and Christmas. Reservations needed for large groups. Charter trips available.
Admission	Adults $4, ages 4-15 $2 (under 4 free). Discounts for groups of 25 or more. Checks and credit cards accepted. Memberships available.
Nearby attractions	Marine World, Sacramento River delta
Mailing address	Bay Area Electric Railroad Association, P. O. Box 193694, San Francisco, CA 94119-3694
Phone	(707) 374-2978

WESTERN RAILWAY MUSEUM

Established in 1960, the Western Railway Museum is operated by the Bay Area Electric Railroad Association. It is located on State Highway 12 in California's Solano County, midway between Fairfield and Rio Vista.

Streetcars and interurbans carry visitors on a 1.5-mile track that circles through the grounds and parallels the former Sacramento Northern Railway interurban line, which is used on occasional weekends by the museum's diesel excursion trains. The cars stop near the carbarns, where visitors can observe the museum's mem-

bers restoring rolling stock. More than 100 pieces of railway equipment — including large collections from the Key System and the Sacramento Northern Railway — are housed at the 25-acre site. Many cars are open for inspection.

The museum is accessible to handicapped and people with baby strollers, but the grounds are not paved. Restaurants and lodging are available in Fairfield and Rio Vista (11 miles), Sacramento and Stockton (45 miles), and San Francisco (55 miles).

Locomotives	Steam
Cars	Coaches, gondolas
Dates open	Museum open daily, 10 a.m. to 5 p.m. Closed New Year's Day, Christmas, and Thanksgiving. Slide show and movie programs on the hour.
Schedule	Excursion trains depart on the hour from 10 a.m. to 5 p.m. weekends and holidays, May through Labor Day (except July 4 weekend).
Admission	Adults $3.00. Children 6-17 $1.00. Group discounts available.
Fares	Adults $4.00. Children 6-17 $2.00 (under 6 free). Charters, special trains, and group rates available.
Memberships	Write for information.
Nearby attractions	Old Sacramento, state capitol, Old Governor's Mansion, Sutter's Fort, State Indian Museum
Mailing address	111 I Street, Sacramento, CA 95814
Phone	State Park offices: (916) 445-4209; recorded information about the railroad museum: (916) 448-4466

CALIFORNIA STATE RAILROAD MUSEUM

Opened in 1981, this museum is located in Old Sacramento, an area of restored and reconstructed buildings from the 1800s containing shops and restaurants. The museum, operated by the California Department of Parks and Recreation, has interpretive and participatory exhibits and includes a roundhouse. The Central Pacific passenger station has been reconstructed to look as it did during the 1870s. Housed in the former Dingley Coffee and Spice Mill, adjacent to the museum's main building, are a large bookstore and gift shop.

In the main building, which covers 100,000 square feet, are exhibited 21 restored locomotives and cars including Southern Pacific No. 1, *C. P. Huntington*, and cab-forward No. 4294; Central Pacific No. 1, *Governor Stanford*; Virginia & Truckee No. 12, *Genoa*, and No. 13, *Empire*; North Pacific Coast No. 12, *Sonoma*; Georgia Northern private car No. 100, *The Gold Coast*; Canadian National sleeping car *St. Hyacinthe*; and Great Northern postal car No. 42.

Excursion trains run along the banks of the Sacramento River on weekends from May through Labor Day. Trains depart on the hour from the Central Pacific passenger depot near Front and K streets and travel to Miller Park, a 7-mile round trip.

Parking is available in a nearby city-operated lot. There are more than a dozen restaurants in Old Sacramento, and two large hotels are within a couple of blocks.

	[1988 information]	**Special events**	Spring and fall meets, last weekends of
Locomotives	50 steam		April and October
Dates open	Second and fourth Sunday of each month, 10	**Nearby attractions**	Orange Empire Railway Museum
	a.m.-3 p.m.	**Mailing address**	P. O. Box 5512, Riverside, CA 92507
Admission	Free; donations appreciated	**Phone**	(714) 683-9628
Memberships	Write for information.		

P & π

RIVERSIDE LIVE STEAMERS, INC.

The Riverside Live Steamers Club was founded in 1965 to operate and maintain a 1½"-scale railroad that had been left to the city by industrialist Joseph L. Hunter. The club rebuilt and expanded the railroad, and the 38 acres of Hunter Park now contain 5,700 feet of 7½"-gauge main line and 3,400 feet of 4¾"-gauge main line, plus servicing tracks for both gauges. The public is welcome to visit and ride on operating days, the second and fourth Sundays of each month. The park is at 1496 Columbia Avenue. Restaurants and motels can be found nearby.

Displays	O, HO, and N scale model railroads	**Memberships**	Write for information.
Dates open	Fridays and first Tuesday of each month,	**Special events**	Railfest (June 23, 1990)
	11 a.m.-4 p.m.; Saturdays and Sundays,	**Nearby attractions**	San Diego Zoo, Pacific Southwest Rail-
	11-5; also Wednesdays and Thursdays		way Museum, Tijuana
	11-4 except between September 9 and	**Mailing address**	1649 El Prado, San Diego, CA 92101
	November 4, 1990	**Phone**	(619) 696-0199
Admission	Adults $1, children under 15 free		

SAN DIEGO MODEL RAILROAD MUSEUM

The San Diego Model Railroad Museum, incorporated in 1980, has four scale model railroads built and operated by three clubs. The San Diego Model Railroad Club, chartered in 1938, has the O scale Cabrillo & Southwestern and the HO San Diego & Arizona Eastern layouts, the latter representing the prototype railroad of the same name. A second HO layout, built by the La Mesa Model Railroad Club, represents the Southern Pacific line over Tehachapi Pass, also used by the Santa Fe. The San Diego Society of N Scale has built a layout that represents a turn-of-the-century proposal to build a railroad east from San Diego.

All the layouts are located on the lower floor of the Casa de Balboa in Balboa Park. The park contains several other museums, the world-famed San Diego Zoo, and a miniature train you can ride. There is a restaurant next to the museum, and motels and restaurants can be found throughout San Diego.

Cars	19 streetcars
Schedule	June-September, daily, 10 a.m.-6:30 p.m. Charter trips available.
Fares	85 cents; 1-day pass $6; 3-day pass $10 (entire Muni system)
Memberships	Market Street Railway Co., P. O. Box 11632, San Francisco, CA 94101
Radio frequency	484.6625
Nearby attractions	Mission Dolores, cable cars — and all San Francisco
Mailing address	San Francisco Municipal Railway, 425 Geneva Avenue, San Francisco, CA 94112
Phone	(415) 673-MUNI, 673-6864

STREETCARS

Number	Type	Original owner or city	Date
1	California	Municipal Railway	1912
106	Deck-roof	Orel, USSR	1912
130	California	Municipal Railway	1914
228	Boat	Blackpool, England	1934
496	W-2	Melbourne, Australia	1930
1834	Peter Witt	Milan, Italy	1928

SAN FRANCISCO HISTORIC TROLLEY FESTIVAL

The San Francisco Historic Trolley Festival was first held in 1983, a cooperative effort of the city and county of San Francisco, the San Francisco Chamber of Commerce, the San Francisco Municipal Railway, and the Market Street Railway Company, a nonprofit organization devoted to promoting and enhancing San Francisco's vintage streetcar service. It consisted of historic streetcars from around the world running between the East Bay Terminal, 1st and Mission Streets, and 17th and Castro, approximately 3½ miles along Market Street (underneath Market Street are two levels of subway tracks carrying the Municipal Railway's light rail vehicles and BART heavy-rail transit trains).

The festival operated each summer through 1987, but construction on Market Street forced the suspension of the festival for 1988. At press time funding had not been approved for the 1990 season; write or call for current information. The Municipal Railway also operates San Francisco's famous cable cars, which run from Market and Powell Streets to Fisherman's Wharf and along California Street between Market Street and Van Ness Avenue.

The cable car barn and powerhouse at 1201 Mason Street, corner of Washington (phone 474-1887), contains a museum and offers a closeup look at the machinery that moves the cables cars.

Cars	2 streetcars
Schedule	Daily, 9 a.m.-3:30 p.m., every 10 minutes, subject to cancellation in inclement weather
Fares	25 cents per person age 5-64; age 65 and over 10 cents
Nearby attractions	Great America; Roaring Camp & Big Trees; Santa Cruz, Big Trees & Pacific; San Francisco, Santa Cruz
Mailing address	P. O. Box 5129, San Jose, CA 95150
Phone	(408) 293-BARN (293-2276); (408) 287-4210 for schedule information

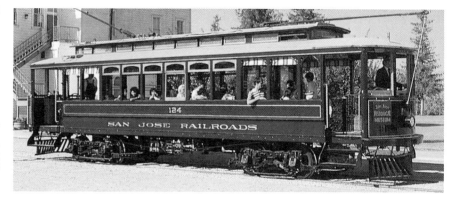

STREETCARS

Number	Original place of operation	Builder	Date
1	Santa Clara		
73	San Jose		1913
124	San Jose	American Car Co.	1912
129	Sacramento	American Car Co.	1913
168	Portugal		
2001	Milan, Italy		

SAN JOSE TROLLEY CORPORATION

The San Jose Trolley Corporation was founded in 1982 to provide old streetcars to operate on new streetcar tracks — at that time still just a proposal — in downtown San Jose. Two restored streetcars, 124 and 129, began operating on November 18, 1988. They run on the downtown loop of San Jose's light rail system, on First, Second, San Carlos, and Devine Streets, every 10 minutes from 9 a.m. to 3:30 p.m. Runs begin and end at the Convention Center/Library stop, but cars receive and discharge passengers at all regular stops on the loop. The lifts that allow the handicapped access to the new LRVs do not work with the historic cars. Tickets can be purchased from machines at each stop. Tickets and passes of the Santa Clara County Transportation Agency are valid on the historic cars.

Restoration is in progress on four more cars at the San Jose Trolley Barn at 635 Phelan Avenue in Kelley Park. Volunteers are at work daily 9 a.m. to 5 p.m.; Thursdays till 9 p.m.

Locomotives	Steam outline
Cars	Open excursion cars
Dates open	Memorial Day-Labor Day and Palm Sunday-Easter, daily; mid-March to late October, weekends. Park opens at 10 a.m.
Admission	$18.95, children 3-6 $9.45 (2 and under free), age 55 and up $11.95. Parking $4. Checks and credit cards accepted. Group discounts available. Admission includes all rides.
Memberships	Write for information.
Nearby attractions	Winchester Mystery House, San Francisco, Santa Cruz
Mailing address	P. O. Box 1776, Santa Clara, CA 95052
Phone	(408) 988-1800 for recorded information

GREAT AMERICAN SCENIC RAILWAY

Running around the perimeter of the Great America theme park in Santa Clara is the Great American Scenic Railway. The 6-minute train ride offers a good view of the park and its various rides, particularly The Edge, The Demon, and The Grizzly Thrill. The train, which is narrow gauge (36"), operates only during good weather. The park also includes a trolley which runs between Orleans Place and Hometown Square. Numerous rides use the flanged-wheel-on-rail principle but don't quite qualify for the purposes of this book as "trains." There are numerous restaurants and snack bars in the park; lodging is available in Santa Clara. Great America is 45 miles southeast of San Francisco and 3 miles northwest of San Jose. Take either the Bayshore Freeway (U. S. 101) or Mountain View-Alviso Road (State Route 237) to Great America Parkway.

Displays	SP 2-6-0 No. 1629, station
Dates open	Sundays 2-4- p.m.
Admission	Free; donations welcome
Nearby attractions	William S. Hart Park and Museum
Mailing address	P. O. Box 875, Newhall, CA 91322
Phone	(805) 254-1275

SAUGUS TRAIN STATION

The Southern Pacific Railroad gave its station building at Saugus, California, to the Santa Clarita Valley Historical Society in 1980. It was moved to a new site and has become a museum and headquarters of the society. On display there is SP 2-6-0 No. 1629, moved in from Gene Autry's Melody Ranch nearby. Restoration of the entine is under way. The station is at 24107 San Fernando Road, a little north of the junction of I-5, the Golden State Freeway, and State Route 14, the Antelope Valley Freeway.

Locomotives	2 steam, 1 gasoline-powered railcar
Cars	15"-gauge gondola and hopper cars, with non-passenger-carrying cars mixed in
Dates open	Weekends year-round 10:30 a.m. to 5 p.m.; daily, June 15-Labor Day
Fares	Adults $2.40. Senior citizens 65 and up $1.60. Children 16 months-16 years $1.80. Group discounts available.
Nearby attractions	Jack London house, General Vallejo's house, Sebastiani winery, northernmost California mission
Mailing address	P. O. Box 656, Sonoma, CA 95476
Phone	(707) 938-3912

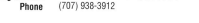

SONOMA TRAIN TOWN RAILROAD

Train Town is a 10-acre railroad park located on Broadway (Highway 12), 1 mile south of the town square in Sonoma, California. Construction began in 1958 and the railroad has been in operation since 1968. The park includes thousands of trees, lakes, animals, bridges, tunnels, and historic structures. Visitors may take a 1¼-mile, 20-minute journey aboard a 15"-gauge train. The train passes Lakeville, a 1/4 scale replica of an old-time mining town. Train Town's grounds are paved. Restaurants and lodging are available in Sonoma, approximately 45 minutes north of San Francisco.

Locomotives	0-4-0T steam locomotive, 44-ton diesel
Cars	Ex-California Western diesel railbus No. 200, former Southern Pacific coaches, open car
Schedule	First and third Sundays of each month plus July 4 and Labor Day, trains leave every half hour between 10 a.m. and 4 p.m.
Fares	Free, but donations are welcome.
Nearby attractions	Sunol Regional Park, wine country, Great America, Marine World, Africa U. S. A.
Mailing address	P. O. Box 2247, Niles Station, Fremont, CA 94536-0247

NILES CANYON RAILWAY

The Pacific Locomotive Association was formed in 1961 and began operating the Castro Point Railway in 1969. Its lease for the land containing the museum's storage area was not extended after 1985, so in 1986 the group established the Niles Canyon Railway. The train journeys through a rustic, winding river canyon between Sunol and Brightside, 2 miles. The museum includes maintenance and storage facilities for locomotives and rolling stock. Steam loco-

motives in the collection include Quincy Railroad 2-6-2T No. 3, Pickering Lumber Co. Heisler No. 5 and Shay No. 12, and Clover Valley Lumber Co. 2-6-6-2T No. 4. The 6-acre grounds are unpaved.

The railway is about 45 minutes from San Francisco. Sunol is between Fremont and Livermore, near the intersection of I-680 and California Route 84. Restaurants and lodging are available in Niles, Pleasanton, and Fremont.

Sunol

Cars	Former Southern Pacific and Burlington Northern streamlined coaches, lounge, diner, and parlor car
Schedule	(1990) Leave Willits 8 a.m./Eureka 8 a.m. May 18/20 and 26/27, June 9/10, 15/17, and 23/24, July 1/7, 8/9, 20/22, and 28/29, August 4/5, 17/19, and 25/26, September 8/9, 15/16, and 21/23, October 6/7 and 13/14. Leave Eureka 8 a.m. for one-day round trip to Fort Seward May 19 and August 18.
Fares	Adults $109 round trip, $78 one way; children 2-12 $49/$35; parlor car, $175/$110. Eureka-Fort Seward round trip, adults $65, children 2-12 $29. Checks and credit cards accepted. Group discounts available.
Nearby attractions	California Western Railroad (Willits), Carson Mansion (Eureka)
Mailing address	P. O. Box 3666, Eureka, CA 95502-3666
Phone	(707) 442-7705; (800) 544-3763 in California

DIESEL LOCOMOTIVES

Number	Type	Former owner	Builder	Date
30, 31	GP38	Conrail	EMD	1967
32, 33	GP38	Conrail	EMD	1969
70	GP7	Central California Traction	EMD	1953

NORTH COAST DAYLIGHT

The Northwestern Pacific Railroad was completed in 1914 from Sausalito, on San Francisco Bay, north through the redwood country to Willits, 278 miles. The topography along the coast was far too rugged to permit construction of a railroad, so the line was built inland. Most of the northern half of the line followed the canyon of the Eel River, remote when it was built and even today far from paved roads. Because of the lack of roads in the area, passenger service between Willits and Eureka continued until Amtrak took over the nation's passenger service in 1971, and in the 1960s the *Red-wood* gained a measure of fame as a scenic train ride.

Southern Pacific, owner of the NWP, sold the line north of Willits in 1984 to the Eureka Southern Railroad, which started operating the North Coast Daylight in 1987. The schedules are arranged for a weekend trip, usually operating north from Willits on Saturdays and returning on Sundays (a few trips are scheduled to allow two nights in Eureka). Ticket price includes continental breakfast and luncheon in both directions, and free transportation is provided to several hotels and motels in Eureka.

Locomotive	1 steam-outline
Cars	Open ore-style
Admission	Parking $4 (admission free)
Fares	Adults $1.75; children 6-15, 95 cents. Similar prices for other attractions.

Schedule	Daily except Christmas, 9 a.m.-5 p.m.
Special events	Palm Sunday weekend, Mother's Day weekend, Columbus Day weekend
Mailing address	P. O. Box 638, Yermo, CA 92398
Phone	(619) 254-2252

CALICO & ODESSA RAILROAD

Calico Ghost Town is a mining camp that was once the largest silver producer in southern California. It has been restored by the San Bernardino County Parks Department. The grounds are paved, but access may be difficult for the handicapped.

The Calico & Odessa Railroad has a mile of 30"-gauge track; the train ride takes about 8 minutes. Yermo is on I-15 about 10 miles east of Barstow. Food and lodging can be found in Barstow.

Locomotives	1 steam
Cars	Coaches, open excursion car
Displays	HO scale model railroad
Schedule	Memorial Day weekend-Labor Day weekend, Saturdays, Sundays, Memorial Day, and Labor Day, leave Yreka 10 a.m.; June 20-Labor Day, Monday-Friday, leave Yreka 9:30 a.m. Charter trips available.
Fares	Adults, $9, children under 12 $4.50. Checks and credit cards accepted.
Radio frequency	161.070
Special events	Murder on the Blue Goose (late July); Wild

	Goose Chase (runners race the train from Yreka to Montague)
Nearby attractions	Siskiyou County Museum, Klamath National Forest Museum, Marble Mountain Wilderness Area, Mount Shasta
Mailing address	P. O. Box 660, Yreka, CA 96097
Phone	(916) 842-4146

STEAM LOCOMOTIVE

Number	Type	Former owner	Builder	Date
19	2-8-2	Choctow River Lumber Co.	Baldwin	1915

YREKA WESTERN RAILROAD

The city of Yreka and the Yreka Western Railroad cooperate in running the "Blue Goose" excursion train, named for YW's emblem. The train runs from a station at 300 East Miner Street, just east of the I-5 interchange, to Montague, 8 miles east, where the YW connects with Southern Pacific. The round trip takes 3 hours. Yreka is on I-5, 20 miles south of the Oregon border. There are motels and restaurants within walking distance of the station.

CUMBRES & TOLTEC SCENIC RAILROAD

Please see the listing for Chama, New Mexico.

Cars	Open cars
Schedule	April-October. Departures, rain or shine, 8 a.m.-8 p.m.
Dates open	March-November, 8 a.m.-8 p.m. Shorter hours for train and museum during off season.
Fares	Adults $3.95, children 5-11 $2.50
Admission	Adults $2, children 5-11 $1. Credit cards accepted. Group discounts available.
Nearby attractions	Rafting, horseback riding, Buckskin Joe (old Western town)
Mailing address	P. O. Box 8, Canon City, CO 81215
Phone	(719) 275-5485

ROYAL GORGE SCENIC RAILWAY AND MUSEUM

Established in 1959, this 15"-gauge railway operates from a depot 1 mile off Highway 50 on Royal Gorge Road, 8 miles west of Canon City, Colorado. The train of open cars runs 1½ miles to the rim of Royal Gorge Canyon at Point Alta Vista, then returns. Royal Gorge Bridge, 1053 feet above the Arkansas River, is the world's highest suspension bridge. Narration is provided during the 30-minute round trip.

Also on the grounds is the Steam Train and Antique Car Museum, which features 3" scale working steam engines (including an 18,000-pound Mallet) and a diesel switcher. Other displays include 22 steam whistles and mint-condition antique and classic automobiles.

The grounds are accessible to handicapped or people with baby strollers, and free parking is available for cars, campers, and buses. Children must be accompanied by adults; pets are allowed aboard the train. Restaurants and lodging can be found in Canon City.

Locomotives	4 steam (one 0-4-0, two 0-4-4-0s, and one 0-4-0+0-4-0)
Cars	Open excursion cars
Schedule	Daily, Memorial Day weekend through first weekend in October. Departures every 45 minutes, 10 a.m.-5 p.m.
Fares	Adults $5.25, children under 13 $3. Group discounts available. Checks accepted.
Nearby attractions	Palace Hotel with dinner and vaudeville show, Imperial Hotel with dinner and Victorian melodrama, Homestead Parlor House
Mailing address	P. O. Box 459, Cripple Creek, CO 80813
Phone	(719) 689-2640

CRIPPLE CREEK & VICTOR NARROW GAUGE RAILROAD

The Cripple Creek & Victor is located in Cripple Creek, Colorado, a former gold mining town. The 2'-gauge steam-powered train departs every 45 minutes from Cripple Creek Museum — the old Midland Terminal Depot — at 5th and Bennett Avenue and carries passengers south out of Cripple Creek past the old Midland Terminal wye, over a reconstructed trestle, and past historic mines, including the deserted mining camp of Anaconda. Stops are made during the 4-mile, 45-minute round trip for interesting scenery and an echo valley.

Restaurants and lodging are available in Cripple Creek or Colorado Springs, 40 miles to the east. Visitors should dress appropriately for Colorado's mountain weather.

Cripple Creek

Dates open	Daily except New Year's Day, Thanksgiving, and Christmas; Monday-Saturday 9 a.m.-5 p.m. May-October, 10-5 rest of year; Sunday 11-5
Admission	Adults $4, age 62 and over $3.50, children 12-18 $2, 5-11 $1. Group discounts available. Reservations are required for groups.
Nearby attractions	Children's Museum, Larimer Square (shopping), Union Station
Mailing address	1416 Platte Street, Denver, CO 80202
Phone	(303) 433-3643

FORNEY TRANSPORTATION MUSEUM

The Forney Transportation Museum was established in 1961 and is housed in the former Denver Tramway Power House, east of Interstate 25 between exits 211 (West 23rd Avenue and Water Street) and 212C (West 32nd Avenue). The museum displays more than 400 transportation items.

Among the highlights of the collection are steam locomotives (including Union Pacific Big Boy No. 4005), business cars, cabooses, a dining car, four railroad paintings by Denver artist Don Milgrim, and one-of-a-kind automobiles.

The locomotives are outside the museum. While the Forney Transportation Museum is accessible to handicapped or people with baby strollers, there are stairs, and quite a bit of walking is involved. There are motels within a mile and restaurants within half a mile.

Locomotives	Diesels
Cars	Ex-Canadian National "Tempo" coaches, parlor cars, and cafe-lounge cars
Schedule	Saturdays in December, Saturdays and Sunday January through mid-April, plus extra trips during the holidays: leave Denver Union Station 7:30 a.m., leave Winter Park 4:15 p.m. Charter trips available.
Fares	Adults $25 coach, $40 first class. Children 2 and under free. Reservations are required. Checks and credit cards accepted. Tickets are also available at Ticketmaster outlets in Colorado. Group discounts available.
Mailing address	555 17th Street, Suite 2400, Denver, CO 80202
Phone	(303) 296-4754

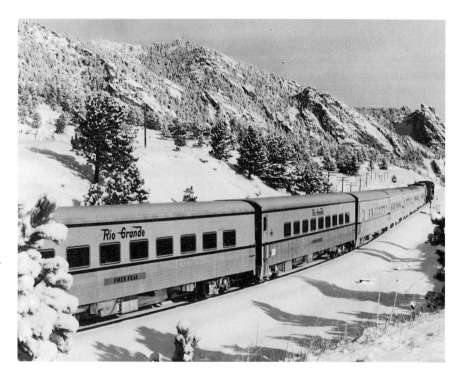

BUDWEISER SKI TRAIN

The Budweiser Ski Train, successor to the Rio Grande Ski Train, operates from Denver to Winter Park. The ski slopes and lifts at Winter Park are right at trainside. The 2-hour, 57-mile train ride climbs the Front Range of the Rockies, one of the most scenic stretches of railroad in North America, then travels through the 6.2-mile Moffat Tunnel. Restaurants and hotels can be found within walking distance of the stations in Denver and Winter Park.

Cars	Open trolley car
Schedule	Through October, every half hour 11 a.m.-5 p.m.; October, Saturdays, Sundays, and holidays; daily June-August, weather permitting. Charter trips available
Fares	Adults $2, children and seniors $1. Group discount available.
Memberships	$15 per year
Nearby attractions	Forney Transportation Museum, Children's Museum, Larimer Square (shopping), Union Station, Mile High Stadium
Mailing address	Denver Rail Heritage Society, 2785 North Speer Boulevard, Suite 220, Denver CO 80211
Phone	(303) 458-6255

PLATTE VALLEY TROLLEY

The Denver Rail Heritage Society operates a replica of an old-time open streetcar along 1¼ miles of track on the west bank of the Platte River. Car stops are located at 15th Street and the Platte River, under Speer Boulevard at Confluence Park behind the Forney Transportation Museum, the Children's Museum, and Old West Colfax Avenue near the Sports Complex. Take Exit 211 from I-25, and go north two blocks on Water Street. The car was built in 1986 by the GOMACO Trolley Company of Ida Grove, Iowa. Pending the erection of overhead trolley wire it is powered by a diesel generator set furnishing current to the traction motors. The Rocky Mountain Railroad Club is restoring Denver & Inter-mountain car 25 for service on the line. Special trips west toward Lakewood are planned for during the summer of 1990. There are restaurants adjacent to the north terminal of the line.

50-COLORADO   **Denver**

Locomotives	6 steam
Cars	Coaches, roofed gondola-type cars, snack car, parlor car; private cars available for charter.
Schedule	May 5-October 28, 1990. One to four trains daily, leaving Durango 7:30, 8:30, 9:30, and 10:15 a.m., getting back to Durango at 4, 5:15, 6:15, and 6:55 p.m. Reservations required. Charter trips and private cars are available.
Fares	Silverton: adults $37.15; children 5-11 $18.65 (under 5 free if not occupying seat); parlor car $63.85. Checks accepted; bank-guarantee card required if paying at the station. Parking at Durango: cars $5, RVs $7.
Nearby attractions	Mesa Verde National Park
Mailing address	479 Main Avenue, Durango, CO 81301
Phone	(303) 247-2733

LOCOMOTIVES

Number	Type	Former owner	Builder	Date
Steam				
473, 476, 478	2-8-2	Denver & Rio Grande Western	Alco	1923
480, 481	2-8-2	Denver & Rio Grande Western	Baldwin	1925
497	2-8-2	Denver & Rio Grande Western	Baldwin	1902

DURANGO & SILVERTON NARROW GAUGE RAILROAD

The longest-lived portion of the Denver & Rio Grande Western's network of narrow gauge track was a 45-mile line from Durango to Silverton, Colorado. By the early 1950s train service on that line consisted of a mixed freight and passenger train that operated once a week. Then tourists discovered the Silverton train. In the mid-1950s weekend operation began, and by 1964 business had increased to the point that the railroad had to schedule two trains each day and build new passenger cars. In 1968 the Rio Grande abandoned its narrow gauge line from Antonito, Colo., through Durango to Farmington, New Mexico, isolating the Durango-Silverton line.

Charles Bradshaw began negotiations to purchase the Durango-Silverton line in 1979; the sale was completed in 1981 and the oper-

ation was named the Durango & Silverton Narrow Gauge Railroad. The DSNGRR has added locomotives and cars to its roster, and at the height of the summer season Durango now sees four daily train departures.

About one-third of the trip is through a broad portion of the valley of the Animas River. At Rockwood the valley narrows to a canyon which the railroad follows, sometimes high above the river and sometimes at water level. The canyon widens just south of the former mining town of Silverton. A layover of 2¼ hours provides ample time to visit the cafes and shops of Silverton before reboarding the train to return to Durango. Overnight layovers are possible in Silverton; trips may begin and end there by using an early-morning bus to Durango.

Car	1 streetcar
Schedule	Noon to 6 p.m. weekends and holidays, mid-April through October, weather permitting. Charter trips available.
Fares	Adults $1, children (through age 12) 50 cents, age 60 and over 75 cents
Memberships	Memberships available in Fort Collins Municipal Railway Society.
Nearby attractions	Rocky Mountain National Park
Mailing address	P. O. Box 635, Fort Collins, CO 80522
Phone	(303) 224-5372

FORT COLLINS MUNICIPAL RAILWAY

Trolleys began operating in Fort Collins in 1907. When service ceased in 1951, the cars were the last Birney cars in scheduled service in North America. The Fort Collins Municipal Railway Society was formed to restore a portion of this streetcar system. Volunteers rebuilt almost every piece of wood, glass, and light metal on single-truck Birney car No 21. The car runs on a restored route along West Mountain Avenue from City Park to the edge of the business district. The 3-mile round trip takes 20 to 25 minutes. Restaurants and lodging are available in Fort Collins, approximately 65 miles north of Denver.

Cars	Open excursion cars	
Schedule	Daily, rain or shine, Memorial Day weekend through Labor Day weekend. Leave Silver Plume 10:20 a.m., 11:40, 1 p.m., 2:20, and 3:40. Leave Georgetown 11 a.m., 12:20 p.m., 1:40, and 3. Charter trips available.	
Fares	Adults $9.50 (plus $3 for the optional mine tour). Children 4-15 $5 (plus $1.50 for mine tour); under 4 free. Group discounts available. Credit cards and checks accepted.	
Nearby attractions	Loveland Pass, Central City	
Mailing address	P. O. Box 217, Georgetown, CO 80444	
Phone	(303) 569-2403 (in season), (303) 279-6101 (Denver — recorded information), (303) 670-1686 (Denver — reservations year-round)	

LOCOMOTIVES

Number	Type	Former owner	Builder	Date
STEAM				
8	3-truck Shay	West Side Lumber Co.	Lima	1922
12	3-truck Shay	West Side Lumber Co.	Lima	1926
14	3-truck Shay	West Side Lumber Co.	Lima	1916
40	2-8-0	Int'l Rys of Central America	Baldwin	1920
44	2-8-0	Int'l Rys of Central America	Baldwin	1921
DIESEL				
15	47 ton	Oahu Ry & Land Co.	GE	1943

GEORGETOWN LOOP RAILROAD

The Georgetown Loop was opened in 1884 as part of the Colorado Central (later Colorado & Southern) narrow gauge line from Denver and Golden to Silver Plume. The railroad was abandoned in 1939. A 3-mile portion of the railroad including the loop and 100-foot-high Devil's Gate Bridge was reconstructed in the mid-1970s. The 6-mile round trip takes 70 minutes.

Trips start at either Georgetown or Silver Plume, Colorado, approximately 50 miles west of Denver on Interstate 70; take exit 226 for Silver Plume or 228 for Georgetown. Parking for buses, RVs, and campers is at Silver Plume, as is the gift shop. The Georgetown Loop Railroad is operated by West/Rail under concession within the Georgetown Loop Historic Mining & Railroad Park, administered by the Colorado Historical Society.

Reservations are suggested for the optional 80-minute guided walking tour of the Lebanon Silver Mine (jackets are recommended). The mine tour is not available on the 3:40 trip from Silver Plume and the 3 o'clock trip from Georgetown. Restaurants and lodging are available in Georgetown.

Dates open	Daily except New Year's Day, Thanksgiving, and Christmas, 9 a.m. to 5 p.m. (to 6 p.m. in June, July, and August)
Admission	Adults $3. Children under 16 $1.50. Family ticket for parents and children under 16 $6.50. Group discounts available. Credit cards and checks accepted.
Memberships	Colorado Railroad Historical Foundation — write for information.
Special events	Six three-day weekends of narrow gauge steam runs; Santa Claus train first weekend in December
Nearby attractions	Buffalo Bill's grave and museum, Coors Brewery, School of Mines Geological Museum
Mailing address	P. O. Box 10, Golden, CO 80402
Phone	(303) 279-4591

LOCOMOTIVES

Number	Type	Former owner	Builder	Date
STEAM				
346	2-8-0	Denver & Rio Grande	Baldwin	1881
DIESEL				
3	0-4-0	U. S. Gypsum	Plymouth	1948
GALLOPING GOOSE				
2		Rio Grande Southern	RGS	1931
6		Rio Grande Southern	RGS	1934
7		Rio Grande Southern	RGS	1936

COLORADO RAILROAD MUSEUM

The Colorado Railroad Museum is the largest railroad museum in the Rocky Mountains. It is housed in an 1880-style masonry depot at 17155 West 44th Avenue, Golden, at the foot of Table Mountain, 12 miles west of downtown Denver.

Inside the museum are displays of rare old papers, photos, and artifacts relating to railroads that served Colorado and adjoining states. Outside, throughout the 12-acre grounds, are narrow gauge and standard gauge locomotives, cars, trolleys, and other railroadiana from the 1870s to the present. Included are Denver & Rio Grande Western 2-8-0 No. 346, Burlington 4-8-4 No. 5632 and business car 96, Colorado Midland observation car 111, Santa Fe observation car *Navajo*, Fort Collins streetcar No. 22, and three Rio Grande Southern "Galloping Goose" motor cars.

Trains operate six weekends a year, led by No. 346, Colorado's oldest operating narrow gauge steam locomotive. The Galloping Geese are used on some of these trips. The trains make a 1-mile, 20-minute round trip through the museum's grounds.

The Denver HO Model Railroad Club meets Thursday evenings in the museum's basement, with an operating session the first Thursday of every month; the public is welcome to attend at no charge.

Locomotives	5 steam, 1 diesel
Cars	Open excursion cars
Schedule	Daily, except when raining, Memorial Day to Labor Day. Good-weather weekends in April, May, September, and October. Charter trips available.
Fares	Adults $2.50. Senior citizens age 65 and up and children 5-12 $1.50 (under 5 free). Checks accepted. Group discounts available.
Special events	July 4 celebration
Nearby attractions	Colorado Railroad Museum, Forney Transportation Museum
Mailing address	1540 Routt Street, Lakewood, CO 80215
Phone	(303) 232-9262

LOCOMOTIVES

Number	Type	Builder	Date
STEAM			
1	0-4-0T	Orenstein & Koppel	1901
3	0-4-0T	Hannover	1923
6	2-truck Shay	Lima	1920
8	0-8-0T	Hartmann	1918
9	0-4-0T	Henschel	1939
DIESEL			
4	0-4-0	Plymouth	1934

HIGH COUNTRY RAILROAD

Established in 1972, the High Country Railroad operates from Heritage Square on U. S. Highway 40 in Golden, 1½ miles west of the junction with U. S. 6. Heritage Square is a 160-acre amusement park and artisans' shopping center.

The 2'-gauge High Country Railroad makes a 2-mile, 15-minute loop around Heritage Square, offering views of Golden and Denver.

Heritage Square has paved grounds, and is accessible to handicapped or people with baby strollers. There are several restaurants in Heritage Square; lodging is available nearby in Golden and Denver.

Golden

Cars	8 open cars
Displays	Colorado & Southern 2-8-0 No. 641, built by Brooks in 1906
Schedule	June-September, daily at 9:30 a.m. and 2 p.m.
Fares	Adults $16.50, children 3-12 $9.75. Credit cards and checks accepted. Group discounts available.
Nearby attractions	Matchless Mine, 1893 fish hatchery, mining and historical districts
Mailing address	P. O. Box 916, Leadville, CO 80461
Phone	(719) 486-3936

DIESEL LOCOMOTIVES

Number	Type	Former owner	Builder	Date
1714	GP9	Burlington Northern	EMD	1955
1918	GP9	Burlington Northern	EMD	1957

LEADVILLE, COLORADO & SOUTHERN RAILROAD

The Leadville, Colorado & Southern operates on 11½ miles of former Colorado & Southern track between Leadville and Climax, Colorado. The route was part of the narrow gauge Denver, South Park & Pacific. In 1937 it was orphaned when the rest of the Denver-Leadville line, by then part of the Colorado & Southern, was abandoned.

The Leadville-Climax line was converted to standard gauge in 1941, and it was operated by steam locomotives until 1962. The last steam locomotive used on the line is on display at the station in Leadville.

The line is the highest in the U. S., climbing to 11,120 feet on a 2 percent grade. There are numerous sharp curves. The station is at 326 East 7th Street in Leadville. Food and lodging are available within a block.

Locomotives	8 diesel-powered passenger cars
Displays	Steam locomotive No. 5 at Manitou station
Schedule	Daily, May through October. June-August, eight departures from 8 a.m. to 5:20 p.m. May, September, and October, departures at 9:20 a.m. and 1:20 p.m. Reservations are necessary; they can be made directly or through most motels in the area.
Fares	Adults $17, children 5-11 $8 (under 5 free if held on lap). Group discounts available.
Radio frequency	161.550
Special events	Occasional steam-up of locomotive No. 4
Nearby attractions	Cheyenne Mountain Zoo, Will Rogers shrine
Mailing address	P. O. Box 1329, Colorado Springs, CO 80901
Phone	(303) 685-5401, (303) 685-1045 (off-season)

LOCOMOTIVES

Number	Type	Builder	Date
STEAM			
4	Vauclain compound	Baldwin	1897
DIESEL CARS			
14-17	Single-unit	Swiss Locomotive Works	1963-1968
18, 19, 24, 25	Twin-unit	Swiss Locomotive Works	1976-1989

P &. 🎁 ▪️

MANITOU & PIKE'S PEAK RAILWAY

The Manitou & Pike's Peak Railway was incorporated in 1888, with financial backing from Zalmon Simmons, of Simmons mattress fame. Operations began June 30, 1891. It is the highest cog railway in the world, and one of only two in North America. The track is standard gauge (4'8½").

The Swiss-built trains leave from the depot at 535 Ruxton Avenue, Manitou Springs, Colorado, 6 miles west of Colorado Springs, off Highway 24. During the 18-mile round trip the train travels to the summit of Pike's Peak, 14,110 feet above sea level. Here the train makes a sightseeing stop; a gift shop, information desk, and concession counter are located in the Summit House. The round trip takes about 3¼ hours. Because of the thin air at the summit, people with severe cardiac or respiratory problems are advised against riding this train. Minors must be accompanied by an adult. Trains may be canceled in inclement weather, and warm clothing is recommended at all times.

The Manitou & Pike's Peak is accessible to handicapped or people with baby strollers. Staff is on the premises year-round, and restaurants and lodging are available in Manitou Springs and Colorado Springs.

Locomotives	2 diesels
Cars	Ex-Reading/SEPTA coaches
Schedule	Not set at press time. Charter trips available.
Fares	Not set at press time. Group discounts are available. Checks accepted.
Special events	Canaan Railroad Days, end of July and beginning of August
Nearby attractions	Mount Riga State Park, other state parks and state forests, Tanglewood (home of the Berkshire Music Festival)
Mailing address	P. O. Box 1146, Canaan, CT 06018
Phone	(203) 824-0339; 824-0850 year-round

HOUSATONIC RAIL ROAD COMPANY

The Housatonic Rail Road, established in 1983, operates excursion trains over 16 miles of the former Berkshire line of the New Haven Railroad along the Housatonic River between Canaan and Cornwall Bridge, Connecticut. The round trip takes a little over 3 hours. The last regular passenger trains on the route, weekend-only New York-Pittsfield, Massachusetts, trains, were discontinued when Amtrak took over the nation's passenger trains in 1971.

Passengers ride in former Reading Company coaches purchased from Southeastern Pennsylvania Transportation Authority; up front is either a GP9 or an RS-3m, both former Conrail locomotives. Trains operate from the Canaan Union Station on U. S. 44 in the center of Canaan.

Schedules and fares for the 1990 season had not been established by press time, but it was anticipated that trains would operate from July 1 to November 1. Canaan is in the northwest corner of Connecticut on U. S. Routes 7 and 44. There are restaurants in Canaan; lodging is available in Great Barrington, Mass., 12 miles from Canaan.

	Displays	Over 95 streetcars and interurbans, including 3 open cars
	Dates open	Sundays April-November, plus Saturdays and holidays May-October, plus weekdays Memorial Day-Labor Day, also weekends November 24-December 16, 1990: 11 a.m.-5 p.m. Trolleys operate at least every 30 minutes. Charter trips are available.
	Fares	Adults $4, children 2-11 $2 (under 2 free), 62 and over $3. Group discounts available.
	Memberships	Branford Electric Railway Association
	Special events	New York Transit Days, Workin' on the Railroad Days, Old-Time Music Days, Oktoberfest, Halloween, Santa Days
	Nearby attractions	Valley Railroad, Connecticut Trolley Museum, Fort Nathan Hale, Yale University, Peabody Museum, Mystic Seaport
	Mailing address	17 River Street, East Haven, CT 06512
	Phone	(203) 467-6927

CARS

Number	Type	Original owner or city	Builder	Date
193	Suburban	Connecticut Company	Jewett	1904
356, 357	Lightweight	Johnstown Traction	St. Louis	1926
629	Lightweight	Third Avenue Railway	Third Avenue Ry	1939
1414	Open	Connecticut Company	Osgood Bradley	1911
2001	Lightweight	Montreal Tramways	CC&F	1929
4573	Convertible	Brooklyn Rapid Transit	Laconia	1906

SHORE LINE TROLLEY MUSEUM

The Branford Electric Railway Association was incorporated in 1945 to preserve and operate trolley cars, which were fast disappearing from the American scene. The association purchased a short piece of track in East Haven and Branford, Connecticut, and its first cars moved onto the property from New Haven in March 1947. The museum was opened to the public in 1953, and in 1959 it was given the Sprague Memorial Visitors Center by the family of Frank Julian Sprague, a native of nearby Milford who was considered the father of electric transportation. The museum was placed on the National Register of Historic Places in 1983. Trolleys operate over 1½ miles of track from East Haven to Short Beach through woodlands and salt marshes and over two major trestles. The round trip, which includes a guided tour of the carbarn, takes about 55 minutes. The museum can be reached from Exit 52 of the Connecticut Turnpike or from U. S. 1. Restaurants and lodging can be found in East Haven, Branford, and New Haven, 4 miles west.

East Haven

Locomotives	3 diesel (ex-New Haven RS3, U25B, and FA1)
Displays	Approximately 50 locomotives and cars
Dates open	Weekends May-December
Admission	Free (special fare on Railfan Day); donations appreciated
Memberships	Regular, $25 per year
Special events	Railfan Day, Members' Day
Nearby attractions	Shore Line Trolley Museum, Mystic Seaport, Mystic Aquarium, Connecticut River Foundation at Steamboat Dock, New London Submarine Museum, Gillette Castle State Park, Ocean Beach
Mailing address	P. O. Box 97, Essex, CT 06426
Phone	(203) 767-0494

RAILROAD MUSEUM OF NEW ENGLAND

The Railroad Museum of New England (formerly the Connecticut Valley Railroad Museum) is a nonprofit organization that currently shares facilities with the Valley Railroad at Essex but is moving to a new site in Willimantic. The museum, which concentrates on the presentation and display of equipment and artifacts, has a large collection of locomotives and cars from New England's railroads. It is open most weekends May through December.

Essex is approximately 30 miles east of New Haven and 40 miles southeast of Hartford on state highways 9 and 153, 4 miles north of the Connecticut Turnpike (I-95).

Food and lodging are available in Essex and Old Saybrook; lodging is also available in Ivoryton. The grounds are not paved, but they are accessible to the handicapped and people pushing baby strollers.

Locomotives	3 steam, 1 diesel	**Special events**	Murder Mystery Train (May 19 and September 22, 1990; reservations required), Halloween Ghost Train (October 26, 1990), Jazz Festival, Christmas trains	
Cars	Ex-Lackawanna, Central of New Jersey, and New Haven heavyweight coaches and parlor car			
Displays	The collection of the Railroad Museum of New England is on display at Essex.	**Nearby attractions**	Shore Line Trolley Museum, Mystic Seaport, Mystic Aquarium, Connecticut River Foundation at Steamboat Dock, New London Submarine Museum, Gillette Castle State Park, Ocean Beach	
Schedule	May-December, weekends and holidays at 11:15 a.m. and 1:15, 2:45, and 4:15 p.m., with earlier and later trains and weekday operation added for different parts of the season — write or call for detailed information. Boat cruises operate May-October.	**Mailing address**	P. O. Box 452, Essex, CT 06426	
		Phone	(203) 767-0103	
Fares	Train and boat: adults $12.95, children 2-11 $5.95 (under 2 free); train only: adults $7.95, children 2-11 $3.95; extra fare for parlor car, $2.95. Age 65 and over 10 percent discount. Checks accepted. Group discounts available. Charter trips available.			

LOCOMOTIVES

Number	Type	Former owner	Builder	Date
STEAM				
40	2-8-2	Aberdeen & Rockfish	Alco (Brooks)	1920
97	2-8-2	Birmingham & Southeastern	Alco (Cooke)	1924
1647	2-8-2	Purchased new	Tang-Shan	1989
DIESEL				
0800	44-ton	Long Island	General Electric	1950

VALLEY RAILROAD

In 1968 the New Haven abandoned the southern portion of its rural branch along the Connecticut River from Hartford to Old Saybrook, Conn. The Valley Railroad was chartered, and the state purchased the track from Penn Central in 1969. Excursion trains began operating between Essex and Deep River, 2½ miles, on July 29, 1971. In 1973 service was extended up the river to Chester, 3½ miles from Essex.

Valley Railroad trains consist of well-restored, well-maintained coaches and a parlor car pulled by a steam locomotive, re-creating the atmosphere of a 1920s branchline railroad. The locomotive roster includes a 2-8-2 built in 1989 by the Tang-Shan works in China. The excursion trains connect with boat cruises at Deep River. The train ride takes 55 minutes; the train-and-boat combination takes 2 hours and 10 minutes.

Essex is approximately 30 miles east of New Haven and 40 miles southeast of Hartford on state highways 9 and 153, 4 miles north of the Connecticut Turnpike (I-95). Food and lodging are available in Essex and Old Saybrook; lodging is also available in Ivoryton. The grounds are not paved, but they are accessible to the handicapped and people pushing baby strollers.

Cars	6 streetcars
Displays	42 streetcars, rapid transit cars, and electric locomotives, including the first locomotive built by General Electric
Dates open	Memorial Day-Labor Day, Monday-Friday 10 a.m.-4 p.m., Saturday 10 a.m.-6 p.m., Sundays noon-6; weekends noon-5 the rest of the year
Fares	Adults $4, children 5-15 $2, 62 and older $3. Checks accepted. Group discounts are available; reservations are needed for charter trips.
Memberships	Connecticut Electric Railway Association
Special events	Rails to the Darkside, October 26-31, 1990, evenings 6:30-9:30 (weekdays) or 6:30-11 (weekends); Winterfest — the right of way is decorated with lights, and cars operate evenings November 23, 1990-January 1: Sunday-Thursday 6-9, Fridays and Saturday 6-10:30
Nearby attractions	New England Air Museum, Old Newgate Prison, Basketball Hall of Fame, Mark Twain House
Mailing address	P. O. Box 360, East Windsor, CT 06088
Phone	(800) 223-6540 in Connecticut, (800) 252-2372 elsewhere, (203) 627-6540 year-round

CARS

Number	Type	Original owner or city	Builder	Date
4	Observation trolley	Montreal Tramways	Montreal Tramways	1924
451	Interurban PCC	Illinois Terminal	St. Louis Car	1949
836	Steel closed car	New Orleans Public Service	Perley Thomas	1922
840	Open car	Connecticut Company	J. M. Jones	1905
1326	Wood closed car	Connecticut Company	Osgood Bradley	1910
2600	Steel closed car	Montreal Tramways	Canadian Car	1929

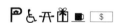

CONNECTICUT TROLLEY MUSEUM

The Connecticut Trolley Museum, operated by the Connecticut Electric Railway Association, Inc., was established in 1940. The first trolley museum in the U. S. to own property, it is located on Connecticut Route 140 (North Road) in the Warehouse Point section of East Windsor half a mile east of Exit 45 of I-91. The museum operates streetcars and interurbans on 1½ miles of former Hartford & Springfield Railway track. In addition, a 1910-vintage Climax geared locomotive is steamed up and run occasionally. On the grounds of the Connecticut Trolley Museum is the Connecticut Fire Museum.

Restaurants and motels can be found nearby and in Hartford and Springfield, Massachusetts, each about 12 miles from the museum.

Locomotives	3 steam, 2 diesel, 1 diesel railcar
Cars	Ex-Lackawanna coaches
Schedule	Sundays, May-October, 12:30, 2, and 3:30 p.m. to Mt. Cuba; last Sunday of the month, noon and 2:30 to Hockessin. Reservations required for special events, caboose rentals, and charters.
Fares	Mt. Cuba, adults $5, children 2-12 $3 (under 2 free); Hockessin, $10/$5. Checks and credit cards accepted. Group discounts available.
Memberships	Historic Red Clay Valley, Inc.
Special events	Theme or reduced fare on most Sundays — mothers ride free on Mother's Day, fathers on Father's Day, and so forth. Spring Steam Specials end of April; Autumn Leaf and Santa Claus Specials.
Nearby attractions	Longwood Gardens, Winterthur, Hagley Museum, Historic New Castle, Brandywine River Museum, Delaware Museum of National History, Ashland Nature Center
Mailing address	c/o Historic Red Clay Valley, Inc., P. O. Box 5787, Wilmington, DE 19808
Phone	(302) 998-7032 Sundays when railroad operates; (302) 998-1930 year-round

WILMINGTON & WESTERN RAILROAD

The Wilmington & Western operates excursion trains over 10 miles of track between Marshallton and Hockessin, Delaware. The line's history goes back to a previous Wilmington & Western Railroad chartered in 1867 and completed in 1872 from Wilmington along Red Clay Creek to Landenberg, Pennsylvania. The road was soon in financial difficulty, and in 1883 it was absorbed by the Baltimore & Ohio, which was building a line from Baltimore to Philadelphia. By the 1960s the line had been cut back to Hockessin and saw a local freight train three days a week. In 1959 a group of men formed Historic Red Clay Valley, Inc., purchased a Canadian National steam locomotive and some coaches, and reached agreement with B&O to allow operation of steam-powered excursion trains on the branch. Operation began in 1966. In 1982 HRCV purchased the line and in 1984 formed the Wilmington & Western Railway to operate freight service. Trains operate from Greenbank station, northwest of the intersection of State Routes 2 and 41, about 5 miles west of downtown Wilmington. Trains normally make a 1-hour round trip to the Mt. Cuba Picnic Grove, 5 miles each way; on special occasions trains operate to Hockessin, 10 miles from Greenbank. The Greenbank station area includes a gift shop, snack bar, and picnic area. The grounds are not paved, but arrangements can be made to accommodate handicapped persons. There are restaurants nearby on Highway 2; lodging is available in and around Wilmington.

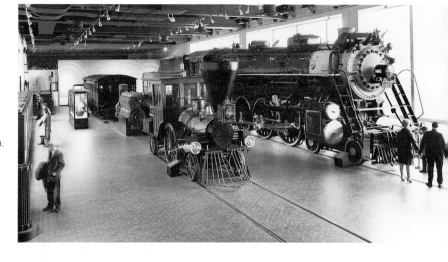

Dates open	Daily except Christmas, 10 a.m.-5:30 p.m.
Admission	Free
Memberships	National Associates program, telephone (202) 357-2700
Nearby attractions	All of Washington
Mailing address	Washington, DC 20560
Phone	(202) 357-2700

SMITHSONIAN INSTITUTION

The Smithsonian's Railroad Hall is located in the National Museum of American History on the National Mall. Exhibits depict the history of American railroad locomotives, freight cars, passenger cars, and transit vehicles primarily through large scale models.

There are full-size exhibits, too, dominated by Southern Railway Ps4 No. 1401, a 4-6-2. Other locomotives on display include the Cumberland Valley 2-2-2 *Pioneer* (1851) and Hawaiian 0-4-2T plantation engine *Olomana* (1883). The boiler and remaining parts of the *Stourbridge Lion*, North America's first locomotive (1829), are displayed; nearby is Camden & Amboy coach No. 3, the oldest 8-wheel passenger car in existence (1836), and a diesel engine from the *Pioneer Zephyr* (1934). The *John Bull*, the oldest operable locomotive in the world (1831), is displayed adjacent to a permanent exhibition, "Engines of Change: the American Industrial Revolution." Within that exhibit a video of the *John Bull* tells the story of its steaming on its 150th birthday in 1981. The narrow gauge 4-4-0 *Jupiter* (1876) is on view in the "1876" exhibition in the Smithsonian's Arts & Industries Building.

The National Museum of American History is on Constitution Avenue between 12th and 14th Streets, not far from the Smithsonian station of the Washington Metrorail system (Blue and Orange Lines).

Dates open	Daily 9 a.m.-6 p.m.
Admission	Adults $18.50, children 3-11 $11.50 (under 3 free). Credit cards accepted. Group discounts available.
Nearby attractions	Bok Tower, Sea World, Walt Disney World
Mailing address	P. O. Box 1, Cypress Gardens, FL 33884
Phone	(813) 324-2111

P 🍴 ♿ 🎁 ☕

CYPRESS JUNCTION

One of the exhibits at Cypress Gardens, a 223-acre theme park off U. S. 27 near Winter Haven, is a large, fully scenicked HO scale model railroad, built and maintained by the Cypress Gardens Model Railroad Society. As many as 20 trains operate at once, and areas of the layout depict different cities and seasons. Restaurants and motels can be found in Winter Haven.

Locomotive	1 steam outline
Cars	Open excursion cars
Dates open	Daily 9 a.m.-5 p.m. Charter train trips available.
Admission	Adults $3, children 4-12 $1.25 (under 4 free), age 65 and over $1.25. There is a parking fee.
Fares	$1 per person
Mailing address	Jacksonville Zoological Society, 8605 Zoo Road, Jacksonville, FL 32218
Phone	(904) 757-4463

P ♿ 🚉 🎁 ☕

OKAVANGO RAILROAD

Circling the 60-acre grounds of the Jacksonville Zoo is the Okavango Railroad. The 1-mile ride takes 20 minutes. The locomotive is a brightly painted, old-time 4-2-4T, something like Southern Pacific's *C. P. Huntington*; passengers ride in open excursion cars. The zoo includes several special areas: Wetlands Discovery, African Adventure, and Birds of Prey Aviary. The zoo is east of I-95 and U. S. 17 in North Jacksonville at 8605 Zoo Road, between Heckscher Drive and the St. Johns River.

	[1988 information]
Locomotives	4 steam
Cars	Open excursion cars
Dates open	Daily from 9 a.m. into the evening
Admission	Adults $26, children 3-11 $19.50. Discount for 3-, 4-, and 5-day tickets.
Nearby attractions	Sea World, Ocala National Forest, John F. Kennedy Space Center, Whistlestop USA
Mailing address	P. O. Box 10,000, Lake Buena Vista, FL 32830-1000
Phone	(305) 824-4321

WALT DISNEY WORLD RAILROAD

The Walt Disney World Railroad offers a 15-minute, 1-mile ride around the Magic Kingdom of Walt Disney World — through Adventureland and Frontierland and past Fantasyland and Tomorrowland. Motive power for the 3'-gauge railroad is a quartet of steam locomotives, a 4-4-0, a 2-6-0, and two 4-6-0s, built by Baldwin for the United Railways of Yucatan. They were purchased in 1969, rebuilt extensively, and converted to burn diesel fuel (they had been oil-burners). Walt Disney World is about 20 miles southwest of Orlando at the junction of I-4 and U. S. 192. Food and lodging are available there.

Locomotives	1 steam, 3 diesel
Cars	Coaches (not air-conditioned)
Displays	Large collection of freight, passenger, and work cars
Dates open	Monday-Friday, 10 a.m.-3 p.m.; weekends and holidays except Thanksgiving and Christmas, 10-5; museum is open at night instead of during the day for a week at Halloween
Schedule	Trains run at 11 a.m. and 12:15, 1:30, 2:30, 3:30, and 4:30 p.m. Charter trips available.
Admission	Weekdays, adults $3, children 3-11 $2 (under 3 free), 60 and over $2.50. Weekends and holidays, adults $5, children $3, seniors $4. Group discounts available.
Memberships	Write for information.
Special events	Flagler Day, arts and crafts fair

Nearby attractions Everglades National Park, Biscayne National Park, MetroZoo, Villa Vizcaya, Miami Seaquarium, Coral Castle, Fairchild Tropical Gardens, Planet Ocean, Weeks Air Museum

Mailing address 12450 S. W. 152 Street, Miami, FL 33177-1402

Phone (305) 253-0063

LOCOMOTIVES

Number	Type	Former owner	Builder	Date
STEAM				
113	4-6-2	Florida East Coast	Alco	1913
DIESEL				
1	S-2	U. S. Army	Alco	1943
167	SW9	Atlantic Coast Line	EMD	1951
1555	RS-3	Long Island	Alco	1955

GOLD COAST RAILROAD MUSEUM

The Gold Coast Railroad was established in 1957 at its present site, but from 1961 to 1985 was located at Fort Lauderdale. It has recently returned to a site adjacent to MetroZoo on Coral Reef Drive (S. W. 152nd Street) just off the Homestead Extension of Florida's Turnpike.

The museum operates trains on 1 mile of track; the 25-minute ride is through pine and palmetto country. The prize exhibit is the Pullman car *Ferdinand Magellan,* which was rebuilt in 1942 for the use of President Franklin D. Roosevelt. Ownership of the car was transferred to the government in 1946. The car was subsequently used extensively by President Truman, very little by President Eisenhower, and on one occasion for campaign purposes by President Reagan. The car has been designated a National Historic Landmark.

The museum's roster of operating locomotives includes two Florida East Coast 4-6-2s, an Atlantic Coast Line SW9, and a Long Island RS3. Steam power is generally used only once a month, either the last weekend or for a special event. The extensive passenger car collection includes a baggage car and a dome observation car from the *California Zephyr*.

The museum grounds are paved and accessible to the handicapped and persons pushing baby strollers. Restaurants and lodging can be found in the nearest town, Cutler Ridge, as well as elsewhere in metropolitan Miami.

Displays	Private car *Rambler*
Dates open	Tuesday-Saturday 10 a.m.-5 p.m., Sunday noon-5, closed Mondays, Christmas, and New Year's Day. Guided tours are offered.
Special events	Open house, first Saturday in February
Admission	Adults $3.50, children 6-12 $1.25. Group discounts are available.
Nearby attractions	Zoo, art museum
Mailing address	P. O. Box 969, Palm Beach, FL 33480
Phone	(305) 655-2833

P & ⛩

HENRY MORRISON FLAGLER MUSEUM

Henry M. Flagler, builder of the Florida East Coast Railway, erected a mansion in Palm Beach for his third wife. The mansion, named Whitehall, was restored in 1960. It is primarily a museum of an opulent life style, but among the exhibits are Florida East Coast memorabilia and Flagler's private car Rambler. The museum is located on the east shore of Lake Worth on Cocoanut Row between the Flager Memorial Bridge (Route A1A) and Royal Palm Way (Route 704). Access for the handicapped is limited to the first floor; baby strollers are not permitted.

Displays	O gauge and standard gauge Lionel layouts
Dates open	Daily 9 a.m.-5 p.m.
Admission	Adults $2.50; children under 11, 50 cents. Checks accepted.Group discounts available. Shell exhibit free.
Memberships	Write for information.
Nearby attractions	Sarasota Jungle Gardens, Ringling Museum, Bellum's Cars and Music of Yesterday
Mailing address	8184 North Tamiami Trail, Sarasota, FL 34243
Phone	(813) 355-8184

P �ⓘ & 🎁

LIONEL TRAIN & SEASHELL MUSEUM

The Lionel Train & Seashell Museum has two Lionel layouts plus a large shelf display of Lionel trains. Standard gauge trains (toy-train "standard gauge" is 2⅛") from the 1920s and 1930s run on a layout measuring 27 x 37 feet. The 14 x 24-foot O gauge layout has mountain scenery and large bridges. A restored 1904-vintage open trolley car serves as the museum's theater. The museum shop sells and services Lionel trains. The museum is on U. S. 41, Tamiami Trail, across from the Sarasota/Bradenton Airport. Food is available as close as next door, and motels are located throughout the area.

Locomotives	2 steam, 5 diesel
Cars	Coaches, dining car
Schedule	Saturdays leave Atlanta 10 a.m., noon, and 2 for 18-mile circle. One Saturday a month trains operate instead to Stone Mountain, leaving Atlanta at 10 and 2. Dinner trains operate on the Atlanta loop Thursdays and to Stone Mountain Fridays and Saturdays — boarding at 7, departure at 7:30 p.m. Charter trips are operated.
Fares	Adults $10 (Atlanta loop) or $12.50 (Stone Mountain), children 2-12 $5 (under 2 free if not occupying a seat). Dinner train, $39.50 plus tax. Reservations are required for the dinner train. Checks and credit cards accepted. Group discounts available.
Nearby attractions	State capitol, Underground Atlanta
Mailing address	Georgia Building Authority, 1 Martin Luther King Jr. Drive S. W., Atlanta, GA 30334
Phone	(404) 656-0769

LOCOMOTIVES

Number	Type	Former owner	Builder	Date
STEAM				
290	4-6-2	Atlanta & West Point	Lima	1926
750	4-6-2	Savannah & Atlanta	Alco	1910
DIESEL				
1	65 ton	U. S. Army	GE	1943
3498, 3499	FP7	Southern	EMD	1950
6901	E8A	Southern	EMD	1951
6902	E8A	New York Central	EMD	1953

NEW GEORGIA RAILROAD

The New Georgia Railroad operates trains over two routes, an 18-mile loop around downtown Atlanta (1½ hours), and from Atlanta to Stone Mountain and return, about 15 miles each way (2½ hours for the daytime excursion; 3½ hours for the dinner train). Trains operate from the bottom floor of the parking deck at 90 Central Avenue, adjacent to Underground Atlanta and one block north of the state capitol. Free parking is available there.

Motive power is either ex-Southern E8 6901 or ex-Savannah & Atlanta 4-6-2 No. 750. Cars include coaches, a commissary car for snacks and souvenirs, and a dining car, all air conditioned. The New Georgia Railroad is operated by the Georgia Building Authority, a state agency, in cooperation with the Atlanta Chapter of the National Railway Historical Society, which owns the locomotives and some of the cars.

Locomotives	Savannah & Atlanta 4-6-2 No. 750, Atlanta & West Point 4-6-2 No. 290, and Southern E8 6901 (usually operating on the New Georgia Railroad in Atlanta)
Cars	2 coaches, baggage car
Displays	Numerous industrial locomotives, several cabooses, nearly two dozen passenger cars
Dates open	Saturdays except when Atlanta Chapter NRHS is operating excursion trains. Reservations required for guided tours, use of the museum library, and excursion trains.
Schedule	0-6-0T No. 97 operates third weekend of each month April-October
Admission	Free; donations appreciated
Fares	Train at museum: adults $2, children $1
Nearby attractions	Stone Mountain State Park, New Georgia Railroad, Six Flags, High Museum (art)
Mailing address	P. O. Box 13132, Atlanta, GA 30324 (Atlanta Chapter NRHS); 3966 Buford Highway, Duluth, GA 30136 (museum)
Phone	(404) 476-2013

STEAM LOCOMOTIVES

Number	Type	Former owner	Builder	Date
9	Heisler	Campbell Limestone	Heisler	1924
97	0-6-0T	U. S. Army/Georgia Power	Porter	1943

SOUTHEASTERN RAILWAY MUSEUM

The Atlanta Chapter of the National Railway Historical Society operates a museum on a 12-acre site at Duluth, Georgia, about 23 miles northeast of Atlanta. The museum is located at the intersection of U. S. 23 and Berkeley Lake Road; from Interstate 85, use Exit 40, Pleasant Hill Road, north to Duluth, and U. S. 23 south a quarter mile to the museum. Atlanta Chapter NRHS occasionally sponsors excursion trains in cooperation with Norfolk Southern. The trains are usually powered by one of Norfolk Southern's steam locomotives; equipment includes open-window and air-conditioned coaches, an open car, and a snack and souvenir car. Write for information on fares and schedules.

The chapter owns several serviceable steam locomotives and passenger cars, which are usually leased to excursion operators, such as the New Georgia Railroad (see previous entry).

Restaurants and lodging can be found in Duluth and nearby Norcross.

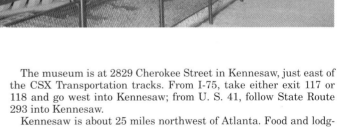

Displays	Western & Atlantic 4-4-0 *General*, Civil War memorabilia
Dates open	March-November, Monday-Saturday 9:30 a.m.-5:30 p.m., Sunday noon-5:30; December-February, every day, noon-5:30; closed New Year's Day, Easter, Thanksgiving, and Christmas
Admission	Adults $2.50, children 7-15 $1, age 65 and over $1.25. Group discounts available.
Special events	Big Shanty Festival in April
Nearby attractions	Kennesaw Mountain National Battlefield Park, Mauldin's Doll Museum
Mailing address	2829 Cherokee Street, Kennesaw, GA 30144
Phone	(404) 427-2117

BIG SHANTY MUSEUM

The story of James J. Andrews' raid is one of the best known of the Civil War. The locomotive the Union forces seized at Big Shanty (now Kennesaw), Georgia, Western & Atlantic's *General*, is the principal exhibit at the Big Shanty Museum, which opened April 12, 1972, 110 years after the Andrews Raid. Other exhibits tell the story of the raid.

The museum is at 2829 Cherokee Street in Kennesaw, just east of the CSX Transportation tracks. From I-75, take either exit 117 or 118 and go west into Kennesaw; from U. S. 41, follow State Route 293 into Kennesaw.

Kennesaw is about 25 miles northwest of Atlanta. Food and lodging can be found nearby as well as in Marietta, 9 miles away.

Cars	Coaches
Dates open	Every day 6 a.m.-midnight
Schedule	June-August, 10 a.m.-8 p.m.; other months, 10 a.m.-5:20 p.m.
Admission	Free; parking $5
Fares	Adults $2.50, children 11 and under $1.50. Credit cards ($15 minimum) and checks accepted. Group discounts available.
Nearby attractions	New Georgia Railroad, White Water
Mailing address	P. O. Box 778, Stone Mountain, GA 30086
Phone	(404) 498-5615, 498-5702 year-round, 498-5690 for recorded information

STEAM LOCOMOTIVES

Name	Type	Former owner	Builder	Date
General II	4-4-0	Red River & Gulf	Baldwin	1919
Texas II	4-4-0	San Antonio & Aransas Pass	Baldwin	1926
Yonah II	2-6-2	Echo Valley Park	Vulcan	1927

STONE MOUNTAIN SCENIC RAILROAD

Stone Mountain, about 15 miles east of Atlanta, is the world's largest exposed granite monolith. It rises 825 feet above the surrounding area. Carved in the north face of the mountain is a memorial to the Confederacy: the likenesses of Jefferson Davis, Robert E. Lee, and Stonewall Jackson.

The area surrounding the mountain is a park with all kinds of entertainment and attractions — museums, antebellum plantation, beach, skating rink, and the like. Circling the base of the mountain is the Stone Mountain Scenic Railroad, which offers a 5-mile, 30-minute ride behind steam locomotives. The park can be reached by taking U. S. Route 78, the Stone Mountain Freeway, east from I-285, or by taking MARTA bus route 120 from downtown Atlanta. Better than those, though, is the New Georgia Railroad, listed a few pages previously.

Food and lodging are available in the park; there are motels near the intersection of U. S. 78 and I-285.

Displays	2 steam locomotives, passenger cars, caboose
Dates open	Tuesday-Saturday 10 a.m.-5 p.m., Sundays 2-4. Closed Mondays, Thanksgiving, Christmas, and New Year's Day.
Admission	Adults $2, children 4-18 $1. Checks accepted. Group discounts available.
Special events	Forest Festival (April), Antique Show (April), Heritage Festival (October)
Nearby attractions	Okefenokee Swamp Park, Jekyll Island, Southern Forest World
Mailing address	Route 5, Box 406A, Waycross, GA 31501
Phone	(912) 285-4260

OKEFENOKEE HERITAGE CENTER

The Okefenokee Heritage Center traces the history of the region surrounding the Okefenokee Swamp in southeastern Georgia. Railroads are a part of that history, and more than half the objects in the collection are related to railroads. In addition to such artifacts as uniforms, tools, lanterns, furniture, and china, and a large variety of documents, there are a 2-8-2 built by Baldwin in 1912, a baggage car, a mail car, a coach, and a caboose.

The museum is 3 miles north of Waycross between U. S. 1 and State Route 50. There are restaurants and lodging in Waycross.

Locomotives	2 steam, 1 diesel
Cars	Open coaches
Displays	Locomotives and cars not in service are kept at Puukolii shops. Telephone the office to arrange a tour of the shops.
Schedule	Daily except Thanksgiving and Christmas. Trains leave Puukoli at 8:55 a.m., 10:15, 11:35, 1:10 p.m., 2:30, and 3:50; they stop at Kaanapali 15 minutes later. Trains leave Lahaina at 9:45, 11:05, 12:40, 2:00, 3:20, and 4:40.
Fares	Adults $9 round trip, children 12 and under $4.50 RT. Credit cards are accepted. Tickets may be purchased at stations, at tour and activities desks, or through travel agents.
Mailing address	P. O. Box 816, Lahaina, HI 96761
Phone	661-0089

LOCOMOTIVES

Number	Type	Former owner	Builder	Date
STEAM				
1	2-4-0	Carbon Limestone	H. K. Porter	1943
3	2-4-0	Carbon Limestone	H. K. Porter	1943
DIESEL				
45		Oahu Railway & Land	Plymouth	1959

LAHAINA KAANAPALI & PACIFIC RAILROAD

Hawaii was served by common-carrier railroads through the 1940s, but after World War Two the trains were replaced by highway transportation — cars and trucks. The last survivor, the Kahului Railroad along the north shore of the island of Maui, was abandoned in 1966, and its rails were used in the construction of the Lahaina Kaanapali & Pacific, which was opened in 1970. The 6-mile, 3-foot-gauge line joins the resort areas of Lahaina and Kaana-

pali; a round trip on the "Sugar Cane Train" takes 65 minutes.

The train travels through fields of sugar cane and along the edge of golf courses and offers views of mountains and the ocean. A double-deck bus provides courtesy transportation between the Lahaina station and the harbor; jitneys connect the station at Kaanapali and the principal hotels. Tour packages that include lunch, boat cruises, and various attractions are available.

Locomotives	2 steam
Cars	Enclosed and open cars
Dates open	June 15-September 3, 1990, daily, noon-8 p.m.
Schedule	Hourly on the half hour
Admission	Adults $8.50. Credit cards and checks accepted.
Fares	Included in admission
Nearby attractions	Farragut State Park
Mailing address	N. 26225 Highway 95, Athol, ID 83801
Phone	(208) 772-0515

LOCOMOTIVES

Number	Type	Former owner	Builder	Date
STEAM				
7		Eureka Nevada Railway	Porter	1915
12	2-6-2	Kahului Railroad	Baldwin	1928

SILVERWOOD THEME PARK

Silverwood is a reproduction of a turn-of-the-century village. In addition to the eating and drinking establishments, there is a large museum of early aircraft and automobiles, an airfield with flying demonstrations, and a 3.2-mile, 3'-gauge railroad, the Silverwood Central Railway.

The train ride through the adjacent forest takes about 20 minutes. The station is a replica of the Boston & Maine station at Greenwood, Massachusetts. Athol is about 15 miles north of Coeur d'Alene on U. S. 95. Silverwood has an RV park; motels and restaurants can be found in Coeur d'Alene.

Displays	Turn-of-the-century station building, local history exhibits
Dates open	Summer, daily 9 a.m.-7 p.m.; spring and fall, daily 9-5; winter, Tuesday-Saturday, 10-3. Closed Thanksgiving, Christmas, and New Year's Day.
Admission	Adults $1, children 16 and under 50 cents
Memberships	$10 per year
Special events	Depot days festival (second Saturday of May)
Nearby attractions	Sierra Silver Mine Tour, 6th Street Melodrama, Wallace District Mining Museum, Wallace District Arts Center, Silver Mountain Gondola
Mailing address	Box 469, Wallace, ID 83873
Phone	(208) 752-0111

NORTHERN PACIFIC DEPOT RAILROAD MUSEUM

The Northern Pacific depot in Wallace, built in 1901 in part with bricks imported from China, was relocated out of the path of a new highway in 1987 and placed in a park at 219 6th Street, at the corner of Pine. In addition to the restored waiting rooms and telegraph office, there are displays interpreting the history of railroading in the Coeur d'Alene mining district. Wallace is on I-90 a few miles west of the Montana border. Restaurants and motels can be found within a block or two of the depot.

Displays	*Pioneer Zephyr*, Santa Fe 4-8-4 No. 2903, New York Central 4-4-0 No. 999, O scale model railroad
Dates open	Weekends and holidays 9:30 a.m.-5:30 p.m., Monday-Friday 9:30-4 (to 5:30 Memorial Day-Labor Day)
Admission	Free; charges for some non-railroad activities and exhibits
Memberships	Write for information.
Mailing address	57th Street and Lake Shore Drive, Chicago, IL 60637-2093
Phone	(312) 684-1414

MUSEUM OF SCIENCE AND INDUSTRY

The Museum of Science and Industry, opened in 1933, is the world's largest and most popular museum of contemporary science and technology. Its exhibits include several locomotives, the world's first diesel-electric streamlined train, and a large O scale model railroad.

The museum is on Lake Shore Drive (U. S. 41). Parking is free.

Chicago Transit Authority bus routes 1 and 6 (from downtown) and 55 (on 55th Street and Garfield Boulevard) serve the museum. Illinois Central Gulf (Metra) trains stop at 57th Street station and Chicago South Shore & South Bend trains stop at 59th Street station, about two blocks west and south of the museum, respectively.

Chicago

Locomotives	1 Heisler steam locomotive, 1 gasoline
Cars	Flatcar, 3 cabooses
Dates open	May 27-28, June 16-17, July 4, July 27-29, August 11-12, September 3, September 29-30 and October 20-21, 1990
Fares	Adults $2.50, children under 10 $1. Checks accepted.
Memberships	Write for information.
Nearby attractions	Stephenson County Historical Museum
Mailing address	Stephenson County Antique Engine Club, P. O. Box 255, Freeport, IL 61032
Phone	(815) 235-2198 when trains are operating; (815) 232-2306 evenings

LOCOMOTIVES

Number	Type	Former owner	Builder	Date
2	Heisler	Louisanna Lumber	Heisler	1912
	Gas-diesel	Unknown	Brookville	1948

SILVER CREEK & STEPHENSON RAILROAD

Several weekends each summer the Stephenson County Antique Engine Club steams up and operates a standard gauge 36-ton Heisler locomotive, reportedly the only one operating in the U. S. Often used in logging operations, the Heisler has cylinders arranged in a V under the boiler driving a longitudinal crankshaft which is connected to the axles with bevel gears.

The 14-acre grounds are half a mile south of Freeport at the corner of Walnut and Lamm Roads. The track is 2 miles long; it crosses Yellow Creek on a 150-foot-long bridge and goes past Indian Garden Nature Preserve. The train ride takes about 20 minutes. Restaurants and motels can be found in Freeport.

Locomotives	2 diesel (steam locomotives are awaiting repair or restoration)
Cars	Combine, coaches, cabooses
Displays	About 60 passenger, freight, and work cars
Schedule	May-October, weekends and holidays, trains leave museum site at 1, 2, 3, and 4 p.m. and leave downtown Monticello 30 minutes later. Charter trips available.
Fares	Adults $5, children 6-12 $3, age 65 and over $3. Checks accepted. Group discounts available.
Memberships	Write for information.
Radio frequency	160.635
Special events	Father's Day Bluegrass Jam, Railroad Days (September 15-16, 1990), Halloween Trains
Nearby attractions	Robert Allerton Park, Bryant Cottage, Illinois Pioneer Heritage Center, Rayville Model Railway Museum
Mailing address	Box 401-H, Monticello, IL 61856
Phone	(217) 762-9011

LOCOMOTIVES

Number	Type	Former owner	Builder	Date
STEAM				
1	0-4-0	Western Ind. Aggr	Alco	1931
191	0-6-0	Republic Steel	Alco	1916
401	2-8-0	Southern	Baldwin	1907
DIESEL				
301	RS3	Long Island (1529)	Alco	
725	F7	Wabash (1189)	GMD	1953

MONTICELLO RAILWAY MUSEUM

The Monticello Railway Museum owns approximately 7 miles of line between Monticello and White Heath. Trains operate from the former Norfolk & Western (Wabash) station in Monticello to the museum site, which is on a 2-mile stretch of former Illinois Terminal line about halfway between Champaign and Decatur, Ill. The museum is located on the south frontage road at Exit 63 of Interstate 75 just north of Monticello. The museum grounds are not paved, but access is possible for the handicapped and persons with baby strollers. At Monticello are a gift shop and several cars containing museum displays. There are restaurants and limited lodging in Monticello; more are available in Champaign and Decatur.

Car	1 streetcar
Schedule	Mid-May to mid-September, in good weather, Tuesdays and Thursdays, on the hour 11 a.m.-6 p.m. Saturdays and Sundays, on the hour noon to 5. Charter trips available.
Fares	Adults $2, children 12 and under $1. Checks accepted. Group discounts available.
Nearby attractions	Rose Garden, four museums, Tinker Swiss Cottage
Mailing address	c/o Riverview Ice House, 324 North Madison Street, Rockford, IL 61107
Phone	(815) 987-8894, 987-8893 year-round

P ⛱ ☕

TROLLEY PLAZA

The Rockford Park District operates a reproduction of an open-air streetcar on a 45-minute round trip alongside the Rock River. The car was donated by the Rockford Rotary Club in 1983; it is powered by a Volkswagen engine modified to run on propane.

The Park District and the City of Rockford negotiated the part-time lease of a portion of a Chicago & North Western line that used to extend to Kenosha, Wisconsin. The car runs from the Riverview Ice House, a skating rink, north past the Sinnissippi Gardens to Auburn Street, then returns.

The Riverview Ice House is at 302 North Madison Street. Handicapped persons can be accommodated with advance notice. Food and lodging are available nearby.

Cars	Chicago L cars, North Shore and South Shore interurban cars
Displays	Electric locomotive, caboose, railway post office streetcar
Dates open	May 13-November 4, 1990, Sundays and holidays 11 a.m.-6 p.m.; July and August, also open Saturdays 12-5
Schedule	Cars run as needed from half an hour after opening to half an hour before closing.
Fares	Adults $2 (two rides for $2.50), children 3-11 $1 (two rides for $1.50), age 65 and over, $1.50 (two rides for $2), all day pass, $6. Checks accepted. Group discounts available. Credit cards accepted for museum store purchases.
Memberships	$15 per year
Special events	Fox River Trolley Fest and Community Picnic (last Saturday in June), Autumn Color Sundays (October 7 and 14. 1990)
Nearby attractions	Blackhawk Park, Haeger Pottery, Fermi National Accelerator Laboratory, Batavia Depot Museum
Mailing address	P. O. Box 315, South Elgin, IL 60177
Phone	(312) 697-4676

CARS AND LOCOMOTIVES

Number	Former owner	Builder	Date
20	Chicago Aurora & Elgin	Niles	1902
715	Chicago North Shore & Milwaukee	Cincinnati	1926
756	Chicago North Shore & Milwaukee	Standard	1930
4451	Chicago Rapid Transit	Cincinnati	1924
5001	Chicago Rapid Transit	Pullman	1947
L-202	Chicago City Railway	CCRy	1908

FOX RIVER TROLLEY MUSEUM

The Fox River Trolley Museum operates 1 mile of the former Aurora, Elgin & Fox River Electric line between Castlemuir (South Elgin) and Coleman Grove (Blackhawk Park). Originally part of an interurban between Elgin and Aurora, the line has been in continuous use since 1896.

Among the electric cars operated by the museum is Chicago Aurora & Elgin interurban car No. 20, built by Niles in 1902; the displays include an 1895 Street Railway Post Office car from Chicago and other historic electric railway cars.

The museum is on Illinois Route 31 (LaFox Street) three blocks south of State Street in South Elgin. There are motels in Elgin, 5 miles away, and restaurants in Elgin and South Elgin.

South Elgin

Locomotives	3 steam, 10 diesel		$2.25 (children under 5 free). Discounts
Cars	Heavyweight coaches, complete Zephyr train, streetcars and interurbans		for senior citizens and groups. Checks and credit cards accepted. Admission
Displays	More than 60 interurbans, streetcars, and transit cars, 18 steam locomotives, 22 diesels, 40 passenger cars, freight and work equipment		price includes rides.
		Memberships	Associate membership $20, family $30
		Special events	Railroad Day (Memorial Day), Trolley
Dates open	Daily Memorial Day to Labor Day: Monday-Friday 10 a.m.-4 p.m.; weekends and holidays 11-5. Also weekends and holidays in May, September, and October, 11-5. Electric cars operate when the museum is open. Steam trains operate weekends and holidays May-September. Charter trips are operated.		Pageant (July 4), Diesel Day (July 15, 1990), Steam Days (first weekend of August), Railfan Weekend (Labor Day weekend), Members' Weekend (September 22-23, 1990)
		Nearby attractions	McHenry County Historical Society, Seven Acres Antique Village, Valley View Model Railroad
Fares	When steam train or Zephyr operates: adults $5.50, children 5-11 $2.75; Railfan and Members' Weekends: adults $7.50, children 5-11 $3.75; other times: adults $4.50, children 5-11	**Mailing address**	Box 427, Union, IL 60180
		Phone	(815) 923-4000; for schedules (800) BIG RAIL (244-7245) in Chicagoland

P & ♿ ⛩ 🎁 ◼

ILLINOIS RAILWAY MUSEUM

The Illinois Railway Museum is one of North America's largest. It is noted for its collections of diesels, Midwestern interurbans (10 pieces of Illinois Terminal equipment alone), and Chicago streetcars and rapid transit cars. Among the locomotives on display are a GG1, a South Shore "Little Joe," 4-8-4s from Grand Trunk and Milwaukee Road, and a Norfolk & Western 2-8-8-2.

The museum was established in 1953 in North Chicago and moved in 1964 to its present site on the eastern edge of the village of Union in McHenry County. On the 56-acre grounds are several carbarns, a well-equipped locomotive shop, a station, a bookstore and gift shop housed in a baggage car, and a Chicago "L" station.

A loop of track takes streetcars and interurbans around the area; steam and diesel trains operate over 3 miles of track along the roadbed of the former Elgin & Belvidere Electric Railway and parallel to a line of the Chicago & North Western.

The museum is about 50 miles northwest of Chicago. Union is just north of U. S. 20 about halfway between Elgin and Rockford; the museum is on Olson Road ½ mile east of the center of Union.

Many of the walkways around the museum and in the carbarns are paved, making access easier for the handicapped and for persons pushing baby strollers. There are restaurants in Union; lodging can be found in Marengo, 3 miles west.

Displays	HO scale model railroad
Dates open	Memorial Day-first weekend in October, Wednesday, Saturday, Sunday, and holidays 1-6 p.m.
Admission	Adults $3, children 5-12 $1.50 (under 5 free). Checks accepted. Group discounts available.
Nearby attractions	Illinois Railway Museum, McHenry County Historical Society, Seven Acres Antique Village
Mailing address	17108 Highbridge Road, Union, IL 60180
Phone	(815) 923-4135

VALLEY VIEW MODEL RAILROAD

Less than a mile north of the Illinois Railway Museum is the Valley View Model Railroad, operated by the Ted Voss family. It is a large, completely scenicked HO scale model railroad with 8 scale miles of track and several trains operating at a time. To reach the Valley View Railroad from the Illinois Railway Museum, follow Olson Road north to Highbridge Road.

INDIANA TIME: Most of Indiana is in the Eastern time zone, but the northwest and southwest corners of the state are in the Central time zone. Areas near Chicago, Evansville, Louisville, and Cincinnati observe daylight time, but the rest of the state does not. To put it another way, since Eastern Standard and Central Daylight time are the same, in summer most of Indiana is on Chicago time.

Locomotives	2 steam, 5 diesel, 1 gasoline
Cars	Coaches with opening windows (mostly ex-Erie Stillwell coaches)
Schedule	May 5-October 28, 1990: Weekends and holidays, leave Connersville 12:01 p.m. Indiana Time (EST), return about 5:30
Fares	Adults $9, children 2-12 $4. Credit cards and checks accepted. Group discounts available. Reservations required for groups.
Radio frequency	160.650
Memberships	Write for information.
Special events	Special runs for school groups by advance reservation on Wednesdays, Thursdays, and Fridays in May. Christmas runs: last weekend of November and first two weekends of December, leave Connersville 5 p.m. Friday and Saturday, 12:01 p.m. Sunday. Fare $12.50 (all ages). Reservations required.

Nearby attractions	Canal House Museum, Brookville Lake, Mary Gray Bird Sanctuary, Whitewater State Park
Mailing address	P. O. Box 406, Connersville, IN 47331
Phone	(317) 825-2054; 825-4550 year-round

LOCOMOTIVES

Number	Type	Former owner	Builder	Date
STEAM				
100	2-6-2	Florala Sawmill Co.	Baldwin	1919
DIESEL				
9	S1	Proctor & Gamble	Alco	1947
25	750 h.p.	Cincinnati Union Terminal	Lima-Hamilton	1951
137	1000 h.p.	Armco	Lima-Hamilton	1949
210	70 ton		GE	1947

P 🎁 $

WHITEWATER VALLEY RAILROAD

In 1865 the Whitewater Valley Railroad was incorporated to build a line from Harrison, Ohio, northwest of Cincinnati, to Hagerstown, Indiana, along the towpath of the Whitewater Valley Canal. The railroad became part of the New York Central System. A new Whitewater Valley Railroad, a tourist railroad, appeared in 1972, and it purchased the line from Penn Central in 1984.

The 16-mile trip from Connersville to Metamora traverses 2 percent grades and offers views of the canal or its remains. A 2-hour layover in Metamora gives time for sightseeing and shopping before the train returns to Connersville. Box lunches are available; they must be ordered at the Connersville station before 11:30 a.m. and will be delivered to the train before departure.

Connersville is about 60 miles from Indianapolis, Cincinnati, and Dayton. The station is on Route 121 (Grand Avenue) about a mile south of the center of Connersville. A gift shop is in the station; various pieces of rolling stock are on display near the station. Restaurants and lodging are available in Connersville; there is a campground half a mile from the station.

Locomotives	3 diesels
Cars	Open-window coaches, air-conditioned RDC
Schedule	(Eastern Daylight Time — Louisville time) Second weekend of May-first weekend of November, Saturday and Sunday, departures at 10:30 a.m. and 1 and 3 p.m.; also at 5 p.m. after Labor Day and on major holidays; also Fridays at 1 p.m. Charter trips available.
Fares	Adults $7, children 4-12 $4 (3 and under free), age 62 and over $6. Credit cards and checks accepted. Group discounts available.
Special events	Train robberies, September 29 and 30, 1990; Christmas Express, December 15, 16, 22, 23
Nearby attractions	Historic buildings, caves, boat rides
Mailing address	P. O. Box 10, Corydon, IN 47112
Phone	(812) 738-8000

DIESEL LOCOMOTIVES

Number	Type	Former owner	Builder	Date
1 (*Betty-Sue*)	45-ton	LNA&C	GE	1951
1230, 1231	SW1200	Norfolk & Portsmouth Belt	EMD	1956

CORYDON 1883 SCENIC RAILROAD

The Louisville, New Albany & Corydon Railroad is a common carrier offering freight service between Corydon, Indiana (once the capital of that state), and a connection with Norfolk Southern at Corydon Junction, 7.8 miles away. On weekends the railroad runs excursion trains over its line.

The scenery includes wooded hills and Big Indian Creek Trestle.

Signs along the way help you identify trees and other interesting vegetation.

Corydon is about 20 miles west of Louisville, Kentucky on I-64. Take exit 105 and follow State Routes 135 and 337 south into Corydon. The station is at Walnut and Water Streets, a block west of the old state capitol.

Locomotives	2 steam, 5 diesel
Cars	Coaches, combine, snack bar car
Displays	Railway Post Office car, diner, coach, sleeper-lounge car
Schedule	FRENCH LICK, WEST BADEN, & SOUTHERN: weekends and holidays April-November, leave French Lick 10 a.m., 1 and 4 p.m. EST
SPRINGS VALLEY ELECTRIC RAILWAY: daily May-October, weekends in April and November, leave every half hour 10-4
Fares	Adults $7, children 3-11 $3.50 (under 3 free), age 65 and over $6. Checks and credit cards accepted. Group discounts available. Reservations required for groups.
Memberships	Write for information.
Special events	Train robberies for Muscular Dystrophy Association, last two weekends of August; Dinner on the Diner, first weekend of November
Nearby attractions	French Lick Springs Hotel, Holiday World Amusement Park, Potaka Lake
Mailing address	P. O. Box 150, French Lick, IN 47432
Phone	(812) 936-2405

INDIANA RAILWAY MUSEUM

The Indiana Railway Museum was established in 1961 and operated in Westport and Greensburg before acquiring 16 miles of Southern Railway track between French Lick and Dubois in 1978. In 1980 the museum was given 2 miles of the former Monon branch to French Lick by the Sheraton Hotel Corporation. The museum's steam train operation, the French Lick, West Baden & Southern Railway, runs from French Lick to Cuzco, 10 miles, through part of the Hoosier National Forest and through one of Indiana's longest railroad tunnels. The round trip takes 1 hour 45 minutes. The train carries a snack bar car. The museum also operates a streetcar between French Lick and West Baden (1 mile) as the Springs Valley Electric Railway. Both depart from the former Monon passenger station, which is owned by the French Lick Springs Hotel.

The museum is at the junction of Routes 145 and 56 in French Lick. The town, which is two hours from Indianapolis and an hour from Louisville, offers a variety of hotels and restaurants.

Locomotives	8 steam
Cars	Open cars
Displays	Steam-powered machinery
Dates open	Weekends and holidays Memorial Day-Labor Day, then Sundays only through October: noon-5 p.m. CDT.
Schedule	Train operation depends on weather and track conditions. Charter trips can be arranged.
Admission	Free, except during Hesston Steam & Power Show: adults $3, children under 13 free
Fares	$1-$2 per person, depending on gauge
Memberships	$15 per year, $30 for families
Special events	Whistle-Stop Days (opening weekend), Hesston Steam & Power Show (Labor Day weekend), Cider Fest
Nearby attractions	Lake Michigan, Indiana Dunes State Park, Washington Park Zoo in Michigan City, Lighthouse Museum
Mailing address	LaPorte County Historical Steam Society, 2940 Mount Claire Way, Long Beach, Michigan City, IN 46360
Phone	(219) 872-7405 (LaPorte County Historical Steam Society), 872-5055 (LaPorte County Tourism)

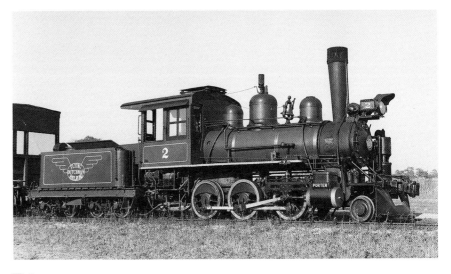

P & 弄 ▣

HESSTON STEAM MUSEUM

In 1957 the LaPorte County Threshermen established a museum of traction engines and other steam-powered machinery at Hesston, east of Michigan City on the Indiana-Michigan border. A steam locomotive was added to the collection in 1964. Subsequently the museum grew through the generosity of Elliott Donnelley.

Trains of four track gauges circle the museum site. A 2½-mile loop of dual-gauge track carries 2'-gauge and 3'-gauge trains, and there are separate 1-mile loops of 14"- and 7½"-gauge track.

The locomotive roster includes a 2'-gauge 0-4-0T from the Dar-jeeling & Himalayan Railway in India and an 0-4-0 built in Czechoslovakia.

Hesston appears on few maps. To reach the museum, use Michigan Exit 1 of I-94, go south on Indiana Route 39 to County Road 1000 North just south of the state line, then east about 2½ miles to the museum.

There are restaurants in Hesston; lodging can be found in LaPorte, 12 miles south; Michigan City, 15 miles west; and New Buffalo, Mich., 6 miles northwest.

Displays	O and HO model railroads, 0-10-0 *Reuben Wells*
Dates open	Tuesday-Saturday 10 a.m.-5 p.m., till 8 p.m. Thursdays; Sundays noon-5; Memorial Day-Labor Day, also open Monday 10-5. Closed New Year's Day, Thanksgiving, and Christmas.
Admission	Adults $4, children 2-17 $3, age 60 and over $3. Group discounts available.
Memberships	Write for information.
Nearby attractions	Indiana Transportation Museum, Indianapolis Zoo, Indianapolis Union Station
Mailing address	P. O. Box 3000, Indianapolis, IN 46206
Phone	(317) 924-5431

THE CHILDREN'S MUSEUM

The Children's Museum of Indianapolis is one of the largest children's museums in the world. In it is the world's largest public display of toy trains; a 1000-square-foot O scale layout; a 350-square-foot HO scale layout; and the locomotive *Reuben Wells*, an 0-10-0 built in 1868 to work the Madison Incline, a 5.9 percent grade north out of Madison, Indiana. The museum is located at 3000 North Meridian Street (U. S. 31) at the corner of 30th Street — I-65 is just west of the museum.

Locomotives	Diesel (E9)
Cars	Budd-built passenger cars
Schedule	Thursdays, Fridays, and Saturdays, 7 p.m.; Sundays 5:30 p.m.; Mondays, Tuesday, Saturdays, and Sundays, 11:30 a.m. Charter trips available.
Fares	Dinner, $49.95 per person; luncheon, $30. Reservations required. Credit cards accepted. Group discount available.
Special events	Special events and excursions are being planned — write for information.
Nearby attractions	Zoo, Union Station
Mailing address	P. O. Box 1243, Indianapolis 46206
Phone	(317) 262-3333

INDIANA DINNER TRAIN

The Indiana Rail Road operates a dinner train, the *Hoosierland Limited*, from Indianapolis 30 miles out to the southwest and back. The round trip takes 3½ hours, long enough for a complete dinner or luncheon. The train is available for boarding and the lounge car is open an hour before departure from the terminal at 1500 South Senate Avenue in Indianapolis. The route the train follows is a former Illinois Central line, purchased by the Indiana Rail Road, a common-carrier freight railroad, in 1986.

Locomotives	1 steam, 2 diesel, 2 electric
Cars	Interurban cars and heavyweight and stainless steel coaches, some air-conditioned
Displays	Approximately 70 cars and locomotives
Dates open	Weekends and holidays April-October, noon-5 p.m. Guided tours by advance arrangement.
Admission	Adults $2.50, children 6-12 $2. Checks accepted. Group discounts available. Reservations required for groups.
Memberships	Write for information.
Special events	Caboose Weekend, Hobo Day, Railroad Festival; each weekend usually has a theme or special feature
Nearby attractions	Conner Prairie Settlement, Indianapolis Zoo, Indianapolis Union Station, Indianapolis Children's Museum
Mailing address	P. O. Box 83, Noblesville, IN 46060
Phone	(317) 773-6000

INDIANA TRANSPORTATION MUSEUM

The Indiana Transportation Museum is located in Forest Park in Noblesville, about 20 miles north of Indianapolis on Route 19. Trains operate over a mile of track along the edge of the park; the ride takes about 15 minutes. The museum's operating locomotives include two electrics, Nickel Plate 2-8-2 No. 587, and a pair of former Milwaukee Road F7 diesels. The grounds are partially accessible to the handicapped. Visitors can find restaurants in Noblesville and lodging in Indianapolis.

Dates open	Visitors are welcome on Saturdays, when members work on the locomotive.
Admission	Free
Memberships	$15 per year
Nearby attractions	Indiana-Erie train ride at Monterey
Mailing address	P. O. Box 75, North Judson, IN 46366
Phone	(219) 223-3834, (219) 542-4221

MIAMI STEAM RAILROAD MUSEUM

The Miami County Steam Locomotive Association was established in 1961 and was given Chesapeake & Ohio 2-8-4 No. 2789, which was placed in a park in Peru, Indiana. In 1985 the association set about to rebuild the locomotive for eventual operation.

The Berkshire type, constructed by Alco in 1947, is one of the few preserved locomotives with a welded boiler. The museum collection includes a variety of freight and passenger cars.

North Judson is in the northwest part of the state, about 15 miles south of U. S. Route 30 and halfway between U. S. 35 and 421. The museum is near the CSX (former Chesapeake & Ohio) tracks, the sole remaining line through the town. All that remains of the New York Central, Pennsylvania, and Erie lines, which all crossed in North Judson, is the Tippecanoe Railroad, which operates the former Erie line to Monterey, 16 miles east.

Food and lodging are available in North Judson.

Locomotives	1 steam, 1 gasoline
Cars	Coaches, open cars, caboose
Schedule	Sundays and holidays Memorial Day to mid-October, also Saturdays July to Labor Day, leave Pleasant Lake 1 and 2 p.m. EST. Charter trips operated.
Fares	Adults $4, children 5-11 $2.50 (under 5 free). Checks accepted. Discounts available for groups of 20 or more.
Memberships	Write for information.
Special events	Father's Day, 101 Lakes Festival, Firecracker Special (July 4), Pleasant Lake Day, fall train robbery, fall color runs, Ghost Train
Nearby attractions	Indiana lake country
Mailing address	P. O. Box 178, Angola, IN 46703
Phone	(219) 825-9182, 833-1804

LITTLE RIVER RAILROAD

The world's smallest standard gauge Pacific-type steam locomotive is the feature attraction of the Little River Railroad. The engine was built by Baldwin in 1911 for a previous Little River Railroad which ran through the Smoky Mountains of eastern Tennessee.

The locomotive now hauls passengers over 3 miles of former New York Central track in the northeast corner of Indiana. Trains depart from Pleasant Lake, 4 miles south of Angola (Exit 148 off Interstate 69), run south to Steubenville, then return. There are restaurants and motels in Angola.

Locomotives	2 diesel, 1 steam
Cars	Ex-South Shore coaches, Rock Island suburban coach, and converted box cars
Displays	Approximately 20 locomotives and cars
Schedule	Memorial Day weekend through October: weekends and holidays, 11 a.m. and 1:30 and 4 p.m.; Monday-Friday 1:30 p.m. Charter trips available.
Fares	Adults $7 diesel, $10 steam; children 5-15 $3 diesel, $4 steam (under 5 free). Checks accepted.
Memberships	$20 per year
Special events	Pufferbilly Days (weekend after Labor Day)
Nearby attractions	Mamie Eisenhower Birthplace and Museum, Ledges State Park, Kate Shelley High Bridge, Kate Shelley Memorial Park and Railroad Museum in nearby Moingona
Mailing address	P. O. Box 603, Boone IA 50036
Phone	(515) 432-4249

LOCOMOTIVES

Number	Type	Former owner	Builder	Date
STEAM				
JS 8419	2-8-2	New	Datong	1988
DIESEL				
1003		Chicago & North Western	EMD	
2254	center-cab	U. S. Air Force	GE	1943

P♿☂🎁☕

BOONE & SCENIC VALLEY RAILROAD

The Fort Dodge, Des Moines & Southern Railroad, an interurban line between Des Moines and Fort Dodge, Iowa, was noted for a high trestle over Bass Point Creek near Boone. In 1971 the Chicago & North Western leased the FDDM&S and in 1983 abandoned most of it. The Boone Railroad Historical Society purchased 11 miles of the line from Boone to Wolf Crossing, including the high bridge, and formed the Boone & Scenic Valley Railroad to operate excursion trains. Trains depart from a station at 11th and Division Streets in Boone and operate over 6 miles of track. The round trip takes 1 hour and 45 minutes; its highlight is the 156-foot-high bridge. The train offers views of the Des Moines River valley. Trains are pulled by diesel locomotives or by a new steam locomotive, the first imported to the U. S. from China and the last built by the works at Datong.

Boone is in central Iowa, 42 miles north-northwest of Des Moines and 15 miles west of Ames. To reach the station from U. S. 30, take Story Street north through the business district, turn left on Tenth, and drive 6 blocks west. Food and lodging can be found in Boone.

Displays	Large Lionel layout
Dates open	Memorial Day to Labor Day, daily, and weekends through September, 9 a.m.-7 p.m. Also open the Friday, Saturday, and Sunday after Thanksgiving, noon-6 p.m. Group tours available with advance notice April-October.
Admission	Adults $3, children 4-12 $1.50 (under 4 free), age 55 and over $2.50. Checks accepted. Group discounts available.
Memberships	Write for information.
Nearby attractions	Adventure Land Park, Maytag Museum
Mailing address	Route 2, Highway 117 North, Colfax, IA 50054
Phone	(515) 674-3813

P ⊼ 🎁

TRAINLAND U. S. A.

In 1964 Red Atwood began collecting Lionel trains. He built two small layouts and began to think of building a large one — which he completed in 1981. The O gauge layout depicts the development of railroads across the U. S. The layout measures 44' by 96' and has 22 trains operating simultaneously. Trainland U. S. A. is on State Highway 117, 2 miles north of Exit 155 of I-80. It is an authorized Lionel repair station. There are restaurants in Colfax and motels in Newton, 10 miles east.

Cars	Coaches
Schedule	Operates only during the Midwest Old Threshers Annual Reunion, a five-day event ending on Labor Day, 9 a.m.-10 p.m.
Admission	Old Threshers Reunion, $6, good for all five days (children under 10 free)
Fares	Adults $1.50, children 75 cents. Children under 6 free. Checks accepted.
Radio frequency	152.915
Nearby attractions	Write for information.
Mailing address	Box 102, Mt. Pleasant, IA 52641
Phone	(319) 385-2912

LOCOMOTIVES

Number	Type	Former owner	Builder	Date
STEAM				
1	2-8-0	Coahuilas & Zacatecas	Baldwin	1897
2	2-6-0	New Berlin & Winfield	Baldwin	1906
6	2-6-0	Surrey, Sussex & Southampton	Baldwin	1891
9	Shay	Westside Lumber Co.	Lima	1923
16	0-4-0		Henschel	1951
DIESEL				
	45 ton		Whitcomb	1943

MIDWEST CENTRAL RAILROAD

The Midwest Old Threshers Reunion is an annual event held for five days ending on Labor Day. It is a combination of a fair, antique agricultural equipment show, farm life museum, and campout. The Midwest Central Railroad has a mile of 3'-gauge track on the reunion grounds and operates steam-hauled passenger trains.

The railroad is located in McMillan Park, between Walnut and Locust Streets.

Mt. Pleasant is 25 miles west of Burlington on U. S. Route 34. In addition to the campground of the Old Threshers Reunion there are restaurants and motels in Mt. Pleasant.

Fares	Round trip 75 cents, one way 40 cents, 10-ride ticket, $2.50. Children under 6 free.
Mailing address	Midwest Old Threshers, Threshers Road, Mt. Pleasant, IA 52641
Phone	(319) 385-8937

ELECTRIC CARS

Number	Type	Former owner	Date
320	Interurban	Chicago Aurora & Elgin	1914
381	Streetcar	Waterloo, Cedar Falls & Northern	1930
9	Interurban	Southern Iowa	1915
1718	Open bench	Rio de Janeiro Tramway	1920
1779	Open bench	Rio de Janeiro Tramway	1911
4476	PCC	Toronto Transit Commission	1949

MIDWEST ELECTRIC RAILWAY

Also operating on the grounds of and during the Midwest Old Threshers Reunion is the Midwest Electric Railway, a 1½-mile loop of standard gauge track connecting the campground with the exhibition areas.

Locomotives	2 diesel
Cars	Dining cars
Schedule	Luncheon trips depart at 11:30 a.m. (boarding begins at 11); evening trips depart at 7 p.m. (boarding begins at 6)
Fares	$39.95 per person. Credit cards and checks accepted. Reservations are required. Group discounts available.
Nearby attractions	Waterloo Greyhound Park, Rensselaer Russell House, Grout Museum of History and Science, Cedar Falls Historical Society, UNI Dome
Mailing address	311 E. Braemer Ave., Waverly, IA 50677
Phone	(319) 232-7558 Monday-Friday 9 a.m.- 7 p.m. and Saturday 9-5; (800) 525-04773 for recorded information

℗⑪🚻⛱🎁

STAR CLIPPER DINNER TRAIN

The Star Clipper Dinner Train offers an elegant four-course dinner during a 3-hour excursion through northeast Iowa. The train consists of a pair of F7s sandwiching two full-length, air-conditioned dining room cars converted from streamlined coaches and a kitchen car.

The Star Clipper operates year-round, mostly on weekends during the winter; its schedule expands to most of the week except Monday as the weather warms up. Trains operate primarily from Waterloo and Waverly with late morning and evening departures.

Reservations, menu choice, and payment are required a minimum of two weeks in advance. The Star Clipper is not recommended for small children. Booster chairs, high chairs, and lap sitting are not allowed on the train.

Lodging can be found in Waterloo and Waverly. Sister dinner trains with the same operating format and prices, the Newport Star Clipper and the Michigan Star Clipper, operate in Newport, Rhode Island, and Paw Paw, Michigan, respectively.

MIDLAND RAILWAY

Locomotives	2 diesel
Cars	Coaches and caboose
Displays	GE boxcab diesel, crane, freight cars, memorabilia
Schedule	April 28-October 28, 1990, weekends and holidays, trains depart at 11:30 a.m. and 12:30, 2, 3, and 4 p.m. Charter trips available.
Fares	Adults $5, children 4-12 $2.50, age 62 and over $4.50. Checks accepted. Group discounts available
Radio frequency	161.055
Special events	Maple Leaf Festival (third weekend of October)
Mailing address	P. O. Box 412, Baldwin City, KS 66006
Phone	(913) 594-6982, 371-3410 year-round

PRAIRIE PIONNER DINNER TRAIN

Schedule	Fridays at 7 p.m.; Saturdays and Sundays at 6 p.m.
Fares	$35 per person. Credit cards and checks accepted. Reservations required.
Mailing address	P. O. Box 9386, KansaS City, MO 64133
Phone	(816) 358-8707

DIESEL LOCOMOTIVES

Number	Type	Former owner	Builder	Date
460	44-ton	Atchison, Topeka & Santa Fe	GE	1942
524	NW2	Chicago, Burlington & Quincy	EMD	1947

MIDLAND RAILWAY

The Midland Railway is a passenger-only common carrier operating excursion trains over the north end of its 11-mile ex-Santa Fe line between Baldwin City and Ottawa, Kansas. Trains depart from the station in Baldwin City and traverse 3½ miles of the line through rolling farmland. A round-trip ride takes 45 minutes. Equipment includes a Great Northern caboose and two Rock Island heavyweight coaches.

Also operating on the Midland Railway is the Prairie Pioneer Dinner Train, which makes a 2-hour round trip. Equipment includes a former Atlantic Coast Line lounge car and a Santa Fe baggage car converted to a kitchen car.

Baldwin City is about halfway between Lawrence and Ottawa, on U. S. Highway 56, 4 miles east of U. S. 59. The station is at 15th and High Streets, next to the grain elevator.

There are restaurants in Baldwin City; motels can be found in Lawrence and Ottawa.

Locomotives	2 diesel
Cars	2 dining cars, 1 kitchen car
Schedule	April-December, Tuesday-Sunday; Charter trips available. Children age 5 and older welcome on daytime trips; evening excursions are limited to those age 14 and up.
Fares	$44.95 per person. Credit cards accepted.
Nearby attractions	The Stephen Foster Story (outdoor musical drama)
Mailing address	P. O. Box 279, Bardstown, KY 40004
Phone	(502) 348-7300

MY OLD KENTUCKY DINNER TRAIN

The R. J. Corman Railroad Corporation, which operates the former Bardstown Branch of the Louisville & Nashville, runs a dinner train out of Bardstown. The train takes 2 hours to run the length of the line to Limestone Springs, then return, 35 miles in all.

Power for the train is a pair of red-and-silver FP7s. The cars are Budd-built stainless steel equipment. Handicapped access is partial: there is a lift for moving wheelchairs on and off the train, but the rest rooms are not fitted for wheelchair access.

Bardstown is 44 miles south-southeast of Louisville on U. S. Routes 31E and 150. The station in Bardstown is at 602 North Third Street.

Locomotives	4 diesel
Cars	Passenger cars of all types
Dates open	May-October, weekends and holidays, 1-4 p.m.
Admission	Adults $2, children $1. Checks accepted.
Memberships	$20 per year
Special events	Christmas train
Mailing address	P. O. Box 15065, Covington, KY 41015-0065
Phone	(606) 491-RAIL; 341-0303 year-round

DIESEL LOCOMOTIVES

Number	Type	Former owner	Builder	Date
1	switcher	Indiana & Ohio Power Co.	Brookville	1949
332	VO-1000	Patapsco & Back Rivers	Baldwin	1947
5888	E8	Pennsylvania	EMD	1951
9408	SW1	Pennsylvania	EMD	1947

THE RAILWAY EXPOSITION CO.

The Railway Exposition Co. has a collection of more than two dozen passenger cars of all types. Some are already available for charters and excursion service, while others are being restored.

The museum site, where the cars are stored, is at 315 West Southern Avenue at 35th Street in Covington. Follow Kentucky Route 17 south from Covington or north from Exit 80 of I-275 to Latonia Avenue. Turn east on Latonia, then bear left on Southern Avenue.

Covington is across the Ohio River from Cincinnati, Ohio. Food and lodging can be found throughout the metropolitan area.

Covington

Locomotives	1 steam, 3 diesel
Cars	Coaches, some air conditioned
Displays	Approximately 75 locomotives and cars
Dates open	May 17 to mid-June 1990, at Ormsby Station; July 4 through Thanksgiving at the new location at New Haven, Kentucky: Saturdays, 8:30 a.m.-5 p.m., Sundays 12:30-5:30; June-August: Tuesday-Saturday 11-5, Sundays 10-5
Schedule	Write for schedules.
Fares	New Haven to Boston, adults $10 round trip, children 3-12 $7, age 65 and over $9. Checks and credit cards accepted. Group discounts available.
Memberships	Associate membership $20, active membership $25; write for information on other categories.
Mailing address	P. O. Box 240, New Haven, KY 40051
Phone	(502) 549-5470

KENTUCKY RAILWAY MUSEUM

The Kentucky Railway Museum opened in 1957 on River Road in Louisville. A 1964 flood prompted a search for a new location on higher ground, and in 1977 the museum moved to LaGrange Road (Route 146) and Dorsey Lane in suburban Jefferson County east of Louisville. In early summer 1990 the museum will move again, to New Haven, about 40 miles south of Louisville.

The collection includes Louisville & Nashville 152, a 4-6-2 built in 1905 by Rogers, and an ex-Santa Fe CF7, both of which are used in excursion service. The museum has an extensive collection of passenger cars. It operates excursion trains on its own track between New Haven and Boston, once part of a Louisville & Nashville route from Louisville to Corbin. New Haven is 14 miles south of Bardstown on U. S. Route 31E. Boston is 13 miles west of Bardstown on U. S. 62. Write or call for information before you visit.

Cars	Ex-Lackawanna electric cars
Schedule	Round trips Paris to Maysville, May 19, October 20-21 (overnight), and December 8, 1990; round trip Maysville to Paris October 6; one-way to Maysville October 5, to Paris October 12
Fares	Adults $30, children 3-12 $20 (under 3 and not occupying a seat free). Reservations are advised. Checks accepted. Group discount available.
Memberships	Write for information.
Nearby attractions	Historic Washington, horse farms
Mailing address	P. O. Box 867, Paris, KY 40361
Phone	(606) 293-0807, 849-2756

STEAM LOCOMOTIVE

Number	Type	Former owner	Builder	Date
11	2-6-2	Reader Railroad	Baldwin	1925

KENTUCKY CENTRAL RAILWAY

The Kentucky Central Railway, operated by the Kentucky Central Chapter of the National Railway Historical Society, operates between Paris and Maysville on the rails of the Transkentucky Transportation Railroad (a former Louisville & Nashville branch).

Round trips, 50 miles each way, take 7 to 8 hours. Snacks are available on the train. The Paris station is on U. S. Route 460 on the north side of town. There are restaurants in Paris and motels in Lexington, 17 miles southwest.

Paris

Locomotive	1 diesel (Alco S2)
Cars	Open excursion cars
Schedule	April 11-October 28, 1990: weekends in April, May, and September and daily May 28-Labor Day and in October, trains depart Stearns at 11 a.m. and 3 p.m. Additional train at 1 p.m. holiday weekends (also June 30-July 1) and weekends in October. April, May, and September, Wednesday-Friday, train departs Stearns 11 a.m. Charter trips available.
Fares	Adults $6.95, children 3-11 $3.95 (under 3 free). Group discounts available. Checks and credit cards accepted.
Nearby attractions	Cumberland Falls State Park, Blue Heron, Yahoo Falls, Natural Arch, Lake Cumberland
Mailing address	P. O. Box 368, Stearns, KY 42647
Phone	(800) 462-5664

BIG SOUTH FORK SCENIC RAILWAY

The Big South Fork Scenic Railway operates excursion trains over the rails of the Kentucky & Tennessee Railway into the Big South Fork National River and Recreation Area. Trains run from the community of Stearns, built as a company town by the Stearns Coal & Lumber Company in 1901, down into the gorge of the Cumberland River.

In a little over 5 miles the train descends 600 feet, passes through a rock tunnel, and arrives at Blue Heron, an interpretive center that explains coal mining 50 years ago. The round trip takes about 3 hours.

Stearns is a few miles north of the Tennessee-Kentucky state line and just east of the Central-Eastern time zone boundary. It is on Kentucky Route 92, 5 miles west of U. S. 27 and about 25 miles west of I-75. Restaurants and motels can be found in Stearns.

Cars	Coaches
Displays	Freight cars, cabooses, Alabama State Docks 0-6-0
Dates open	May 19-November 4, 1990, open Saturdays 9 a.m.-4 p.m. and Sundays noon-4. Trains run at 10, 1, and 4 Saturdays and 1 and 4 Sundays. Charter trips operated.
Admission	Adults $6, children $4, Seniors $5. Checks accepted. Group discount available.
Memberships	Write for information.
Special events	Train robberies, Halloween Special
Radio frequency	160.275
Nearby attractions	Kentucky State Horse Park, Bluegrass Horse Farms, Headley-Whitley Museum,
Mailing address	Shakertown, state capitol P. O. Box 27, Versailles, KY 40383
Phone	(606) 873-2476; 281-2476 during non-business hours

LOCOMOTIVES

Number	Type	Former owner	Builder	Date
STEAM				
717	0-6-0T	U. S. Army	Porter	1947
DIESEL				
2043	MRS-1	U. S. Army	Alco	1953

BLUEGRASS RAILROAD MUSEUM

The Bluegrass Railroad Museum operates excursion trains from its museum grounds, on U. S. Route 62 a mile west of Versailles, to the Kentucky River, 5 miles away. The 11-mile round trip takes about 1½ hours. Refreshments are available on the train. The line traverses remote, rugged countryside and ends at Young's High Bridge, a steel bridge 281 feet high and 1600 feet long. Rolling stock and memorabilia are on display at the museum site. There are restaurants in Versailles, and motels in Lexington, 8 miles east.

Displays	Lionel trains, other trains and toys
Dates open	Wednesday-Saturday 10 a.m.-5 p.m. and Sunday 1-5
Admission	Adults $3, children 5-11 $1.50 (under 5 free), age 60 and over $2.50. Group discounts available. Checks accepted for admission. Credit
Nearby attractions	cards accepted in gift shop. Kentucky State Horse Park, Bluegrass Horse Farms, Headley-Whitley Museum, Shakertown, state capitol
Mailing address	279 Depot Street, Versailles, KY 40383
Phone	(606) 873-2497

NOSTALGIA STATION

Nostalgia Station is a toy and train museum located in a former Louisville & Nashville depot. The exhibits include a reproduction of a Lionel standard gauge store display and an actual Lionel O gauge store display.

It is located on Depot Street at the corner of Douglas, just off Bypass 60 in Versailles, which is about 10 miles west of Lexington and 10 miles southeast of Frankfort, the state capital. Nostalgia Station offers toy train repair and appraisal services.

Displays	Southern Pacific 0-6-0 124, Amtrak coach, Missouri Pacific caboose
Dates open	Year-round Monday-Friday, 8 a.m.-5 p.m.
Admission	Free; donations appreciated
Memberships	Individual $2.50, families $5
Special events	Louisiana Railroad Days (second weekend in April)
Nearby attractions	All Saints Episcopal Church, Dog Trot Museum, Sabine National Wildlife Refuge, Creole Nature Trail, Toledo Bend Dam
Mailing address	P. O. Box 997, DeQuincy, LA 70633
Phone	(318) 786-2823

P &. 저 🎁

DEQUINCY RAILROAD MUSEUM

DeQuincy, Louisiana, got its start as a railroad town — it is the junction of Kansas City Southern's main line from Kansas City to Port Arthur, Texas, with a 23-mile branch to Lake Charles, La., and also with a Union Pacific (ex-Missouri Pacific) line from New Orleans. The museum was established in 1976, a year after the KCS donated its station building and grounds to the city for a park.

On display in the museum are photos, models, hardware, and other railroad memorabilia. DeQuincy is about 50 miles northeast of Beaumont, Tex., at the junction of Louisiana Routes 12 and 27. The museum is in downtown DeQuincy on Lake Charles Avenue. The 5-acre museum grounds include playground equipment for children.

There are restaurants in DeQuincy, and lodging is available in nearby Sulphur and Lake Charles.

Displays	Illinois Central caboose, railroad artifacts and photographs
Admission	Adults 50 cents, children 25 cents
Nearby attractions	New Orleans
Mailing address	P. O. Box 8412, New Orleans, LA 70182
Phone	(504) 288-6489 for recorded information

ᗊ �& 🎁

GRETNA DEPOT

The former Southern Pacific depot at Gretna, Louisiana, houses the Louisiana Railroad Museum. Part of the collection is Illinois Central caboose 9959, built in 1951. The museum is at 4th and Huey P. Long Avenues in Gretna. Gretna is across the Mississippi River from New Orleans.

Displays	Toy trains, memorabilia, and photos	**Nearby attractions**	Kenner City Museum, Louisiana Wildlife and Fisheries Museum, Science Center and Planetarium, New Orleans Saints Hall of Fame, New Orleans
Dates open	Year-round		
Schedule	Tuesday-Saturday 9 a.m.-5 p.m., Sunday 1-5. Closed holidays.		
Admission	Adults $1.50; children 50 cents; seniors citizens $1. Checks and credit cards accepted. Group discounts available.	**Mailing address**	519 Williams Boulevard, Kenner, LA 70062
		Phone	(504) 468-7223

ᗊ &🚻🎁

LOUISIANA TOY TRAIN MUSEUM

The Louisiana Toy Train Museum was established in 1989. The museum is at 519 Williams Boulevard in Kenner, between U. S. 61 (Airline Highway) and the Mississippi River, half a mile from New Orleans International Airport and right next to the Kansas City Southern and Illinois Central Gulf line. Inside over 22,000 items are on display, including toy trains, photos, and memorabilia. A "Boy's Train," one of two in the U. S., is part of the collection. Several cabooses located behind the museum may be reserved for special events such as birthday parties. There are numerous hotels, motels, and restaurants near the museum.

Cars	Heavyweight coaches
Displays	Cabooses, snow plow, and other rolling stock at Belfast; museum at Brooks
Schedule	March-May, September, and October, weekends; June-August, Tuesday-Sunday: depart Belfast for Waldo at 10 a.m. and 12:30 and 2:45 p.m. Fridays, Saturdays, and Sundays in July and August, depart Belfast for Brooks at 5:30 p.m.
Fares	To Waldo, adults $6.95, children under 12 $4.95, age 60 and over $4.95. Credit cards and U. S. checks accepted. Reservations recommended. Group discounts available.
Radio frequency	160.710
Special events	Hobo Days, Train Show
Nearby attractions	Acadia National Park, Penobscot Marine Museum, Maine coast
Mailing address	11 Water Street, Belfast, ME 04915
Phone	(207) 338-2931

DIESEL LOCOMOTIVES

Number	Type	Former owner	Builder	Date
50	70 ton	Belfast & Moosehead Lake	GE	1947
53	70 ton	Berlin Mills	GE	1948
54	70 ton	Berlin Mills	GE	1947

BELFAST & MOOSEHEAD LAKE RAILROAD

The Belfast & Moosehead Lake Railroad connects the coastal city of Belfast with Guilford Transportation Industries' ex-Maine Central line at Burnham Junction, 33 miles inland. B&ML discontinued regular passenger service in 1960 but began running excursion trains in 1987. Power for the excursion train is drawn from B&ML's stable of General Electric 70-ton diesels; passengers ride in former Southern Railway coaches.

The trains are not readily accessible to the handicapped, but the crew will lift wheelchair-bound passengers aboard. Trains make round trips to Waldo and Brooks, 7½ and 12½ miles from Belfast, respectively. The trips take 1¼ and 2½ hours, 14 miles each way, at 1 p.m. Tuesdays and Thursdays, June-September, and on Saturdays during September and October.

There is a small museum and souvenir shop in the station at Brooks. Restaurants and motels can be found in Belfast, which is on U. S. Route 1 about 40 miles south of Bangor.

Locomotives	3 steam
Cars	Coach, open car, caboose
Displays	3 box cars, 1 coach, antique autos
Dates open	Daily 10 a.m.-5 p.m. June 9-October 7, 1990
Schedule	Train operates every half hour.
Admission	Adults $5, children 12 and under $2. Checks and credit cards accepted. Group discounts available.
Memberships	Individuals $15, families $25
Special events	Father's Day, Antique Engine Meet (June 30-July 1, 1990), Antique Auto Days (July 21-22, 1990), Children's Day (August 19, 1990), Maine Narrow Gauge Railroad Day (September 23, 1990), Fall Foliage Festival (October 6-7, 1990)
Nearby attractions	Boothbay Playhouse Theatre Museum, Grand Banks Schooner Museum, Fort Edgecomb, Lincoln County Jail and Museum
Mailing address	Box 123, Boothbay, ME 04537
Phone	(207) 633-4727

BOOTHBAY RAILWAY VILLAGE

In most of the U. S. "narrow gauge" meant rails 3' apart. In Maine it was a foot less. The last two decades of the nineteenth century saw a number of 2'-gauge railroads built into rural Maine. Boothbay Railway Village, established in 1965, evokes the atmosphere of turn-of-the-century Maine, with a 1-mile circle of 2'-gauge track around a re-created rural hamlet.

The train ride takes about 15 minutes; the trains are powered by German-built four-wheel tank engines (a tank engine carries its water in tanks placed over or alongside the boiler and its fuel in a bunker behind the cab instead of in a separate car, a tender, behind the locomotive).

Access to the 8-acre museum grounds is somewhat limited for the handicapped or those pushing a stroller.

The museum is on Route 27 in Boothbay, 10 miles south of Wiscasset; Wiscasset is about 50 miles east of Portland. Staff members are on the premises year-round.

Restaurants and lodging are available in nearby Boothbay Harbor, a summer resort community.

SEASHORE TROLLEY MUSEUM

Now in its 52nd year, Seashore was the first successful railway preservation effort, beginning with Biddeford & Saco Railway open car No. 31. The collection now numbers over 200 mass-transit vehicles representing most major geographic areas of the U. S. as well such foreign cities as Berlin, Glasgow, Hamburg, Liverpool, Nagasaki, and Sydney. Cars operate over more than a mile of the roadbed of the former Atlantic Shore Line interurban. Shuttle cars link the visitor center with the exhibit barns.

The museum is located about 80 miles northeast of Boston, halfway between Portsmouth, New Hampshire, and Portland, Maine. You can reach the museum easily from Exits 3 and 4 of the Maine Turnpike. From Kennebunk proceed north 2.8 miles on U. S. Route 1. At the flashing yellow signal, turn right (east) onto Log Cabin Road and drive 1.7 miles to the museum. From Kennebunkport take North Street from the west end of Maine Street; it's 3.2 miles to the museum. Lodging and restaurants can be found in Kennebunkport, a summer resort area.

Cars	More than 30 restored electric cars, with many more under restoration, plus work equipment and freight cars
Dates open	Daily April 28-October 14, 1990, plus weekends through October and the first weekend in December. Hours: 10 a.m.-5:30 p.m. (last ride 4:30), weekdays June 2-September 9, 1990, and weekends May 26-October 8, 1990; 11 a.m.-3 p.m. weekdays in late May and September and weekends In May and October; 1:15-3:15 (ride and tour only at 1:30) last weekend of April, weekdays in May, and October 9-12.
Schedule	Rides every half hour. Charter trips available.
Admission	Adults $5.50, children 6-16 $3.50 (children under 6 free), $18 maximum per family, age 60 and over $4.50. Friday evening trolley ride (July and August) $2. Group rates available. Checks and credit cards accepted.
Memberships	$17.50 per year
Special events	Annual meeting weekend, May 26-28, Members weekend, October 6-8, 1990 — many extra cars operate those weekends; Christmas Prelude, December 1-2 1990, noon-6 p.m.
Nearby attractions	Beaches, Wedding Cake House, Brick Store Museum, President Bush's summer home
Mailing address	P. O. Drawer A, Kennebunkport, ME 04046
Phone	(207) 967-2712

P &. 开 🎁

Locomotives	2 diesel, 1 gasoline
Cars	Coaches
Displays	Freight cars, maintenance equipment
Dates open	First and third Sunday of each month, May to November
Schedule	Trains run at 11 a.m., 1 p.m., and 3 p.m.
Fares	Adults $2, children 6-12 $1, under 6 free
Memberships	$10 per year
Special events	Old Home Days (third weekend of August)
Nearby attractions	Rangeley Lakes, Sugarloaf Ski Area
Mailing address	P. O. Box B, Phillips, ME 04966
Phone	(207) 639-2881

P & 🎁

SANDY RIVER RAILROAD

The 2'-gauge Sandy River Railroad was opened from Farmington north to Phillips in 1879. It and its successor, the Sandy River & Rangeley Lakes, served northwest Maine until 1935; at its peak the SR&RL had more than 120 miles of track.

In 1969 the Sandy River Railroad was reestablished in Phillips. SR&RL freight and passenger cars have been restored, and train rides are offered on a short piece of track laid along the SR&RL roadbed.

Phillips is on State Route 4 about 65 miles north of Lewiston. The park is at Sanders Station on Mill Hill Road. Restaurants and lodging can be found in Farmington, 18 miles southeast.

Phillips

Displays	Replicas and originals of B&O's earliest locomotives and cars, Camelback and Shay locomotives, early diesels, wide range of steam locomotives, exhibits showing development of track, signals, and bridges, HO scale model railroad
Dates open	Wednesday-Sunday, 10 a.m.-4 p.m. Closed Monday and Tuesday. Call for holiday schedule.
Admission	Adults $4, students 7-18 $3 (under 7 free), age 65 and over $3. Checks accepted.
Nearby attractions	Baltimore Streetcar Museum, Fort McHenry, Harbor Place, H. L. Mencken House, Babe Ruth's Birthplace, Ellicott City B&O Railroad Station Museum
Mailing address	901 West Pratt Street, Baltimore, MD 21223-2699
Phone	(301) 237-2387

P & 🎁

B&O RAILROAD MUSEUM

The Baltimore & Ohio Railroad, now part of CSX, was the first common carrier railroad in the U. S. and the first to offer scheduled freight and passenger service. The museum was established in 1953 by the historically conscious B&O, and at that time its collection covered the B&O's history from a replica of the Tom Thumb of 1829 to a recently retired passenger diesel. The collection soon included items from other railroads, and it kept expanding.

The chief building of the museum is a full-circle roundhouse that was part of B&O's Mount Clare shop complex; the entrance to the museum is through the former Mount Clare station, which was the first railroad station in the U. S. The B&O Museum is on Pratt Street in Baltimore. Access is easiest from the southwest: Frederick Road and U. S. 1 intersect Pratt Street about a mile west of the museum, and Washington Boulevard aims right at the museum.

Cars	13 streetcars
Dates open	Year-round, Sunday noon-5 p.m.; June-October, Saturday noon-5 Groups can be accommodated at any time, but reservations 3 weeks in advance are necessary. Groups planning to visit during regular hours should notify the museum 2 weeks ahead.
Admission	Free
Fares	Adults $1, children 4-11 50 cents, all-day pass $3. Checks accepted. Groups are given two rides for a single fare.
Memberships	Write for information.
Nearby attractions	B&O Railroad Museum, Fort McHenry, Ellicott City B&O Railroad Station Museum
Mailing address	P. O. Box 4881, Baltimore, MD 21211
Phone	(301) 547-0264

BALTIMORE STREETCAR MUSEUM

Three blocks northwest of the Amtrak station in Baltimore at 1901 Falls Road is the Baltimore Streetcar Museum. Its collection is limited to streetcars used in Baltimore because of a unique track gauge, 5'4½". Cars operate on ⅝ mile of track along Falls Road past the former Maryland & Pennsylvania Railroad roundhouse and freight station. In addition to the streetcars (2 horse-drawn and 11 electric) visitors may view an audiovisual presentation titled *Rails*

Into Yesterday depicting the history of street rail transportation in Baltimore.

To reach the museum by car, take the North Avenue exit from the Jones Falls Expressway (I-83), go east over the viaduct to Maryland Avenue, turn right (south), and at the next corner, Lafayette Avenue, turn right again, and then take a third right onto Falls Road.

Baltimore

Displays	HO scale model railroad, photos, artifacts
Dates open	Mid-April to the second week of December, Saturday 10 a.m.-4 p.m. and Sunday 1-4
Admission	Adults $2, children 5-12 $1 (under 5 free), age 60 and over $1. Checks and credit cards accepted. Group discounts available.

Memberships	Write for information.
Special events	Railroad Days (first weekend in October, 1990), Victorian Christmas (weekend after Thanksgiving), History Days (mid April)
Nearby attractions	Harpers Ferry National Historic Park,

Antietam Battlefield Park, Appalachian Trail, Maryland Midland Railway

| Mailing address | 40 West Potomac Street, Brunswick, MD 21716 |
| Phone | (301) 834-7100 |

BRUNSWICK MUSEUM

In 1886 the Baltimore & Ohio opened its extension from Baltimore to Philadelphia and found it needed a classification yard east of Cumberland, where its lines from Chicago and St. Louis joined, and west of Point of Rocks, where lines diverged for Washington and Baltimore. The B&O chose the town of Berlin, 6 miles east of Harpers Ferry, as the site for the yard. As the yard and engine terminal developed, the population of the town grew from 200 to 5000, and the town was renamed Brunswick.

The Brunswick Museum, established in 1968, displays artifacts and photos of the railroad. On the third floor is a large HO model railroad depicting the B&O between Washington and Brunswick; the second floor includes an exhibit on Brunswick railroaders. The museum is at the corner of Maryland and Potomac Streets, a block and a half south of the bridge that takes Route 17 over the yards, and a block uphill from the railroad. Brunswick is on the Potomac River about 60 miles west of Baltimore and 50 miles northwest of Washington. Food is available in Brunswick; lodging is in Frederick, about 15 miles northeast, and Harper's Ferry.

Displays	Chesapeake Beach Railway memorabilia
Dates open	May-September, daily 1-4 p.m.; April and October, Saturday and Sunday 1-4
Admission	Free
Memberships	$5 annually
Special events	Antique Auto Show third Sunday in May; Christmas Open House first Sunday in

Nearby attractions	December; summer concerts Battle Creek Cypress Swamp, Calvert Marine Museum
Mailing address	P. O. Box 783, Chesapeake Beach, MD 20732
Phone	(301) 257-3892, 855-6472

CHESAPEAKE BEACH RAILWAY MUSEUM

The Chesapeake Beach Railway was opened in 1900 from Seat Pleasant, Maryland, on the District of Columbia border, to Chesapeake Beach, a resort 28 miles southeast on the shore of Chesapeake Bay. Among its backers were two Colorado railroad builders, Otto Mears and David Moffat. The line was abandoned in 1935, having succumbed to the competion of automobiles.

The road's one surviving station at Chesapeake Beach was offered to the Calvert County Historical Society in 1979, and the last Chesapeake Beach passenger car, a coach named *Dolores*, was brought to the station. The museum contains pictures and artifacts of the railway. Chesapeake Beach is southeast of Washington and south of Annapolis on Maryland Routes 260 and 261. The museum is on Mears Avenue. There is a restaurant next to the museum, and lodging can be found in nearby Rose Haven.

Cars	Coaches, caboose
Schedule	April 14-December 23, 1990: Saturdays and Sundays depart Cumberland at 11:30 a.m. and 3:30 p.m. (no 3:30 trains in November); additional trains: May, Tuesdays and Thursdays at 11:30; July-October, Tuesday-Friday at 11:30 and 3:30. May 12 and 19, June 13, July 18, and August 7, 10:30 instead of 11:30.
Fares	Adults $9.50-$14, seniors and students, $8.50-$13.50, children 4-12 $5-8, depending on the month (lowest prices in April and November, highest in October). Checks and credit cards accepted. Group discounts available.
Displays	Baltimore & Ohio and Western Maryland photos and artifacts
Dates open	Saturdays and Sundays, 1-4 p.m.
Admission	Free
Nearby attractions	Chesapeake & Ohio Canal National Historic Park, Rocky Gap State Park, Allegany County Historical Society
Mailing address	Canal Street, Cumberland, MD 21502
Phone	(301) 759-4400; (800) TRAIN-50 (301) 722-2101 for recorded information

LOCOMOTIVES

Number	Type	Former owner	Builder	Date
STEAM				
2138	4-6-2	Canadian Pacific	Montreal	1946
1286	4-6-2	Canadian Pacific	Canadian Locomotive Co.	1948
DIESEL				
40	GP9	Chesapeake & Ohio	EMD	1954

WESTERN MARYLAND SCENIC RAILROAD — WESTERN MARYLAND STATION CENTER

The Western Maryland Scenic Railroad operates trains between Cumberland and Frostburg, 17 miles, over former Western Maryland and Cumberland & Pennsylvania trackage. Cars include two air-conditioned coaches, an open-window coach, and an air-conditioned dining car.

Trains depart from the Western Maryland Station Center on Canal Street in Cumberland and run to Frostburg via the Narrows, Helmstetter's Curve, and Brush Tunnel. Travel time is 45 minutes each way, with a 90-minute layover at Frostburg, where there is a restaurant in the station. Reservations are recommended. Trains are accessible to the handicapped.

The former Western Maryland station in Cumberland houses a museum operated by Western Maryland Chapter, National Railway Historical Society. To reach the Cumberland station from U. S. Routes 40 and 48, take the Downtown Cumberland exit westbound and the Johnson Street exit eastbound.

Restaurants and motels can be found in Cumberland and Frostburg.

Cumberland

Displays	Artifacts and memorabilia, model railroad depicting B&O's early days
Dates open	Year-round, Friday-Monday 11 a.m.-5 p.m.; also Wednesdays and Thursdays from Memorial Day to Labor Day. Open at other times for groups with reservations. Closed Thanksgiving, Christmas, and New Year's Day.
Admission	Adults $3, children 5-12 $1 (under 5 free), persons age 62 and over $2. Checks accepted. Group discount available.
Nearby attractions	B&O Railroad Museum, Baltimore Streetcar Museum, Western Maryland Railway Museum, Maryland Midland Railway
Mailing address	2711 Maryland Avenue, Ellicott City, MD 21043
Phone	(301) 461-1945, 461-1944 for recorded information

ELLICOTT CITY B&O RAILROAD STATION MUSEUM

The first terminus of the Baltimore & Ohio Railroad was Ellicott City, 13 miles from Baltimore. The station at Ellicott City has become a museum, a cooperative project of Howard County and Historic Ellicott City, Inc. In addition to the exhibits and displays, the main station building houses a library and a gift shop.

The freight house contains an HO scale model railroad depicting the early B&O. The turntable area between the two buildings is being excavated by archeologists. One of the buildings is barrier-free; the other has 5 stairs. The museum is at the corner of Maryland Avenue and Main Street (also known as Frederick Road and State Route 144) in Ellicott City, 4 miles west of Exit 13 of I-695, the Baltimore Beltway. Restaurants and antique and specialty shops are nearby. Lodging can be found in Columbia, 5 miles away, and throughout metropolitan Baltimore.

Displays	Western Maryland memorabilia, N scale model railroad	Memberships	$18 per year
Dates open	May-October, Sunday 1-4 p.m.	Special events	Monthly meeting, annual convention
Admission	Free	Mailing address	Western Maryland Ry Historical Society, P. O. Box 395, Union Bridge, MD 21791

WESTERN MARYLAND RAILWAY HISTORICAL SOCIETY MUSEUM

The Western Maryland Railway Historical Society was founded in 1967 to preserve the heritage of the WM, now part of CSX. It has established a museum in the former general office building of the railway at Union Bridge, next to the Maryland Midland station.

On exhibit are Western Maryland artifacts and an N scale model railroad. The museum includes a library and an archives collection, which are available for research by appointment.

Cars	Streamlined coaches, dome diner, open-window coaches, buffet-lounge, business car	Special events	cards accepted. Group discounts available. Westminster Railfest, Union Bridge Volunteer Fire Department Day, Thurmont Catoctin Colorfest, Autumn Gold Special
Schedule	Trains operate selected weekends and some weekdays, April-December; Sundays only January-March. Most depart from Union Bridge at 1 p.m. Charter trips are available.	Nearby attractions	Catoctin Mountain Park, Gettysburg National Military Park, Monocacy Battlefield, Brunswick Museum
Fares	Adults $18 coach, $35 first class. Reservations required. Checks and credit	Mailing address	P. O. Box 478, Union Bridge, MD 21791
		Phone	(301) 775-TRAIN

THE ENTERTRAINMENT LINE

The Maryland Midland was established in 1980 to operate the Taneytown-Walkersville portion of the former Pennsy branch from York, Pennsylvania, to Frederick, Maryland. In 1983 the road acquired the former Western Maryland main line from Westminster to Highfield, Md. The railroad runs Blue Mountain Limited excursions from Union Bridge to Highfield (50 miles, 4 hours). Most trips depart from the Union Bridge station (41 North Main Street); spe-

cial excursions are operated several times a year from other towns along the line. Snacks and souvenirs are available on the train, which offers coach, first class (with buffet), and luxury accommodations. Handicapped persons can be accommodated with advance notice. Union Bridge is between Frederick and Westminster on Maryland Route 75, about 40 miles northwest of Baltimore. Food and lodging can be found in Westminster, Frederick, and Thurmont.

Locomotives	15 streetcars
Dates open	Year-round, weekends noon-5 p.m.; also Memorial Day, July 4, and Labor Day, noon-5, and Wednesdays in July and August, noon-4
Schedule	Cars run every half hour from noon to 4:30 p.m. (3:30 on summer Wednesdays)
Admission	Free
Fares	Adults $1.50, children under 18 $1 (under 2 free). Checks and credit cards accepted. Group discounts available with advance notice.
Memberships	Write for information.
Special events	Parade of Trolleys, third Sundays of April and September; Holly Trolley Illuminations, 5-9 p.m., weekends in December
Nearby attractions	Washington, D. C.
Mailing address	P. O. Box 4007, Silver Spring, MD 20914
Phone	(301) 384-6088

STREETCARS

Number	Type	Original owner or city	Builder	Date
1101	PCC	D. C. Transit	St. Louis	1937
1053	Pre-PCC	Capital Transit	St. Louis	1935
678	Double-truck city car	Third Avenue Ry, New York	TARy	1939
120	Single-truck tram	Graz, Austria	Weitzer	1908
5954	Single-truck tram	Berlin, Germany	Duwag	1924
955	Single-truck tram	Düsseldorf, Germany	Schondorff	1928

NATIONAL CAPITAL TROLLEY MUSEUM

Streetcar service ended in Washington, D. C., on January 28, 1962, and the cars were sent off to second careers in Texas, Spain, and Yugoslavia. By then the National Capital Trolley Museum had been established, and within a decade it was operating cars and building a collection that included a number of cars from Europe. The museum's visitor center houses exhibits depicting the history of Washington's streetcar system. Cars make a 1-mile, 20-minute round trip. The museum is located in Northwest Branch Regional Park at 1313 Bonifant Road, between Layhill Road (Maryland Route 182) and New Hampshire Avenue (Route 650) — or 14 miles due north of the White House. Food and lodging can be found in Wheaton and throughout the metropolitan area.

Displays	³/₄"-scale models, railroadiana
Dates open	Patriots Day (mid April) to the last week-end in June, and Labor day to the first weekend in December, Saturdays, Sundays, and holidays (except Thanksgiving), 10 a.m.-4 p.m.. Last weekend in June to Labor Day, daily 10 a.m.-5 p.m.
Admission	Adults $1; children 5-12, 50 cents (under 5 free); age 60 and over 50 cents. Checks accepted. Group discounts available.
Memberships	$12 per year
Special events	Railroad show, latter part of January
Nearby attractions	Heritage State Park, Fall River Marine Museum, Battleship Cove, Columbia Street Cultural District
Mailing address	P. O. Box 3455, Fall River, MA 02722
Phone	(508) 674-9340; 673-7061 year-round

OLD COLONY & FALL RIVER RAILROAD MUSEUM

The Old Colony & Fall River Railroad Museum is housed in a former Pennsylvania Railroad Class P70 coach directly across from the entrance to Battleship Cove, where U.S.S. *Massachusetts* is on display. The museum contains several ³/₄"-scale models and a collection of New Haven, Penn Central, Conrail, and Amtrak artifacts.

A ramp leads from the parking lot to the entrance, but the door is of ordinary width. The museum is located at 1 Water Street — at the corner of Central Street — southwest of and below the intersection of I-195 and Massachusetts Route 138. Restaurants and motels can be found nearby.

Fall River

Locomotive	1 diesel
Cars	3 restored Lackawanna coaches
Schedule	Saturdays and Sundays June 16-0August 26,1990. Trains make three trips daily between 1 and 4 p.m. Charter trips available.
Fares	Adults $7, children under 12 $4, age 65 and over $6. Fares for shorter run are half those stated.
Memberships	Write for information.
Nearby attractions	Basketball Hall of Fame, Volleyball Hall of Fame, Children's Museum
Mailing address	221 Appleton Street, Holyoke, MA 01040
Phone	(413) 534-1723 (park info); 534-0909 (railroad info, TDD and voice)

P & ⚲

HOLYOKE HERITAGE PARK RAILROAD

The Pioneer Valley Railroad, a short line running from Westfield to Holyoke and Northampton, Massachusetts, and the Holyoke Heritage Park Railroad team up to operate tourist trains from the Holyoke Heritage State Park to the Holyoke Mall at Ingleside, 3 miles, and to Westfield Center, 10 miles. Pioneer Valley provides the rails and the locomotive, and Holyoke Heritage Park Railroad furnishes the passenger cars. Special events are held throughou the operating season.

Holyoke is in central Massachusetts on the Connecticut River Use Exit 16 of I-91, then go north 1 mile on Route 202. Turn righ onto Appleton Street and follow the signs to Heritage State Park Restaurants and lodging are available nearby.

Locomotives	3 diesels
Cars	Coaches
Schedule	June 11-October 22, 1990, Tuesdays, Wednesdays, Thursdays, and Sundays, trains leave Hyannis at 10 a.m. and 12:30 and 3 p.m.; trains leave Sagamore at 11 a.m. and 1:30 and 4 p.m.
Fares	Adults $10.50, children 3-12 $6.50, age 64 and over $9.50. Checks accepted. Group discounts available.
Special events	Railfan's Day (June 23, 1990)
Nearby attractions	Boat cruises, Heritage Plantation, Glass Museum
Mailing address	P. O. Box 7, South Carver, MA 02366
Phone	(508) 866-4526

DIESEL LOCOMOTIVES

Number	Type	Builder	Date
0670	RS-1	Alco	1948
0672	RS-1	Alco	1955
1058	S-4	Alco	1950

CAPE COD SCENIC RAILROAD

    The Cape Cod Scenic Railroad, owned by the Edaville Railroad, operates excursion trains between Hyannis and Sagamore, at the north end of the Cape Cod Canal, with an intermediate stop at Sandwich. The ride takes 37 minutes to Sandwich and 45 minutes to Sagamore. Returning trains leave Sandwich 10 minutes after leaving Sagamore. The Sunday 4 p.m. train from Sagamore may be subject to a 50-minute layover at Sandwich, depending on Amtrak schedules. A continental breakfast is available on the morning trains, and lunch is available on the early afternoon trains. The station in Hyannis is at the corner of Main and Center Streets, a block from the Plymouth & Brockton bus station.

    There are restaurants and motels within walking distance.

Hyannis

Locomotives	5 diesel
Cars	Ex-Lackawanna and Pennsylvania coaches
Displays	Caboose, model railroad
Dates open	Weekends and holidays Memorial Day through October, 10 a.m.-4 p.m.
Schedule	Write or call for train schedule.
Admission	Free
Fares	Adults $7, children 5-12 $4, age 60 and over, $6. Checks and credit cards accepted. Group discounts available.
Memberships	Write for information.
Special events	Halloween party
Nearby attractions	Norman Rockwell Museum, Hancock Shaker Village, Tanglewood (home of the Berkshire Music Festival), Jacob's Pillow Dance Festival, Berkshire Theater Festival
Mailing address	P. O. Box 2195, Lenox, MA 01240
Phone	(413) 637-2210

DIESEL LOCOMOTIVES

Number	Type	Former owner	Builder	Date
6	S-1	Maine Central	Alco	1946
8	110 ton	GE (Pittsfield)	GE	1967
19	80 ton	GE (Schenectady)	GE	1947
67	50 ton	United Illuminating	GE	1957
8619	SW8	New York Central	EMD	1953

BERKSHIRE SCENIC RAILWAY MUSEUM

The Berkshire Scenic Railway Museum, established in 1984, operates excursion trains over the former Berkshire line of the New Haven Railroad along the Housatonic River from Lenox, Massachusetts. The route's last regular passenger trains, which ran weekends only between New York and Pittsfield, Mass., were discontinued when Amtrak took over the nation's passenger service in 1971.

The railway's trackage rights were withdrawn the day before the 1989 season opened, and as this book went to press in early 1990, the railway was negotiating for use of the tracks. Write or call for train schedules.

The railroad's headquarters are in the former New Haven station at Lenox, which is being rehabilitated and contains a small museum and a gift shop. Tickets can be purchased at the museum and gift shop or on the train. Food and lodging can be found throughout the Berkshire area — reservations for lodging are advisable.

Cars	2 open streetcars, 1 closed car
Dates open	Park is open daily year-round; streetcars operate May 26-October 8, 1990, 9 a.m.-5 p.m.
Admission	Free
Fares	Adults $2, children 16 and under free, age 62 and over $1. Reservations are necessary.
Special events	Lowell Folk Festival, July 27-29, 1990
Nearby attractions	Lexington, Concord, Boston
Mailing address	169 Merrimac Street, Lowell, MA 01852
Phone	(508) 459-1000

LOWELL NATIONAL HISTORICAL PARK

Abundant water power and the new technology of the power loom combined in the early 1800s to create America's first industrial city, Lowell, Massachusetts. The textile industry moved to the South after World War Two, and decline overtook Lowell (and many other New England cities). In the 1970s high-tech industry began moving into the area, Lowell began to boom again, and the area of the textile mills and power canals became first a Heritage State Park and then a National Historical Park dedicated to the American industrial revolution and the first planned industrial city.

The park includes restored mills and boarding houses, and boat rides along canals. A mile of a Boston & Maine industrial track was electrified and extended, and three streetcars were constructed by GOMACO of Ida Grove, Iowa, to operate along the track and tie together the areas of the park. The streetcar ride takes 30 minutes.

If you are driving, follow U. S. 3 or Interstate 495 to the Lowell Connector; leave the Connector at Exit 5N, Thorndike Street, and follow signs to the parking area for the historical park.

You can also take a Massachusetts Bay Transportation Authority train from North Station, Boston — hourly on weekdays; every two hours on weekends and holidays. The 26-mile ride takes about 40 minutes.

There are numerous restaurants in and around the park area; lodging is available nearby. The park facilities are partially accessible to the handicapped.

Displays	More than 2000 model trains; 50 operating trains, many of which can be activated by visitors
Dates open	Weekends January-May and September-October, Daily Memorial Day-Labor Day and Thanksgiving-December 31, 10 a.m.-6 p.m.
Admission	Adults $4, children 4-12 $2.50, age 65 and over $3.50. Group discounts available.
Memberships	Write for information.
Special events	Usually one weekend a month has a special theme.
Nearby attractions	Cape Cod, Plymouth, Edaville Railroad
Mailing address	49 Plymouth Street, Middleboro, MA 02346-1197
Phone	(508) 947-5303

A&D TOY-TRAIN VILLAGE AND RAILWAY MUSEUM

More than 2000 toy trains of all kinds from around the world are on display at the A&D Toy-Train Village and Railway Museum. The museum began with a Christmas train set that soon outgrew an apartment, then a basement, then a barn, and is now housed in a former supermarket.

Middleboro is in southeastern Massachusetts between Taunton and Plymouth and between Brockton and Fall River. To reach the museum, go north on Routes 18 and 28, 2 miles from the Middleboro traffic circle, junction of 18 and 28 with U. S. 44. Turn left (west) on Plymouth Street; the museum is at 49 Plymouth Street.

Locomotives	4 steam, 1 diesel
Cars	Wood coaches, open cars, cabooses
Displays	Boston & Maine 2-6-0 and *Flying Yankee*
Dates open	Weekends in May, noon-5 p.m.; daily June-Labor Day 10 a.m.-5:30 p.m.; Labor Day through October weekends 10:30-5 with steam, Monday-Friday 10:30-3 with diesel power; November through first Sunday after New Year's Day, except Thanksgiving and Christmas, weekends 2-9, weekdays 4-9
Schedule	Trains run hourly on the hour.
Admission	Adults $12.50, children 3-12 $6.50, senior citizens $8.50. Admission includes all rides and attractions. Checks accepted. Group discounts available (reservations necessary for groups).
Memberships	Write for information.
Special events	Civil War Weekend (second weekend in June), Railfans Weekend (third weekend in June), Antique and Classic Auto Show (third Sunday in August), Christmas Festival (November-New Year's)
Nearby attractions	Plymouth, Cape Cod, A&D Toy-Train Village, Cape Cod Scenic Railroad
Mailing address	P. O. Box 7, South Carver, MA 02366
Phone	(508) 866-4526

LOCOMOTIVES

Number	Type	Former owner	Builder	Date
STEAM				
3	0-4-4 T	Monson Railroad	Vulcan	1913
4	0-4-4 T	Monson Railroad	Vulcan	1918
7	2-4-4T	Bridgton & Harrison	Baldwin	1913
8	2-4-4T	Bridgton & Harrison	Baldwin	1924
DIESEL				
1			GE	1949

EDAVILLE RAILROAD

When Maine's 2'-gauge Bridgton & Harrison ceased operation in 1941, its rolling stock was purchased by Ellis D. Atwood, who had a large cranberry plantation at South Carver, Massachusetts. Atwood moved the equipment to Massachusetts at the end of World War Two, laid a 5-mile loop of track on the dikes around his cranberry bogs, and set the railroad to work hauling cranberries and sand and, more often, people. Word spread, and soon Atwood was in the tourist-railroad business. Atwood died in 1950, but the Edaville Railroad (the name came from his initials) thrived and grew, adding a museum and various tourist attractions and becoming separate from the cranberry business.

In addition to the 30-minute, 5-mile train ride, Edaville offers children's rides, a petting zoo, and entertainment. The Edaville Railroad is southeast of Middleboro and southwest of Plymouth on Massachusetts Route 58, south of U. S. 44 and north of I-495/State Route 25.

Edaville has a restaurant and a snack bar; food and lodging are available in Plymouth, about 15 miles northeast.

Locomotives	Diesel hood units
Cars	Streamlined coaches, cafe car, round-end observation car
Schedule	May-October, several Sundays a month, plus one December trip. Charter trains available.
Fares	Depend on itinerary. Fares on the Zoo Train to Providence, for example, are adults $21.95, children under 13 $12.95, observation car $24.95. Babies not occupying a seat ride free; persons 62 and over receive a 10 percent discount. Discounts are available for groups of 25 or more. Tickets must be purchased in advance by mail or in person; checks accepted.
Nearby attractions	Old Sturbridge Village
Mailing address	P. O. Box 1188, Worcester, MA 01601
Phone	(508) 755-4000

PROVIDENCE & WORCESTER RAILROAD

The Providence & Worcester was opened between the cities of its name in 1847, and by the turn of the century it was part of the New Haven. In 1970 the P&W requested independence from New Haven successor Penn Central and in 1973 got it. It has purchased several former New Haven and Boston & Maine lines in Rhode Island, Connecticut, and Massachusetts, and has acquired freight rights on Amtrak between Providence & Old Saybrook.

In 1983 the P&W began operating weekend excursion trains using former Union Pacific coaches and dining car and an ex-Northern Pacific observation car. Trains operate up to three Sundays a month to such diverse destinations as Roger Williams Park Zoo in Providence; the Valley Railroad; Mystic Seaport; the U. S. Naval Submarine Base in Groton, Conn.; plus fall foliage and Santa Claus trains. Depending on the destination, trips take 2 to 10 hours.

The trains are air-conditioned and heated and carry a dining car with snack service and an observation car offering first-class service. In addition there is a souvenir shop in one of the coaches.

All trains depart from the P&W yard at 382 Southbridge Street in Worcester, Mass., half a mile from Exit 11 of I-290. Departure time depends on the destination; most are between 8 and 11:30 a.m. Handicapped persons may have difficulty boarding and detraining; advance inquiry is advisable.

Food and lodging are available in Worcester.

Cars	Coaches, open cars
Displays	Passenger and freight cars, historical exhibits in station
Schedule	May-October, trains depart at 10 a.m., noon, and 2, 4, and 6 p.m. Charter trips available.
Fares	Adults $6.50, children 8-14 $4.50, children 2-7 $2.50, age 60 and up $5.50. Group discount available. Checks accepted.
Radio frequency	154.600
Nearby attractions	Mackinac Island, Fort Mackinac, Old Mill Creek, Petoskey State Park Beach
Mailing address	P. O. Box 247, Alanson, MI 49706
Phone	(616) 347-8200

DIESEL LOCOMOTIVE

Number	Type	Former owner	Builder	Date
8419	SW1	Baltimore & Ohio	EMD	1942

LITTLE TRAVERSE SCENIC RAILWAY

The Little Traverse Scenic Railway operates excursion trains on former Michigan Northern (earlier, Pennsylvania Railroad) track between Alanson and Bay View, just east of Petoskey. Alanson is on U. S. Route 31 and Michigan Route 68, 11 miles northeast of Petoskey and 25 miles south of Mackinaw City.

Passengers ride in restored coaches or open cars; a vintage diesel switcher pulls the train. The train ride takes about 80 minutes.

The railway's plans include steam power and a dinner train. Food and lodging are available in Alanson.

Locomotives	6 diesel
Cars	46 freight cars with seats, 2 cabooses
Dates open	Week before Memorial Day-Labor Day, Monday-Saturday 10 a.m.-6 p.m., Sunday 1-6; then weekends through October, 1-5 p.m.
Fares	Adults $2.75, children 12 and under $2.25, age 65 and over $2.50. Group discounts available.
Special events	Valley of Flags (July 4 weekend), Operation Lifesaver (third weekend in August), Halloween Spook Train Ride, Christmas Fantasyland Ride
Nearby attractions	Village of Frankenmuth
Mailing address	7065 Dixie Highway, Bridgeport, MI 48722
Phone	(517) 777-3480

JUNCTION VALLEY RAILROAD

The Junction Valley Railroad has 1½ miles of 14⅛"-gauge track. Quarter-size trains loop around a lake and then pass through woods to a picnic area with concession stands and playground equipment, operating according to regular railroad practices. The ride takes about 20 minutes. Children must be accompanied by adults. Guided tours are available of the railroad's shop, where all the equipment was built, and staff is on premises year-round.

The railroad is located a few miles southeast of Saginaw, Michigan. From Flint and south, leave I-75 at Exit 136, go east to the first traffic signal, then north 6 miles on Dixie Highway. From Saginaw and north, use Exit 144 from I-75 and follow Dixie Highway southeast 2 miles to just beyond Junction Road.

Restaurants and lodging can be found in Bridgeport and Frankenmuth, 5 miles east.

Locomotives	3 diesels, 10 motor cars				
Cars	Fairmont motor cars, gondolas, cabooses				
Displays	Ann Arbor RS1 diesels, motor cars, and other maintenance equipment				

Locomotives	3 diesels, 10 motor cars
Cars	Fairmont motor cars, gondolas, cabooses
Displays	Ann Arbor RS1 diesels, motor cars, and other maintenance equipment
Schedule	Weekends and holidays June-October, frequent departures noon-5 p.m. Charter trips are available on weekends.
Admission	Free
Fares	Adults $5, children 2-12 $2.50. Checks accepted; credit cards accepted at Tecumseh but not at Clinton. Group discounts available.
Memberships	$10 per year
Special events	Promenade the Past in Tecumseh, third weekend in May; Clinton Fall Festival, last full weekend in September
Nearby attractions	Irish Hills, Michigan International Speedway
Mailing address	P. O. Box 434, Clinton, MI 49236-0434
Phone	(517) 456-7677 (456-SMRS); (517) 456-9610 year-round

DIESEL LOCOMOTIVES

Number	Type	Former owner	Builder	Date
57	20-ton	Hayes-Albion Corp.	Plymouth	1938
303	RS2	Ann Arbor	Alco	1950
8201	RS2	New York Central	Alco	1950

SOUTHERN MICHIGAN RAILROAD

The Southern Michigan Railroad runs trains over a former Conrail branch (ex-New York Central) from Tecumseh, Michigan, north to Clinton, 4½ miles, in the summer, and from Tecumseh south to Raisin Center, 6 miles, during October. The line, which was built in 1839, is a typical rural branch traversing fields and woods. Scenic highlights of the trips are the bridges on which the line crosses the River Raisin. Most of the passenger-carrying cars are open, so dress for the weather.

At Clinton the Southern Michigan Railroad Society, which operates the railroad, has a museum containing artifacts, photographs, locomotives, and cars. An interesting aspect of the railroad is a collection of small motor cars that were used to carry track workers and their tools and supplies.

Clinton is in southeast Michigan about 25 miles southwest of Ann Arbor and 45 miles northwest of Toledo, Ohio. The station and museum are at 320 South Division Street, 3 blocks south of U. S. Route 12. In Tecumseh trains stop at the corner of Chicago and Evans Streets, and tickets can be purchased at The Lucky Duck.

The round-trip ride takes about 2 hours. There are restaurants in Tecumseh and Clinton; lodging can be found in Tecumseh.

Locomotives	3 steam
Cars	Open cars; occasionally 2 historic cars
Dates open	Daily 9-5; closed Thanksgiving and Christmas; village building interiors closed January through mid-March
Schedule	Train operates mid-April to November 1
Admission	Adults $10.50 to museum, $10.50 to village; children 5-12 $5.25/$5.25; senior citizens $9.50/$9.50. Combination pass, adult $18, children $9. Credit cards accepted. Group discounts available.
Fares	All ages $1.50 (good all day)
Memberships	Write for information.
Special events	The museum and village have numerous special events but none of them is railroad-oriented.
Nearby attractions	Detroit; Windsor, Ontario
Mailing address	P. O. Box 1970, Dearborn, MI 48121
Phone	(313) 271-1620

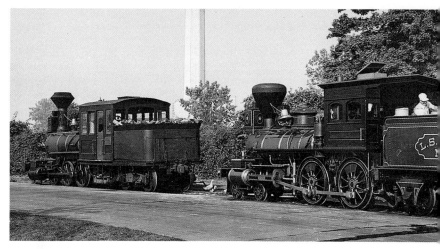

HENRY FORD MUSEUM & GREENFIELD VILLAGE

The Henry Ford Museum & Greenfield Village tells how America changed from a rural, agrarian society to an urban industrial nation, focusing on the period from 1800 to 1950. The museum covers 12 acres, and its collections include transportation, agriculture, power, communication, and domestic arts.

Adjacent to the museum is 240-acre Greenfield Village, consisting of homes and workplaces, many of which were moved there from various parts of the U. S. Henry Ford Museum & Greenfield Village was founded by Henry Ford as a tribute to his friend Thomas Edison and was dedicated in 1929. It is an independent, nonprofit, educational institution not connected with the Ford Motor Company or Ford Foundation.

Steam-powered trains circle Greenfield Village on a 2-mile loop of track. The ride takes about 20 minutes. The museum contains several small, older locomotives, some original, some replicas; a Chesapeake & Ohio 2-6-6-6; several older passenger cars; and a collection of railroad hardware, notably lanterns, rail, and couplers.

Dearborn is 10 miles southwest of Detroit and a 15-minute ride from the Detroit Metropolitan Airport. The museum is located at 20900 Oakwood Boulevard, 2 miles from the Southfield Freeway (Route 39) and 2 miles from Exit 206 of the Detroit Industrial Freeway (I-94).

The museum is accessible to the handicapped; not all the buildings in Greenfield Village are. The museum and the village have several restaurants and snack bars; food and lodging can be found in Dearborn.

Schedule, Fares, and Information

Schedule	Year-round, every 12 minutes, 7 a.m.-6 p.m. Monday-Friday, 10-6 on weekends; on special occasions such as summer ethnic festivals cars operate to 11 p.m. Charter trips available.
Fares	45 cents
Nearby attractions	Greektown, Trapper's Alley, Renaissance Center, Rivertown, Bricktown, Cobo Hall Convention Center, Henry Ford Museum & Greenfield Village
Mailing address	1301 East Warren, Detroit, MI 48207
Phone	(313) 933-1300

STREETCARS

Number	Type	Native City	Date
	Closed	Lisbon, Portugal	1899
	Closed	Lisbon, Portugal	1899
	Closed	Lisbon, Portugal	1899
	Closed	Lisbon, Portugal	1925
	Closed	Lisbon, Portugal	1925
	Closed	Lisbon, Portugal	1899
4	Double-decker	Burton-on-Trent, England	1904
247	Open	Lisbon, Portugal	1901
Nestlé	Closed	Vevey, Switzerland	1895

DETROIT DEPARTMENT OF TRANSPORTATION

Detroit's last streetcar line shut down in 1956, but twenty years later streetcars returned to operate along nine blocks of Washington Boulevard in downtown Detroit. Instead of the streamlined PCC cars that were sold to Mexico came six antique 4-wheel cars from Lisbon, Portugal, five closed cars and one open. They were later joined by other cars, one of them a British double-deck car. It and the open car operate only during the summer.

The line was extended to the Renaissance Center in 1980. The total length of the meter-gauge track is 1 mile; the ride from the Renaissance Center to Grand Circus Park takes 12 minutes.

Food and lodging are available: The trolley runs past three of Detroit's most elegant hotels. The Grand Circus Park underground garage offers the least expensive parking in the area of the trolley.

Detroit

		Cars	Coaches, open cars

Cars Coaches, open cars
Dates open Monday-Friday May 12 to September 3, 1990; weekends Labor Day-October 21, 1990; Thursday-Sunday in December: 10 a.m.-5:30 p.m.
Schedule Hourly departures, Monday-Friday 11-4, weekends and holidays noon-5
Admission Adults $7.25, children 4-12 $6.25 (under 4 free), age 60 and over $4.95. Checks accepted. Group discounts available (reservations are advisable).
Memberships Write for information.
Special events Railfans Weekend, Christmas at Crossroads, Capt. Phogg Balloon Festival, Michigan Storytellers Festival, Harvest Jubilee, Ghost Train
Nearby attractions Flint Cultural Center, Pennywhistle Place, Frankenmuth
Mailing address 5045 Stanley Road, Flint, MI 48506
Phone (313) 736-7100; 736-3220 for recorded information

LOCOMOTIVES

Number	Type	Former owner	Builder	Date
STEAM				
2	4-6-0	Alaska	Baldwin	1920
3*	2-6-0	Quincy & Torch Lake	Brooks	1894
4*	2-8-0	Potosi & Rio Verde	Baldwin	1904
464	2-8-2	Denver & Rio Grande Western	Baldwin	1903
DIESEL				
5	12-ton	American Smelting & Refining	Plymouth	1950
1203	C-C	U. S. Gypsum	Porter	1946

* not in service

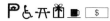

HUCKLEBERRY RAILROAD

A few miles north of Flint, Michigan, the Genesee County Parks and Recreation Commission operates Crossroads Village, a replica of an 1800s-era country town, complete with the 3'-gauge Huckleberry Railroad. The train makes a 45-minute, 10-mile trip through the Genesee Recreation Area. Usual motive power is an ex-Alaska Railroad 4-6-0 or an ex-Rio Grande 2-8-2. Staff is on the premises year-round. The grounds and railroad are fully accessible to the handicapped. Crossroads Village has a cafe and a snack bar.

Restaurants can be found in Genesee and Flint; lodging in Flint. To reach Crossroads Village, use Exit 11, Carpenter Road, from I-475 in the northern part of Flint. Drive east approximately a mile, then turn north on Bray Road.

Displays	Crossing watchman's tower, stationary crane, South Shore interurban cars 13 and 21		Impression 5 Science Museum, air museum, North Lansing Historic Commercial District
Dates open	By appointment	Memberships	Write for information.
Admission	Free; donations welcome	Mailing address	306 East Grand River, Lansing, MI 48906
Nearby attractions	State capitol, state museum, riverwalk,	Phone	(517) 485-9600

MICHIGAN RAILROAD MUSEUM

In the center of the North Lansing Historic Commercial District is the Michigan Railroad Museum. The museum building houses a collection of books, maps, timetables, and other historic items. Just west of the museum building is an outdoor display area.

As this book went to press, the museum was seeking a new location, so a letter or phone call in advance of a visit is advisable.

Food and lodging are available nearby.

Dates open	Mt. Clemens Depot Museum: Sundays year-round except major winter holiday weekends, 2-4 p.m.		6 free). Admission to the Selfridge Military Air Museum is an additional 50 cents for adults, 25 cents for children.
Schedule	Mid-May through September, Sundays, leave Caboose Depot at 1, 2, 3, and 4 p.m. Charter trips operated.	Memberships	Group discounts available; reservations required for groups. Checks accepted. Write for information.
		Mailing address	P. O. Box 12, Fraser, MI 48026
Admission	Mt. Clemens Depot Museum: free	Phone	(313) 466-5035; 463-1863 for recorded information
Fares	Adults $4, children 6-12 $2 (under		

DIESEL LOCOMOTIVE

Number	Type	Former owner	Builder	Date
1807	S-1	U. S. Army	Alco	1941

ELECTRIC CARS

Number	Type	Former owner	Builder	Date
4442, 4450	Transit	Chicago Transit	Cincinnati Car	1924
268	PCC	Detroit/Mexico City	St. Louis Car	1949

MICHIGAN TRANSIT MUSEUM

The Michigan Transit Museum operates 4 miles of track extending east from Mt. Clemens, Michigan, to Selfridge Air National Guard Base. The museum's usual train consists of an Alco S1 switcher and two Chicago elevated cars. Eastbound the locomotive functions solely as a generator providing current for the motors in the two L cars; on the return trip the locomotive pulls the cars.

Trains depart from the Caboose Depot on the east side of Gratiot Avenue (Michigan Route 3) north of downtown Mt. Clemens

between Joy Boulevard and Hall Road (Route 59) — between Exits 237 and 240 of I-94. On Sundays SMART's Gratiot Avenue bus service stops at the Caboose Depot.

The headquarters of the Michigan Transit Museum is in the former Grand Trunk station. The building is at Cass and Grand Avenues west of downtown Mt. Clemens. The museum is accessible to the handicapped; the train ride is not. Food and lodging can be found nearby. Mt. Clemens is about 20 miles northeast of Detroit.

Schedule	Trains operate several times each day on June 2 and 3, July 14, September 1, 2, and 3, and October 13 and 14, 1990.	**Nearby attractions**	Charles village office. Junction Valley Railroad, Huckleberry Railroad, Crossroads Village, Frankenmuth
Fares	Adults $8-$10. Mystery Theater trains, $25; Dinner and Mystery Theater, $55. Credit cards and checks accepted. Reservations are required. Tickets are also available at the Chesaning chamber of commerce and the St.	**Mailing address** **Phone**	P. O. Box 665, Owosso, MI 48867 (517) 723-5797 for ticket information; (517) 725-9464 year-round

STEAM LOCOMOTIVE

Number	Type	Former owner	Builder	Date
1225	2-8-4	Pere Marquette	Lima	1941

SHIAWASSEE VALLEY RAILROAD

The Michigan State Trust for Railway Preservation operates its restored Pere Marquette steam locomotive several times a year on a former Michigan Central (New York Central) line between Owosso, Chesaning, and St. Charles. The trains operate in conjunction with local festivals. Several types of excursions are offered: short day-time trips, murder-mystery theater trains, and dinner-plus-mystery trains. Send a stamped, self-addressed envelope for schedules and prices. Owosso is west of Flint and northeast of Lansing on State Routes 21 and 52. Chesaning is 13 miles north; St. Charles is 8 miles farther. Motels and restaurants can be found nearby.

Locomotives	2 GP-7		
Cars	Ex-Denver & Rio Grande Western open-window coaches	**Fares**	5:30. Charter trips available. Adults $7, children 2-11 $3, age 65 and up $6. Caboose cupola, $3 additional, reservations required. Christmas Tree Trains, adults $15, children $5. Group discounts available. Checks and credit cards accepted
Schedule	April 14-May 20, September 15-30, and November 3-4, 1990, Saturdays and Sundays, 1 p.m. May 26-September 9, Wednesday-Sunday, 1 and 3:30 (also July 2 and 3). October 1-28, Mondays and Tuesdays at 1 p.m., Wednesday-Friday at 1 and 3:30, and Saturdays and Sundays at 1, 3:30, and	**Special events**	Wine and Harvest Festival September 8-9, 1990 ; Christmas Tree Trains

Nearby attractions	St. Julian and Warner wineries
Mailing address	P. O. Box 178, Paw Paw, MI 49079
Phone	(616) 657-7037, 657-5963 for recorded information; Star Clipper dinner train, (800) 828-3423

KALAMAZOO, LAKE SHORE & CHICAGO RAILWAY

The Kalamazoo, Lake Shore & Chicago operates excursion service on its ex-Chesapeake & Ohio line between Paw Paw and Hartford. Most trains cover about half of the line, between Paw Paw and Lawrence, 8 miles. Round trips take 1½ hours. Trains operate most of the year. Specials include snow and ski trains in January and February and Christmas tree trains in late November and December (bring your own saw). Also operating on the KLS&C is the Star Clipper dinner train, which usually departs at 7 p.m. for a 3-hour trip (on certain days, trains depart at noon or 6 p.m.). Reservations are required for dinner trains. Paw Paw is 13 miles west of Kalamazoo. The station is ¼ mile north of Exit 60 (Michigan Route 40) of I-94. There are restaurants and motels in Paw Paw.

Locomotives	1 gasoline, 1 diesel
Cars	Open cars; closed cars in September and October
Schedule	June 15-30, 1990, daily; July 1-August 24, 1990, Friday, Saturday and Sunday; and August 25-October 6, 1990, daily: leaves 10:30 a.m., returns at 5 p.m. July 1-August 24, 1990, Monday-Thursday trains leave at 10 and 11:30, return at 4:30 and 6:30. Charter trips available.
Fares	Train and boat, adults $12, children 6-15 $6 (under 6 free). Checks and credit cards accepted. Group discounts available.
Nearby attractions	Hiawatha National Forest, Pictured Rocks National Lakeshore, Newberry Tahquamenon Logging Museum, Algoma Central Railway
Mailing address	115 East Avenue A, Newberry, MI 49868
Phone	(906) 876-2311; after hours and winter, 293-3806

TOONERVILLE TROLLEY

The Toonerville Trolley is a 24"-gauge railroad that carries tourists 5 miles from the highway to a boat dock, where connection is made with a sightseeing boat on the Tahquamenom River.

The rail portion of the trip begins at Soo Junction, off Michigan Route 28 between Newberry and Hulbert in the eastern part of Michigan's Upper Peninsula. The destination of the boat trip is Upper Tahquamenom Falls. One trip a day is operated from mid-June to the beginning of October, except Monday through Thursday in July and August, when two trips run. Warm clothing is advised for trips toward the end of the season. Snacks are available at Soo Junction and on the boat. Restaurants and lodging can be found in Newberry; the cities of Sault Ste. Marie, Mich., and Ontario, are 57 miles east. Access is possible for the handicapped; however, walking is required at the end of the boat trip.

Cars	2 ex-Reading coaches, open cars, caboose
Schedule	Three trips daily, beginning in July 1990
Fares	Not set at press time. Credit cards accepted. Group discounts available.
Nearby attractions	Sleeping Bear Dunes National Lakeshore, Manistee National Forest, 15"-gauge
Mailing address	steam train at Clinch Park Zoo 9945 Carter Road, Traverse City, MI 49684
Phone	(616) 947-6667

DIESEL LOCOMOTIVES

Number	Type	Former owner	Builder	Date
5258	SW9	Chesapeake & Ohio	EMD	1951
5298	NW2	Manistee & Northeastern	EMD	1949

P ᴅ ⚘ 🎁

LEELANAU SCENIC RAILROAD

The Leelanau Scenic Railroad operates excursion trains from Traverse City north through Leelanau County to Sutton's Bay, Omena, and Northport, Michigan, 31 miles from Traverse City. The line was once part of the Manistee & Northeastern Railway, then was leased to the Chesapeake & Ohio. One of the line's diesels is former Manistee & Northeastern NW2 No. 3, which is being repainted in its original colors. Snacks are available on the train. The railroad's facilities are located half a mile north of the intersection of Michigan Routes 22 and 72 on the northern outskirts of Traverse City. Restaurants and lodging can be found in Traverse City, Sutton's Bay, Omena, and Northport. Traverse City is about two-thirds of the way up the west side of Michigan's Lower Peninsula.

Locomotive	1 steam
Cars	Open cars
Schedule	Memorial Day-Labor Day, 10 a.m.-5:30 p.m., except during rain
Fares	Adults 75 cents; children 5-11 50 cents
Nearby attractions	Clinch Park Zoo, beach, museum
Mailing address	P. O. Box 592, Traverse City, MI 49685-0592
Phone	(616) 922-4910

P ⚘ 🎁 ◼

SPIRIT OF TRAVERSE CITY

Circling the Clinch Park Zoo in Traverse City on a half mile of 15"-gauge track is a train named *Spirit of Traverse City*. The train is pulled by a ¼-scale Atlantic-type steam locomotive. Clinch Park is between Grandview Parkway (U. S. 31) and the marina and beach on Grand Traverse Bay. There are restaurants within a block and motels within a mile.

Locomotives	2 diesel, 1 gasoline
Cars	Coaches, tap car, baggage cars, cabooses
Schedule	April-October, Sundays, 1 and 2:30 p.m. Call to verify schedule for holiday weekends. Charter trips available.
Fares	Adults $5, children 2-10 $4, age 65 and over $4. Group discounts available.
Nearby attractions	Pontiac Silverdome, Henry Ford Museum & Greenfield Village, Detroit
Mailing address	840 North Pontiac Trail, Walled Lake, MI 48088
Phone	(313) 669-1248, depot; (313) 851-7957, office

COE RAIL, INC.

Coe Rail operates excursion trains and freight service on a short piece of former Grand Trunk Western track between Walled Lake and Wixom, Michigan. The usual motive power for the train is an Alco S1; passenger cars include 3 Lackawanna coaches, a 1947-vintage Milwaukee Road tap-lounge car, a baggage car, and the 1920 Box Car Saloon. The hour-long, 10½-mile ride traverses woodlands and a bird sanctuary.

Restaurants can be found nearby. Lodging is available in Novi, West Bloomfield, and Southfield. Walled Lake is northwest of Detroit and southwest of Pontiac, a little north of I-96.

Walled Lake

Locomotive	1 diesel
Cars	2 streetcars, converted box cars
Dates open	April 14 to mid-October, 1990, daily 10 a.m.-7 p.m. Streetcars leave the reception center approximately every hour from 11 to 6.
Schedule	Trolley operates mid-May through September.
Admission	Adults $5.75, children 7-17 $3.50 (under 7 free). Checks accepted. Group discounts available.
Memberships	Write for information.
Special events	Minnesota Ethnic Days, International Polkafest, Fabulous Fifties, Iron Country Hoedown, Golden Years
Nearby attractions	Forest History Center, Hill Annex Mine Tour, Minnesota Museum of Mining, Paulucci Space Theater, Soudan Mine State Park, Hockey Hall of Fame, Hull-Rust Mahoning Mine
Mailing address	P. O. Box 392, Chisholm, MN 55719
Phone	(218) 254-3321; in Minnesota (800) 372-6437

IRONWORLD USA

Ironworld USA is a theme park in Minnesota's Iron Range. It is sponsored by Minnesota's Department of Iron Range Resources and is an outgrowth of the Iron Range Interpretive Center that was established in 1977. Two streetcars from Melbourne, Australia, negotiate a 5 percent grade between the reception center and a transfer station, from which a diesel-powered train carries visitors from the reception center around the rim of an open-pit mine.

The streetcars were refurbished and the passenger cars were converted from box cars by the staff of the Lake Superior Museum of Transportation in Duluth. The 5-acre grounds of the park have paved paths; buildings and trains are fully accessible to the handicapped. Ironworld is 5 miles east of Hibbing on U. S. 169. It is about 1 hour from Duluth and 3 hours from Minneapolis and St. Paul. Lodging can be found nearby in Chisholm and Hibbing.

Displays	Caboose, memorabilia, artifacts
Dates open	May 1-October 1, daily 10 a.m.-4:30 p.m.
Admission	Adults $2, children $1. Group discounts available. Checks accepted.
Special events	Red Rooster Days (Labor Day)
Nearby attractions	Historical museum in nearby Litchfield
Mailing address	651 West Highway 12, Dassel, MN 55325
Phone	(612) 275-2646

OLD DEPOT MUSEUM

In the former Great Northern station at Dassel is the Old Depot Museum. On display are a restored caboose and various memorabilia and artifacts.

Dassel is about 50 miles west of Minneapolis and 35 miles south of St. Cloud at the intersection of U. S. 12 and State Route 15.

Dassel

Cars	Coaches
Displays	GN *William Crooks*, NP *Minnetonka*, DM&IR 227, CMStP&P 10200, rotary snow plow, passenger and freight cars
Dates open	Year-round, daily 10 a.m.-5 p.m., except winter Sundays opens at 1
Schedule	Weekends, leave Duluth Zoo 11 a.m. and 1:30 and 4 p.m. Charter trips operated.
Admission	Museum, including trolley ride: adults $4, children 6-17 $2, age 60 and over $3. Group discounts available. Checks accepted.
Fares	Excursion train: adults $5, children to age 12 $2, age 60 and over $4
Radio frequency	160.380
Memberships	Write for information.
Special events	Mainline excursion trains
Nearby attractions	Canal Park Marine Museum, Duluth-Superior harbor cruise, Glensheen House Tour, Lake County Historical Society Museum

Mailing address 506 West Michigan Street, Duluth, MN 55802
Phone (218) 727-0687

MOTIVE POWER

Number	Type	Former owner	Builder	Date
STREETCARS				
530, 531	Single-truck	Lisbon, Portugal	Company shops	1925
DIESEL LOCOMOTIVE				
46	45-ton	Flambeau Paper	GE	1945

LAKE SUPERIOR MUSEUM OF TRANSPORTATION

Duluth Union Depot saw its last pre-Amtrak train in May 1969. The building, a fine example of French Norman architecture, was designated a National Historic Site in 1971 and was purchased from the Burlington Northern that same year. It soon became the property of St. Louis County, and work began to renovate the building and transform it into a cultural center. The building now serves as an art museum and a theater — and houses an excellent railroad museum.

A train shed covers the station's track area, protecting the locomotives and cars on display and allowing year-round viewing of the displays. Locomotives displayed include Great Northern 4-4-0 *William Crooks*; Northern Pacific's first engine, *Minnetonka*; Duluth, Missabe & Iron Range 2-8-8-4 No. 227; and Milwaukee Road boxcab electric 10200.

The collection is filled out by numerous passenger and freight cars and pieces of maintenance-of-way equipment. Two 4-wheel streetcars from Lisbon, Portugal, operate on ¼ mile of track on the museum grounds.

The museum is in downtown Duluth, easily accessible from I-35. Food and lodging are available within one block. The museum is accessible to the handicapped, and tours for the sight- or hearing-impaired are available if requested in advance.

The Lake Superior & Mississippi Railroad, an affiliate of the museum, operates excursion trains on certain summer weekends. They operate from the Duluth Zoo on a 1½-hour trip over 5½ miles of track along the St. Louis River. To reach the zoo, take Exit 251A, Cody Street, from I-35 northbound; Exit 251B, Grand Avenue, from I-35 southbound.

Car Schedule	RDC Daily June 20-August 31, 1990; weekends during fall. Saturdays and Sundays, leave Duluth at 10 a.m. for Two Harbors. Monday-Friday, leave Duluth 9:30 and 11 a.m., and 12:30, 2, 3:30, and 5 p.m. for trip along Duluth waterfront. Charter trips available.
Fares	Two Harbors: adults $12, children age 3-15 $8, age 60 and over $11. Weekend train ride in Duluth: adults $6, children $4, seniors $5. Group discounts available.
Nearby attractions	Lake Superior Museum of Transportation, Canal Park Marine Museum, Duluth-Superior harbor cruise, Glensheen House Tour, Lake County Historical Society Museum, Depot Museum (Two Harbors)
Mailing address	P. O. Box 244, Duluth, MN 55801
Phone	(218) 726-9098

NORTH SHORE SCENIC RAILROAD

Operating from the Lake Superior Museum of Transportation (formerly Duluth Union Depot) is the North Shore Scenic Railroad. Saturdays and Sundays it offers a 1-hour round trip on 5 miles of track along Duluth's waterfront. Monday through Friday the train operates to Two Harbors, about 27 miles northeast of Duluth, a 5-hour trip, including time in Two Harbors.

Equipment for the train is a Budd Rail Diesel Car formerly on the roster of the Reading Company; former Lake Superior & Ishpeming 2-8-2 No. 14 is scheduled to enter service in October 1990.

Food and lodging are available within a block of the Lake Superior Museum of Transportation.

Duluth

Cars	Open cars, cabooses
Dates open	Memorial Day-Labor Day, daily 10 a.m.-6 p.m.
Schedule	Trains run every 20 minutes.
Admission	Weekends, adults $8.95, children 15 and under $6.95, age 62 and over $6.95; $2 less on weekdays. Checks accepted. Group discounts available.
Fares	Included in admission
Nearby attractions	St. Croix State Park, Hinckley Fire Museum
Mailing address	Box 590, Hinckley, MN 55037
Phone	(612) 384-7600; (800) 228-1894 in Minnesota

STEAM LOCOMOTIVES

Number	Type	Former owner	Builder	Date
4514	2-6-0	United Fruit Co.	Porter	1909
7036	2-4-0	Fairmont & Baltimore Coal & Coke	Porter	1926

MISSION CREEK 1894 THEME PARK

Operating on 2 miles of 3'-gauge track at Mission Creek 1894 Theme Park are two steam locomotives built by H. K. Porter. The park includes a village with shops and restaurants, a fort, an Ojibwa village, and a trading post. Mission Creek is right off I-35 at Hinckley, which is about 75 miles north of St. Paul and 75 miles southwest of Duluth.

There are restaurants and motels within a quarter mile of the park.

Schedule	Memorial Day weekend to Labor Day: Monday-Friday 6:30 p.m.-dusk; Saturdays 3:30-dusk; Sunday and holidays 12:30-dusk; Labor Day through October: Saturday 3:30-dusk and Sunday 12:30-dusk, weather permitting. Charter trips available.
Fares	75 cents per person. Checks accepted. Group discounts available.
Memberships	Write for information.
Nearby attractions	Tyrone Guthrie Theater, Hennepin County Historical Society and Museum, state capitol (in St. Paul), Bandana Square Shopping Center (railroad displays and model railroad), Milwaukee Road Minnehaha depot in Minnehaha Park
Mailing address	P. O. Box 1796, Pioneer Station, St. Paul, MN 55101
Phone	(612) 228-0263; 522-7417 year-round

STREETCARS

Number	Type	Former owner	Builder	Date
78	Single-truck	Duluth Street Railway	LaClede Car Co.	1893
265	Double-truck	Duluth Street Railway	TCRT Snelling Shops	1915
1300	Double-truck	Twin City Rapid Transit	TCRT Snelling Shops	1908

COMO-HARRIET STREETCAR LINE

The primary operating exhibit of the Minnesota Transportation Museum is the 1-mile Como-Harriet streetcar line at West 42nd Street and Queen Avenue South in Minneapolis. Three cars operate over a restored portion of track between Lake Harriet and Lake Calhoun. A duplicate of the original Lake Harriet depot serves as a museum and gift shop. To reach the site from downtown, follow Hennepin Avenue and Route 20. From the south use the Xerxes Avenue South (Route 31) exit from Route 62.

Displays	O scale model railroad
Dates open	Monday-Friday, noon-9 p.m., Saturdays 10-6, Sundays 1-5
Admission	Free; donations welcome
Memberships	Write for information.
Nearby attractions	Children's Museum, Como Park (zoo and conservatory), State Fairgrounds
Mailing address	Box 26, Bandana Square, 1021 Bandana Boulevard East, St. Paul, MN 55108
Phone	(612) 647-9628

P ⓘ ♿ ⛲ 🎁 ■

TWIN CITY MODEL RAILROAD CLUB

The former Northern Pacific Como passenger car shops in St. Paul have become Bandana Square, a shopping, residential, and recreational complex. Several locomotives and cars are displayed there. At the north end of the second floor is a 3500-square-foot O scale model railroad built and operated by the Twin City Model Railroad Club.

Bandana Square is about 3 miles northwest of downtown St. Paul and about a mile northeast of the Amtrak station. It is on Energy Park Drive between North Snelling Avenue (Minnesota Route 51) and North Lexington Parkway. Food and lodging are available in Bandana Square.

Locomotives	2 F7 diesels
Cars	Dining cars, dome lounge cars
Schedule	Mid-February through December, open at 6:30 p.m., departure at 7:30 Friday and Saturday; open at noon, departure at 12:30 on Sundays. As business warrants, trains are operated on Tuesday, Wednesday, and Thursday. Reservations required.
Fares	$47.50. Checks accepted. Group discounts available.
Nearby attractions	St. Croix River, Taylors Falls, Stillwater & St. Paul Railroad
Mailing address	P. O. Box 573, Stillwater, MN 55082
Phone	(612) 430-3000

MINNESOTA ZEPHYR LIMITED

Minnesota Zephyr operates a dinner train out of Stillwater, Minnesota, about 15 miles east of St. Paul on Route 36. The train carries dome lounge cars, for before-dinner cocktails and hors d'oeuvres, and dining cars, where dinner is served.

During dinner the train travels past wooded bluffs along the St. Croix River on 7 miles of track owned by the Minnesota Transportation Museum. Minnesota Zephyr's 1990 plans include a depot museum at Stillwater and afternoon trips.

Stillwater

Cars	Streamlined and suburban coaches, combine, observation car			
Schedule	Weekends and holidays Memorial Day to mid-October. Phone for train schedule.			
Fares	Adults $6, children 12 and under $4, age 65 and over $4. Checks accepted. Group discounts available.			
Memberships	Write for information.			
Nearby attractions	St. Croix River, historic town of Stillwater			
Mailing address	Minnesota Transportation Museum, P. O. Box 1796, Pioneer Station, St. Paul, MN 55101			
Phone	(612) 228-0263			

LOCOMOTIVES

Number	Type	Former owner	Builder	Date
STEAM				
328	4-6-0	Northern Pacific	Alco	1907
DIESEL				
102	NW2	Lake Superior Terminal & Transfer	EMD	1948
105	SW1200	Lake Superior Terminal & Transfer	EMD	1957

STILLWATER & ST. PAUL RAILROAD

The Minnesota Transportation Museum operates excursion trains on the Stillwater & St. Paul Railroad, a 6-mile former Northern Pacific line running west from Stillwater. The line, built in 1870, is a scenic one and climbs a stiff grade out of the valley of the St. Croix River. Stillwater is on State Routes 36 and 95 about 15 miles east of St. Paul.

Restaurants are within walking distance; motels can be found about 2 miles away in Stillwater.

Displays	Duluth & Iron Range 2-6-0 No. 3, ore car, and caboose; DM&IR 2-8-8-4 No. 229
Dates open	April 16-October 31, 1990, daily 10 a.m.-6 p.m.
Admission	Free
Nearby attractions	Lighthouse, ore dock and harbor activity, Lake Superior Museum of Transportation, North Shore Scenic Railroad
Mailing address	P. O. Box 313, Two Harbors, MN 55616
Phone	(218) 834-4898

DEPOT MUSEUM

At Two Harbors, Minnesota, on the shore of Lake Superior 27 miles northeast of Duluth, the Lake County Historical Society has a railroad museum in the Duluth, Missabe & Iron Range depot (built in 1907 by the Duluth & Iron Range). Photos and artifacts on exhibcover not only railroads but logging and lake shipping.

On display outside are Duluth & Iron Range 2-6-0 No. 3, which came from Duluth to Two Harbors in 1883 by lake barge, and Duluth, Missabe & Iron Range Yellowstone No. 229, one of the largest and heaviest locomotives ever built.

To reach the museum, turn off 7th Avenue (U. S. 61) at Waterfront Drive, and drive toward the lake. Food and lodging are available in Two Harbors.

Displays	0-6-0, hardware, and artifacts
Dates open	Monday-Saturday 9 a.m.-5 p.m., Sundays, 1-5 p.m.
Admission	Adults $1, children 3-11 50 cents (under 2 free). Checks accepted.
Nearby attractions	Holmes County State Park
Mailing address	P. O. Box 605, Vaughan, MS 39179
Phone	(601) 673-9864

P & ⛪

CASEY JONES MUSEUM

Casey Jones was an engineer on the Illinois Central Railroad who was killed in a collision at Vaughan, Mississippi, on April 30, 1900. Jones would have been forgotten but for a ballad written by Wallace Saunders, a friend of his who was an engine wiper.

The song became enormously popular, and Casey Jones became part of American folklore. The Mississippi Bureau of Recreation and Parks operates a museum at Vaughan in a depot moved there from Pickens, a few miles north. Vaughan is 33 miles north of Jackson, Miss., and a mile east of Exit 133 of I-55. Food and lodging can be found in Canton, about halfway between Vaughan and Jackson.

Displays	[1988 information]	**Special events**	Christmas Open House
Dates open	Frisco memorabilia and artifacts	**Nearby attractions**	Wilson's Creek Battlefield National Park,
	Saturday 10 a.m.-5 p.m.; Sunday 2-5; June-		Mark Twain National Forest, Ozark Moun-
	August also Wednesday-Friday 10-5; other		tains
	times by appointment	**Mailing address**	P. O. Box 276, Ash Grove, MO 65604
Admission	Free; donations appreciated	**Phone**	(417) 672-3110
Memberships	$25 per year		

P & 🎁

FRISCO RAILROAD MUSEUM

On June 1, 1986, the Frisco Railroad Museum opened, the only museum and archive center devoted specifically to the St. Louis-San Francisco Railway. The principal lines of the Frisco, which became part of the Burlington Northern in 1980, extended from St. Louis southwest through Oklahoma into Texas and from Kansas City southeast to Birmingham, Alabama, and Pensacola, Florida. The hub of the system was Springfield, Missouri.

The museum contains an extensive collection of Frisco artifacts; particularly notable are dining car china and crew uniforms. The museum is at 500 Walker Street in Ash Grove, 15 miles northwest of Springfield. To reach the museum, follow Calhoun Avenue south two blocks from U. S. 160, then turn southeast on Main Street, which merges into Walker Street after four blocks. There is a restaurant in Ash Grove; motels can be found in Springfield.

Cars	Open cars	**Phone**	(417) 338-2611, 338-8210 year-round, 338-8100 for
Dates open	April 14-October 28, 1990, daily; closed		recorded information
	Mondays and Tuesday through May 15,		
	and closed Tuesdays after October 9		
Admission	Adults $17.50, children 11 and under		
	$9.95. Checks and credit cards accepted.		
Fares	Train ride is included in admission.		
Nearby attractions	Mark Twain National Forest, Table Rock		
	State Park, lakes, country music		
Mailing address	Branson, MO 65616		

STEAM LOCOMOTIVES

Number	Type	Builder	Date
13	2-4-0	Orenstein & Koppel	1940
43	2-4-0	Orenstein & Koppel	1934
76	2-4-0		1940

P & 🌲 🎁 ◗

SILVER DOLLAR CITY

Silver Dollar City is a pioneer theme park in southwestern Missouri. Trains drawn by German-built locomotives offer a 20-minute ride on 1½ miles of 2'-gauge track. During the year there are numerous special events and festivals celebrating such things as folk music, flowers, and quilting. Silver Dollar City is about 35 miles south of Springfield, off U. S. Routes 65 and 160. Hotels and motels are plentiful in Branson, the nearest town.

Locomotive	1 steam
Cars	Open cars
Dates open	Weekends only in April, May, September, and October; daily June-August
Admission	Adults $18.50, children 3-11 $13. Credit cards and checks accepted. Discounts available for elderly and handicapped. Parking $3.
Fares	Admission includes all rides.
Special events	Country fair (fall weekends), Halloween
Nearby attractions	Wabash, Frisco & Pacific Mini-Steam Tourist Railway, National Museum of Transport, Meramec Caverns
Mailing address	P. O. Box 60, Eureka, MO 63025
Phone	(314) 938-5300

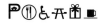

SIX FLAGS OVER MID-AMERICA

A 3'-gauge railroad runs around the perimeter of Six Flags Over Mid-America, a theme park. Power for the train is a propane-burning steam locomotive built in 1970 by Crown Metal Products.

Passengers ride in open cars; a caboose brings up the rear of the train. The ride covers 1¼ miles and takes 20-25 minutes. Six Flags Over Mid-America is north of U. S. 50/I-44, about 30 miles west of St. Louis.

There are several motels within a mile of the park.

Locomotives	5 steam, 1 gasoline
Cars	Flat cars with benches, 6 passenger cars, freight cars
Dates open	Sundays May–October, frequent trains from 1 to 4:15 p.m., weather permitting. Charter trips available before 1 p.m. trip.
Fares	$2 per person (children under 3 free). Checks accepted. Group discounts available.
Memberships	$15 per year; students $7.50
Radio frequency	151.955
Special events	Steam-up for NRHS convention, June 15, 1990; 50th anniversary celebration, June 24, 1990
Nearby attractions	National Museum of Transport, Six Flags Over Mid-America
Mailing address	1569 Ville Angela Lane, Hazelwood, MO 63042-1630
Phone	(314) 587-3538

LOCOMOTIVES

Number	Type	Builder	Date
STEAM			
171	4-4-0	International Miniature Train	1907
180	4-4-0		1922
300	4-4-2	V. A. Schmidt	1958
350	4-4-4	Wagner Brothers	1959
400	4-6-2	Jackson-Rigby	1925
GASOLINE			
802	SW-11	Clarence Poeling	1982

WABASH, FRISCO & PACIFIC MINI-STEAM TOURIST RAILWAY

The Wabash, Frisco & Pacific is a 12"-gauge steam-powered railroad that operates as authentically as possible. The railroad was begun in 1939 at a site near the St. Louis airport. Rising land values forced relocation in 1959, and in 1961 a new railroad was built along the Missouri Pacific's original roadbed. Trains operate over more than a mile of track up and down grades, over bridges, and through woodlands along the Meramec River. Unique to the Wabash, Frisco & Pacific is the crossing of Grand Avenue, protected by full-size flashers.

Glencoe is 25 miles west-southwest of downtown St. Louis on Route 109, north of I-44/U. S. 50. Follow Route 109 north 3 miles to Old State Road. Turn right on Old State Road, go one block east to the Glencoe post office, then turn right again on Washington Avenue. Follow Washington and Grand approximately half a mile to the Wabash, Frisco & Pacific station. Food and lodging are available in Eureka 3 miles away. There is a soda vending machine at the station. Access to the trains may be difficult for the handicapped, but train crews offer assistance as needed.

Locomotive	1 steam (ex-Crab Orchard & Egyptian 2-4-2)
Cars	Ex-Illinois Central coaches, ex-Missouri Pacific caboose, ex-Baltimore & Ohio caboose
Schedule	April-October, Saturdays and holidays leave Jackson for Gordonville at 10 a.m. and 1 p.m., for Delta at 3 p.m. (dinner train first and third Saturday of the month); Sundays to Gordonville at 1 and 2:30, to Dutchtown at 4. Reservations are recommended.
Fares	Gordonville, adults $7, children 3-10 $5; Dutchtown, $10/$7; Delta, $15/$10. Children under 3 free. Group discounts available. Checks and credit cards accepted.
Nearby attractions	Bollinger Mill State Historical Site, Trail of Tears State Park, Cape Girardeau River Heritage Museum, Glenn House, Oliver House
Mailing address	P. O. Box 244, Jackson, MO 63755
Phone	(314) 243-1688

ST. LOUIS, IRON MOUNTAIN & SOUTHERN RAILWAY

The name of a long-ago predecessor of the Missouri Pacific was revived for a tourist railroad operating over the rails of the Jackson & Southern Railroad, a short line established to operate a former MP branch from Delta to Jackson, Missouri. The St. Louis, Iron Mountain & Southern operates trains from Jackson to Gordonville, 5 miles, to Dutchtown, 9 miles, and to Delta, 18 miles; round trips take 1 hour, 2 hours, and 4 hours, respectively. Trains depart from the intersection of Highways 25, 72, and U. S. 61 in Jackson. Jackson is about 110 miles south-southeast of St. Louis on I-55 and about 6 miles northwest of Cape Girardeau.

Restaurants and motels can be found in Jackson and Cape Girardeau.

Displays	One of the largest collections of locomotives and cars in the U. S.
Dates open	Daily 9 a.m.-5 p.m.; closed Thanksgiving, Christmas, and New Year's Day
Admission	Adults $3, children 5-12 $1.50 (under 5 free), age 65 and over $1.50. Credit cards and local checks accepted. Group discounts available; reservations required for groups.
Memberships	Transport Museum Association — write for information.
Nearby attractions	Wabash, Frisco & Pacific Railway, Six Flags Over Mid-America
Mailing address	3015 Barrett Station Road, St. Louis, MO 63122
Phone	(314) 965-7998

NATIONAL MUSEUM OF TRANSPORT

The rescue and preservation of a mule-drawn streetcar in 1944 was the beginning of the National Museum of Transport. The museum soon acquired other exhibits and its collection became one of the largest and most diverse in the U. S. In 1979 operation of the museum was taken over by the St. Louis County Department of Parks & Recreation.

The locomotive collection ranges from industrial switchers and a Reading inspection locomotive with a 2-2-2 wheel arrangement to a Union Pacific Big Boy and a Norfolk & Western 2-8-8-2. The electric locomotives represent both interurbans and standard railroads, and among the diesels are Baltimore & Ohio 50, the first non-articulated mainline diesel passenger locomotive; Burlington 9908, *Silver Charger*, the last of the shovel-nose Zephyr units; and one unit of Electro-Motive 103, the Model FT demonstrator that was the first large mainline freight diesel. The passenger car, freight car, and trolley collections are similarly extensive; in addition the museum has collections of automobiles, buses, and trucks.

The museum is located on a section of the original right of way of the Missouri Pacific, northwest of the intersection of I-270 and I-44. Using I-270 from the north, take the Big Bend Road exit, go west to Barrett Station Road, then north to the museum. From the south, take the Dougherty Ferry Road exit, go west to Barrett Station Road, then south to the museum. (Neither exit from I-270 has ramps in all directions.) Food and lodging are available throughout the area.

Locomotives	4 diesel
Cars	Coaches, flatcars with benches, cabooses
Schedule	April-October, second Sunday of the month, departures at 1, 2, 3, and 4 p.m.
Fares	Free, except for hayride; donations accepted
Memberships	$15 per year
Special events	Moonlight Train Ride, Hayride on the Train (second Sunday in November)
Nearby attractions	Gateway Arch, Missouri Botanical Garden
Mailing address	4351 Holly Hills Boulevard, St. Louis, MO 63116
Phone	(314) 752-3148

ST. LOUIS & CHAIN OF ROCKS RAILROAD

The St. Louis Water Works Railway was opened between the Baden section of St. Louis and a water works at Chain of Rocks in 1902. The railroad soon developed into a steam-powered freight railroad and a streetcar line with a scenic route serving a large city park. Passenger service was discontinued in 1955. A group of railroad enthusiasts looking for a site for an operating museum approached the St. Louis Water Department, which was amenable — even enthusiastic — about the project. Excursion trains began running in 1972, and the St. Louis & Chain of Rocks Railroad was organized in 1976.

Trains operate on 3 miles of track along Riverview Boulevard

between Burlington Northern Junction and Mississippi River Dam No. 27, the largest rock-fill dam in the U. S. At the south end of the run there is a distant view of the St. Louis skyline and the Gateway Arch.

The boarding area is at Briscoe Station on Riverview Boulevard at Lookaway Drive, 1 mile south of the I-270 bridge over the Mississippi River. Take the Columbia Bottom Road-Riverview Drive exit from I-270 at the west end of the Mississippi River bridge, and drive south along Riverview to the station.

Food and lodging are available throughout the area; lemonade is available at the station.

Schedule	Two or three all-day excursions between May and October — write for information.
Fares	Approximately $65 for adults, depending on the trip; $5-$10 less for children
Nearby attractions	National Museum of Transport; Wabash, Frisco & Pacific; St. Louis & Chain of Rocks Railroad, Six Flags Over Mid-America
Mailing address	115 St. Georges Place, Webster Groves, MO 63119
Phone	(314) 962-1653

ST. LOUIS STEAM TRAIN ASSOCIATION

St. Louis-San Francisco Railway 4-8-2 No. 1522, built by Baldwin in 1926, is owned by the National Museum of Transport but is operated several times a year by the St. Louis Steam Train Association. The trips are usually under the sponsorship of the St. Louis Chapter of the National Railway Historical Society. Write for specific information on dates and fares. The locomotive is usually stored (and viewable) at St. Louis Union Station, which is now a hotel and shopping complex.

Displays	Milwaukee Road electric locomotive E57B
Nearby attractions	Upper Musselshell Historical Museum, fishing, hunting
Mailing address	Save the Engine Committee, Box 261, Harlowton, MT 59036
Phone	(406) 632-5554

FISCHER PARK

For years North America's longest stretch of electrified track was the 440 miles of the Milwaukee Road (Chicago, Milwaukee, St. Paul & Pacific Railroad) between Harlowton, Montana, and Avery, Idaho. (The Milwaukee Road had another portion of electrified line from Othello, Washington, to Tacoma and Seattle, 216 miles.) Electric operation began in 1916 and ended in 1974. Electric locomotive

E57B, built in 1916, was the last Milwaukee Road electric to operate. It was donated to the city of Harlowton and was placed on display at Fischer Park at Central Avenue and U. S. 12.

The city is on U. S. Routes 12 and 191 about halfway between Billings and Great Falls. Food and lodging are available within three blocks of the park.

Locomotives	Speeders
Cars	Open cars
Displays	Turn-of-the-century cars and locomotives
Dates open	Memorial Day-Labor Day
Schedule	Trains operate mid-June to Labor Day, hourly 10 a.m.-6 p.m., weather permitting. Charter trips available.
Admission	Age 12 and over $3 (under 12 free), age 65 and

over $2.50. Includes train ride. Credit cards accepted. Group discounts available.

Nearby attractions	Virginia City, Nevada City, Nevada City Open Air Museum, Yellowstone National Park
Mailing address	P. O. Box 338, Virginia City, MT 59755
Phone	(406) 843-5377

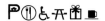

BOVEY RESTORATIONS

One of the attractions of Nevada City, Montana, a restored gold-mining town near Virginia City, is the Alder Gulch Short Line, which carries passengers over 1½ miles of track between Nevada City and Virginia City. At Nevada City is a railroad museum which includes 4 locomotives and 25 freight and passenger cars, among them 5 Soo Line passenger cars of the early 1900s, the chapel car

Saint Paul, and possibly the largest collection of cars built by Barney & Smith. Staff is on the premises year-round. Food and lodging are available in Virginia City and in the Nevada City restoration. Virginia City is on State Route 287 southwest of Bozeman and southeast of Butte and about 70 highway miles from each.

154-MONTANA   **Harlowton   Virginia City**

Locomotives	1 steam, 2 diesel
Cars	Coaches
Dates open	Monday-Saturday, 9 a.m.-5 p.m.
Admission	Free
Schedule	Trains operate last week of April through October, leave Fremont 1 p.m. Saturday and 2 p.m. Sunday (to Hooper), and 2 p.m. Tuesday-Friday (to Nickerson); additional trips are operated Memorial Day-Labor Day. Reservations are advised. Charter trips available.
Fares	To Hooper: adults $10, children $6; to Nickerson: $6/$4. Children under 3 free. Checks and credit cards accepted. Group discounts available.
Memberships	Write for information.
Radio frequency	160.245
Nearby attractions	Fremont Lakes State Recreation Area, Louis E. May County Museum
Mailing address	1835 North Somers Avenue, Fremont, NE 68025
Phone	(402) 727-0615 ,(800) 942-7245

LOCOMOTIVES

Number	Type	Former owner	Builder	Date
STEAM				
1702	2-8-0	U. S. Army	Baldwin	1942
DIESEL				
1219	SW1200	Chicago & North Western	EMD	1962
1121	SW1200	Soo Line	EMD	1955

P & 禾 🎁

FREMONT & ELKHORN VALLEY RAILROAD

The Fremont & Elkhorn Valley was established in 1985 by the Eastern Nebraska Chapter of the National Railway Historical Society; the F&EV is Nebraska's state railroad museum. Trains run over former Chicago & North Western rails from Fremont north through the Elkhorn Valley to Nickerson, 6 miles, and Hooper, 15 miles. During the summer most trains are pulled by 2-8-0 No. 1702,

a former U. S. Army locomotive previously owned by the Reader Railroad in Arkansas. Hooper's 1890s Main Street is listed on the National Register of Historic Places.

The station and ticket office are at 1835 North Somers Avenue in Fremont. Food and lodging can be found in Fremont, which is about 35 miles northwest of Omaha on U. S. routes 30, 77, and 275.

Fremont

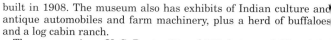

Locomotive	1 steam
Cars	Coach, freight cars
Dates open	May-October, daily 9 a.m.-6 p.m.; November-April, Monday-Saturday 9-5, Sunday 1-5
Schedule	Train operates May-October; Monday-Saturday at 11 a.m., noon, 1:30 p.m., and 3:30, also 4:30 if needed; Sunday continuously from 11
Admission	May-October, adults $6, children 7-16 $3.50 (under 7 free). November-April, adults $4, children 7-16 $2. Checks accepted.
Fares	Adults $2, children 7-16 $1
Memberships	Individual, $20 per year; family, $25
Special events	Memorial Day and July 4th celebrations
Nearby attractions	Harold Warp Pioneer Village
Mailing address	3133 West Highway 34, Grand Island, NE 68801
Phone	(308) 381-5316

P & ⛟ 🎁 ▣

STUHR MUSEUM OF THE PRAIRIE PIONEER

The Stuhr Museum, operated by Hall County, interprets prairie life of the latter half of the nineteenth century with two year-round exhibit buildings and a re-creation of a small prairie town. Part of the town exhibit is the 3'-gauge Nebraska Midland Railroad, which offers a 3-mile ride around the museum grounds.

The train is pulled by former White Pass & Yukon No. 69, a 2-8-0

built in 1908. The museum also has exhibits of Indian culture and antique automobiles and farm machinery, plus a herd of buffaloes and a log cabin ranch.

The museum is on U. S. Routes 34 and 281, between I-80 and the city of Grand Island. Restaurants and motels can be found in Grand Island, 3 miles north.

Locomotives	2 steam	**Fares**	Train: Adults $2, children 2-12 $1.50	**Mailing address**	Children's Museum
Cars	Open coaches, caboose		(under 2 free)		3701 South 10th Street,
Dates open	Daily, April-October	**Memberships**	Zoo, write for information.		Omaha, NE 68107
Schedule	Train operates weekends only in April, May,	**Special events**	Membership Day — zoo members may	**Phone**	(402) 733-8401; 733-8400 for
	September, and October; daily June-August		ride train free all day.		recorded information
Admission	Zoo: Adults $4.50, children $2.50 (under 6	**Nearby attractions**	Union Pacific Historical Museum, General		
	free), senior citizens $3. Group discounts		Dodge House, Western Heritage Muse-		
	available.		um, Sarpy County Historical Museum,		

OMAHA ZOO RAILROAD

Circling the grounds of the Henry Doorly Zoo in Omaha is 3 miles of 30"-gauge track, home rails for a pair of steam locomotives, one a ⅝ scale replica of Union Pacific 119 (one of the participants in the 1869 Golden Spike ceremony) and the other an 0-6-2T built in 1890 and first used in Austria and later in Romania.

The railroad is operated by the Omaha Zoological Society; it is maintained with the help of the Union Pacific, which is headquartered in Omaha.

The zoo is one block southeast of the 13th Street (U. S. 73-75) exit of I-80 near the Missouri River.

Dates open	Monday-Friday, 9 a.m.-5 p.m.; Saturday 9-1. Closed Sundays and holidays.
Admission	Free
Nearby attractions	Omaha Zoo Railroad, General Dodge House, Western Heritage Museum, Sarpy County Historical Museum, Children's Museum
Mailing address	1416 Dodge Street, Omaha, NE 68179
Phone	(402) 271-3530

UNION PACIFIC HISTORICAL MUSEUM

The Union Pacific Railroad claims a closer connection to the history of the United States than any other railroad. UP was one of the two companies that built the first railroad to the Pacific; completed in 1869, that railroad was the sole thread that connected East and West for more than a decade.

UP founded its museum in 1921 when it discovered in a vault silverware, purchased decades earlier, which had been used on Abraham Lincoln's funeral car. The museum has recently been refurbished. Its displays cover the history of UP; exhibits include a re-creation of Lincoln's funeral car, artifacts from the driving of the Golden Spike, a model of a centralized traffic control panel, and an O scale model railroad.

The museum is in UP's general office building at 1416 Dodge Street in downtown Omaha.

Locomotives	2 steam, 1 motor car
Cars	Open cars
Displays	4 locomotives, 1 motor car, numerous freight and passenger cars
Dates open	Wednesday-Sunday, year-round, 8:30 a.m.-4:30 p.m.
Admission	$1
Memberships	Write for information.
Special events	Steam-ups — Memorial Day, July 4, Labor Day, and Nevada Day (October 31); handcar races (May 19-20, 1990)
Nearby attractions	Lake Tahoe, Reno, Virginia City, Virginia & Truckee Railroad
Mailing address	Capitol Complex, Carson City, NV 89710
Phone	(702) 687-5168

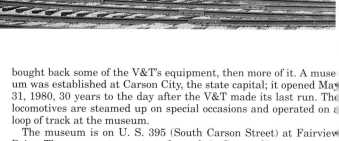

NEVADA STATE RAILROAD MUSEUM

The Virginia & Truckee Railroad was built to serve the gold and silver mines of Virginia City, Nevada. The mines were played out by 1900, and the V&T hung on until 1950, occasionally selling an antique locomotive or car to a Hollywood movie studio. It was the archetypal western short line — not much mileage, not much business, not much income.

When the movie studios hit hard times, the state of Nevada bought back some of the V&T's equipment, then more of it. A museum was established at Carson City, the state capital; it opened May 31, 1980, 30 years to the day after the V&T made its last run. The locomotives are steamed up on special occasions and operated on a loop of track at the museum.

The museum is on U. S. 395 (South Carson Street) at Fairview Drive. There are restaurants and motels in Carson City.

Locomotives	1 steam, 2 diesel
Cars	Wood baggage car and coach; gondola fitted with benches
Displays	Freight, passenger, and maintenance-of-way cars
Schedule	May 18-October 20, 1990, weekends and occasional Wednesdays. The steam train operates Saturdays (usually at 2:30 and 4:30 p.m.) and Sundays (usually at 10:30 a.m. and 1 p.m.) two or three weekends a month. Saturdays and holidays either the Hiline excursion (departure 6:30 p.m.) or the combination trip (4:30 and 6:30) operates. The Hiline trip also operates on occasional Wednesdays at 2:30. Saturday departures are 1 hour earlier in September and October. Charter trips available.
Fares	Adults $2, children 5-11 50 cents (under 5

free), age 65 and over $1. Keystone route: Adults $12, children 5-11 $4, teenagers and seniors $10. Hiline: $8/$3/$6. Combination: $14/$4/$10. Credit cards and checks accepted. Reservations are advised. Group discounts available.

Memberships	Friends of the Nevada Northern Railway, P. O. Box 40, East Ely, NV 89315
Special events	Railfair — Saturday and Sunday of Memorial Day weekend, July 4th, Christmas Train
Nearby attractions	Lehman Caves at Great Basin National Park, ghost towns, and areas for picnics, camping, fishing, and hunting
Mailing address	P. O. Box 40, East Ely, NV 89315
Phone	(702) 289-2085

NEVADA NORTHERN RAILWAY MUSEUM

The Nevada Northern Railway was completed in 1906 from Ely, Nevada, north to a connection with the Southern Pacific at Cobre. The principal reason for the road's existence was the copper mine at Ely. When the mine and smelter shut down in 1983 the railroad ceased operation; the railroad's owner, Kennecott Copper Corp., donated the East Ely station and several pieces of rolling stock to the city of Ely and the White Pine Historical Railroad Foundation to form the nucleus of a railroad museum. Among the rolling stock was 4-6-0 No. 40 — when the Nevada Northern replaced its passenger train with a bus in 1941 it carefully preserved the steam locomotive and the two cars, bringing them out from time to time for excursions.

The museum is in the East Ely depot at East 11th Street and

Avenue A; it includes NN's shops, which have changed little since the railroad began operation.

Trains operate over two different routes, the 7-mile Keystone route past downtown Ely to the Keystone mining district, and the 5-mile Hiline that was built to carry ore to the smelter at McGill. Round trips on each take 1½ hours. The steam locomotive usually pulls the Keystone train; an Alco RS-3 is assigned to the Hiline and to late-afternoon trips that cover both routes. Access for the handicapped is somewhat limited, but the staff will assist passengers as needed.

Ely is at the junction of U. S. Routes 6, 50, and 93 in east-central Nevada. Lodging and food are available in Ely. The nearest cities are Reno, Las Vegas, and Salt Lake City, all 250-300 miles away.

Locomotive	1 steam
Cars	Gondolas, caboose
Displays	Freight and passenger cars; shop is open to view
Schedule	May 26-September 30, 1990, daily, every 40-45 minutes from 10:30 a.m. to 5:45 p.m. Charter trips available.
Fares	Adults $3.50, children 5-12 $1.75 (under 5 free). Group discounts available. Checks accepted.
Nearby attractions	Mine tours, historic mansion tours, Nevada State Railroad Museum, Reno, Lake Tahoe
Mailing address	P. O. Box 467, Virginia City, NV 89440
Phone	(702) 847-0380

VIRGINIA & TRUCKEE RAILROAD

The Virginia & Truckee Railroad ceased operation on May 31, 1950; its line to Virginia City had been abandoned in 1939. In the mid-1970s a mile and a half of track was restored from Virginia City through a tunnel to Gold Hill, and an excursion train began operation through the heart of the Comstock Lode mining area. The track has since been extended another quarter mile. The train is powered by 2-8-0 No. 29, built by Baldwin in 1916 and once the property of the Longview, Portland & Northern.

The station (actually a coach, standing in for a station building) is on F Street south of Washington Street in Virginia City. There is a parking lot on the east side of F Street. Tickets can also be purchased at V&T Car 13, which is on C Street opposite the post office. Several freight and passenger cars are on display.

Food and lodging are available in Virginia City; Reno and Carson City are about a half hour away.

Cars	Ex-Lackawanna M.U. cars
Displays	Wolfeboro Railroad 2-6-2 No. 250 (Baldwin, 1926)
Schedule	July 1 through Labor Day, daily at 9 and 11 a.m. and 1, 3, 5, and 7 p.m.; weekends during May, daily Memorial Day-June 30 and Labor Day through October, 11 a.m. and 1 p.m.; additional trips Saturdays at 3 and 7 p.m. Charter trips available.
Fares	Adults $7, children $4.50; 7 p.m. trip $8. Group discounts available.
Radio frequencies	160.470, 161.550
Special events	Santa trains, weekends November 24-December 23, 1990
Nearby attractions	Loon Mountain, Lost River, White Mountains, Mt. Washington Cog Railway, Conway Scenic Railroad
Mailing address	P. O. Box 9, Lincoln, NH 03251
Phone	(603) 745-2135

DIESEL LOCOMOTIVES

Number	Type	Former owner	Builder	Date
1008	S-1	Portland Terminal	Alco	1949
1186	S-3	Boston & Maine	Alco	1952

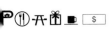

HOBO RAILROAD

The Hobo Railroad offers a 15-mile, 1½-hour round trip on former Boston & Maine track along the Pemigewasset River, crossing the river several times and affording views of the White Mountains. Breakfast, lunch, and dinner are available on the train. Reservations are suggested. The Hobo Railroad is on the Kancamagus Highway at Exit 32 of I-93. Lincoln is about 65 miles north of Concord and 25 miles south of Littleton. Food and lodging are available there.

Locomotives	2 steam (1 Climax, 1 Heisler)
Cars	Open excursion cars
Displays	1930 Reo rail bus, small switch engine
Dates open	Weekends Memorial Day through June, daily in July and August, weekends to mid-October, 10 a.m.-5 p.m.
Schedule	Steam train operation begins July 1. Departures at 11:30 a.m. and 12:30, 1:30, 2:30, 3:30, and 4:30 p.m. Charter trips available.
Admission	Adults $6, children 6-12 $4 (under 6 free). Credit cards accepted.
Fares	Admission includes train ride.
Nearby attractions	Loon Mountain, Lost River, White Mountains, Mt. Washington Cog Railway, Conway Scenic Railroad
Mailing address	Box 1, Lincoln, NH 03251
Phone	(603) 745-891

WHITE MOUNTAIN CENTRAL RAILROAD

At Clark's Trading Post in Lincoln, New Hampshire, two geared steam locomotives operate passenger trains on the White Mountain Central, 1¼ miles of track along the Pemigewasset River and through a covered bridge.

Other attractions at Clark's include an ice cream parlor, a maple cabin, performing bears, and numerous other tourist attractions. Staff is on the premises year-round.

Clark's Trading Post is on U. S. 3 at Exit 33 of I-93. Lincoln is about 65 miles north of Concord and 25 miles south of Littleton. Food and lodging are available in Lincoln.

Locomotives	3 diesel
Cars	Coaches
Displays	Cabooses, milk car, baggage car
Schedule	May 26-June 10, 1990, weekends and holidays; June 23-Labor Day, daily: train leaves Weirs Beach on the hour from 10 a.m. to 4 p.m.; leaves Meredith at 9:30, 11:30, 1:30, and 3:30.
	September 4-28, 1990, Monday-Friday, train leaves Weirs Beach 11, 1, and 2, leaves Meredith 1:30; weekends leaves Weirs Beach on the hour 11-4, leaves Meredith 11:30, 1:30, and 3:30.
	September 29-October 21, 1990, Monday-Friday, train leaves Weirs Beach on the hour 11-2; leaves Meredith 11:30 and 1:30; weekends and holidays, leaves Weirs Beach on the hour 10-4, leaves Meredith 9:30, 11:30, 1:30, and 3:30. Charter trips available.
Fares	2-hour ride, Meredith-Lakeport, boarding at either Meredith or Weirs Beach: adults $7, children 5-12 $4 (under 4 free). 1-hour ride, Weirs-Meredith or Weirs-Lakeport, $6/$3. Group discounts available.
Nearby attractions	Lake Winnipesaukee, M/V *Mount Washington*, White Mountains
Mailing address	RFD 4, Box 317, Meredith, NH 03253
Phone	(603) 279-3196

WINNIPESAUKEE RAILROAD

The Winnipesaukee Railroad operates excursion trains over former Boston & Maine track between Lakeport and Meredith, in the lake region of central New Hampshire. The basic pattern of operation is round trips from Meredith south along the shores of Paugus Bay and Meredith Bay to Lakeport, 9 miles, stopping at Weirs Beach in both directions. Passengers may board at Meredith or Weirs Beach.

Free parking is provided only at Meredith. Refreshments are available on the train; food and lodging can be found throughout the area.

Meredith

NEW HAMPSHIRE-163

	[1988 information]
Locomotives	8 steam
Cars	Coaches
Displays	*Old Peppersass*, world's first cog railway locomotive
Schedule	Mid-April to mid-November, daily, hourly departures as needed. Call for specific schedule information. Charter trips available.
Fares	$27 round trip to summit for persons age 16 and over, children 6-15 $13.50, 10 percent senior citizen discount. Credit cards accepted. Discounts available for groups of 20 or more with advance reservation.
Nearby attractions	White Mountains, Conway Scenic Railroad
Mailing address	Summer: Mt. Washington, NH 03589; winter: P. O. Box 932, Littleton, NH 03561
Phone	(603) 846-5404

P ♿ ⛩ 🎁 ☕

MT. WASHINGTON COG RAILWAY

The Mt. Washington Cog Railway opened in 1869, the first mountain-climbing cog railroad in the world. It ascends to the summit of Mt. Washington, highest peak in the Northeast (6288 feet) with an average grade of 25 percent — 1 foot up for every 4 feet forward. During the 3¼-mile trip the train climbs 3760 feet. On a clear day the view from the top encompasses all six New England states.

Only coal-burning steam locomotives are used; most were built in the late 1800s and early 1900s, but the two newest ones date from 1972 and 1983. Trains operate from Base Station, east of U. S. 302 about halfway between North Conway and Littleton. The trip to the summit and back takes about 3 hours.

Train operations depend on weather conditions. The weather at the summit is never warm; take a jacket or a sweater.

There is a restaurant at the base and a snack bar at the summit. Food and lodging are available throughout the area.

Cars	Coaches, extra-fare parlor-observation
Displays	Maine Central 2-8-0, roundhouse, turntable, freight and passenger cars
Dates open	May-October, 10 a.m.-5:15 p.m.
Schedule	Weekends May through early June, daily mid-June to late October, also Thanksgiving weekend, and weekends before Christmas: leave North Conway 11 a.m. and 1, 2:30, and 4 p.m.; also 7 p.m. on Tuesdays, Wednesdays, Thursdays, and Saturdays in July and August. Charter trips available.
Fares	Adults $7, children 4-12 $4.50 (under 4 free). Group discounts available.
Radio frequency	161.250
Special events	Railfan's Day (second Saturday after Labor Day)
Nearby attractions	Storyland, Heritage New Hampshire, Attitash Alpine Slide, Wildcat Mountain Gondolas, Mt. Washington
Mailing address	P. O. Box 1947, North Conway, NH 03860
Phone	(603) 356-5251

LOCOMOTIVES

Number	Type	Former owner	Builder	Date
STEAM				
7470	0-6-0	Grand Trunk Railway	GTRy	1921
DIESEL				
15	44-ton	Maine Central	GE	1942
1055	S-4	Portland Terminal	Alco	1950
4266	F7A	Boston & Maine	EMD	1949

P &. ⊼ 🎁 ▣ $

CONWAY SCENIC RAILROAD

The railroad line that eventually became the Conway Scenic Railroad reached the village of North Conway, New Hampshire, in 1872 under the banner of the Portsmouth, Great Falls & Conway Railroad. The village was a growing summer resort, and the railroad erected there a large, ornate wooden depot. The PGF&C became part of the Eastern Railroad in 1878, and the Eastern was absorbed by the Boston & Maine in 1890. B&M's Conway Branch fared better than most other branch lines. North Conway developed into a winter sports area in the 1930s and passenger traffic increased, but in December 1961 the last passenger train left North Conway, and freight service ended in October 1972.

After long negotiations Boston & Maine sold the North Conway property, including the depot, and 7 miles of track to three men who formed the Conway Scenic Railroad. Operation began in August 1974. Conway Scenic's trains operate on 5½ miles of track between North Conway and Conway, traversing farmland and offering views north to Mt. Washington and south to Mt. Chocorua. The round trip takes about 1 hour. Food and lodging are available in North Conway, a resort town; the station is at the center of town. The railroad is notable for having a complete branchline terminal, with station, roundhouse, and turntable. North Conway is about 140 miles north of Boston and 60 miles northwest of Portland, Maine.

North Conway

Displays	HO scale model railroad
Dates open	July 1-Labor Day: daily 10 a.m.-5:30 p.m.; Memorial Day-June 30 and Labor Day-December 31: Thursday, Friday, and Saturday 10-5. Other times by appointment.
Admission	Adults $3, children 2-12 $2 (under 2 free). Checks accepted. Group discounts available.
Memberships	Write for information.
Nearby attractions	Lake Winnipesaukee, Motor Ship Mount Washington
Mailing address	P. O. Box 205, Wolfeboro Falls, NH 03896
Phone	(603) 569-5384

KLICKETY-KLACK RAILROAD

The Klickety-Klack Railroad is a large, scenicked HO scale model railroad. Visitors may operate many of the trains and animated accessories by pushing buttons.

The railroad occupies a 30 x 76-foot building at the junction of State Routes 28-109A and 109 in Wolfeboro Falls. Associated with the railroad is a hobby and gift shop.

Restaurants and lodging can be found in Wolfeboro, less than a mile west.

Cars	Open-platform coach, excursion flatcar, caboose		
Displays	Assorted locomotives and cars not in service or awaiting restoration		
Schedule	Mid-April through October, weekends and holidays; July and August, daily: every 30 minutes, noon-5 p.m.. Steam locomotives are used only on weekends May through mid-October.		
Admission	State Park, $2 per car weekends Memorial Day-Labor Day, $1 weekdays		
Fares	$1.50 per person (children under 3 free). In-state checks accepted.		
Memberships	Write for information.		
Special events	Andrews Raid reenactment on Father's Day, Railroader's Day (September 9, 1990), Christmas Express first three weekends in December		
Nearby attractions	Beaches		
Mailing address	P. O. Box 622, Farmingdale, NJ 07727-0622		
Phone	(201) 938-5524		

LOCOMOTIVES

Number	Type	Former owner	Builder	Date
STEAM				
3L	4-4-0T	Cavan & Leitrim (Ireland)	Stephenson	1887
6	Shay	Ely-Thomas Lumber Co.	Lima	1927
26	2-6-2	Surrey, Sussex & Southampton	Baldwin	1920
DIESEL				
1	12 ton	Haws Refractories	Plymouth	1942
40	25 ton	Midvale Steel Corporation	Whitcomb	1940
7751	25 ton	U. S. Army	GE	1942

NEW JERSEY MUSEUM OF TRANSPORTATION

The Pine Creek Railroad of the New Jersey Museum of Transportation is a 3'-gauge line at Allaire State Park. Trains operate over a ¾-mile loop of track and offer a 1½-mile, 10-minute ride through woods and fields. The state park includes Historic Howell Works, a restored iron mining community of the early 1800s.

Farmingdale is west of Asbury Park and southeast of Freehold.

To reach Allaire State Park, take Exit 31 (Route 547, about halfway between U. S. 9 and the Garden State Parkway) from I-195; then go north a short distance to Route 524.

The park contains a restaurant and a snack bar; food and lodging are available in Freehold, Lakewood, Belmar, and Manasquan.

Cars	Ex-Lackawanna and Central of New Jersey coaches
Displays	0-6-0T, Mack locomotive, caboose, several private cars
Schedule	Weekends and holidays, April-December, leave Ringoes 10:45 a.m. and 12:15, 1:45, 3:15, and 4:45 p.m. for Flemington, leave Flemington 45 minutes later; Sundays, May-October, leave Ringoes 12:15, 1:45, 3:15, and 4:45 for Lambertville, leave Lambertville 45 minutes later; Monday-Friday, July and August, leave Ringoes 12:30, 1:30, 2:30, and 3:30, leave Flemington 30 minutes later; Saturday nights, June-August, leave Flemington 7 p.m., leave Ringoes 7:30, arrive Lambertville 8, leave Lambertville 10:30 p.m., arrive Ringoes 11, arrive Flemington 11:30. Charter trips available.
Fares	Adults $5, children 4-12 $2.50 (under 4 free). Checks and credit cards accepted. Group rates available.
Nearby attractions	Delaware & Raritan Canal State Park, Washington Crossing State Park, outlet stores in Flemington
Mailing address	P. O. Box 200, Ringoes, NJ 08551
Phone	(201) 782-9600

LOCOMOTIVES

Number	Type	Former owner	Builder	Date
STEAM				
6	2-8-0	Great Western Railway	Alco	1937
DIESEL				
42	CF7	Santa Fe	EMD/AT&SF	1978
56	T-6	Pennsylvania	Alco	1953
57	RS-1	Washington Terminal	Alco	1947
4666	Motor car	Pennsylvania	Brill	1930

P & 木 🎁 ▣

BLACK RIVER & WESTERN RAILROAD

The Black River & Western was incorporated in 1961. In 1965 it leased a portion of the Pennsylvania Railroad's Flemington Branch from Flemington to Ringoes, New Jersey, and began excursion service. In 1970 it acquired the rest of the branch from Ringoes to Lambertville and began operating freight service. In 1976 the BR&W expanded again by acquiring Central of New Jersey track between Flemington and Three Bridges.

The primary route for BR&W's passenger trains is between Ringoes and Flemington, 6 miles north. On summer Sundays trains also operate between Ringoes and Lambertville, 7 miles southwest on the Delaware River. Charter trips can be operated to Three Bridges.

Restaurants and lodging can be found in Flemington; there are also restaurants in Lambertville.

Displays	Cabooses, passenger cars, large Lionel layout, railroadiana
Dates open	April-October, Sundays noon-4 p.m.
Admission	Free, donation of $1 for adults, 50 cents for children suggested. Checks accepted.
Memberships	Write for information.
Special events	Railroad Festival in October
Nearby attractions	Morris Museum, General Washington's Morristown Headquarters, Jockey Hollow National Historic Site, Waterloo Village in Stanhope
Mailing address	P. O. Box 16, Whippany, NJ 07981
Phone	(201) 887-8177

WHIPPANY RAILWAY MUSEUM

The Whippany Railway Museum was chartered in 1973. In 1985 it acquired its present name and moved to new quarters in the former freight house of the Morristown & Erie Railway at Whippany, New Jersey. The building, which dates from 1904, contains a gift shop, a collection of railroadiana, and a Lionel train layout. Nearby are approximately a dozen pieces of rolling stock owned by museum members and other railroad associations.

The museum is at 1 Railroad Plaza at the intersection of Route 10 and Whippany Road. To reach the museum by car, take Exit 35 (Route 10 East) from I-287 about halfway between Morristown and I-80. It is also accessible by bus or taxi from the NJ Transit commuter rail station in Morristown — the distance is about 2 miles. There are restaurants in Whippany and restaurants and lodging in Morristown.

Whippany

Locomotives	9 steam (4 active), 1 diesel (used for switching)	**Nearby attractions**	Great Sand Dunes, Rio Grande National Forest, Carson National Forest, Jicarilla Apache Reservation		
Cars	Coaches, snack and souvenir car, open observation car	**Mailing address**	P. O. Box 789, Chama, NM 87520		
Schedule	Memorial Day weekend to mid-October: leave Chama 10:30 a.m., return 4:30 p.m.; leave Antonito 10, return at 5. Charter trips available.	**Phone**	(505) 756-2151		

Fares — Round trip to Osier from either Chama or Antonito: adults $29, children 11 and under $11; through trip with return by van: adults $43.50, children $21; overnight trip, adults $121, children $55. Checks and credit cards accepted.

Memberships — Friends of the Cumbres &Toltec Scenic Railroad, P. O. Box 222, Chama, NM 87520.

STEAM LOCOMOTIVES

Number	Type	Former owner	Builder	Date
484, 487, 488, 489	2-8-2	D&RGW	Baldwin	1925

P ⊕ ⊼ 🎁 ☕

CUMBRES & TOLTEC SCENIC RAILROAD

When the Denver & Rio Grande Western abandoned its 3'-gauge line between Antonito and Durango, Colorado, in 1968, the states of New Mexico and Colorado purchased a 64-mile segment of the line between Antonito and Chama, N. Mex., and the locomotives and cars necessary to operate the line. The line is now operated by Kyle Railways for the two states. It is the longest and highest narrow gauge steam railroad in the U. S.

The line from Chama (elevation, 7,863 feet) climbs a 4 percent grade to the summit at Cumbres (10,015 feet) and descends to Osier (9634 feet). The climb from Antonito (7,888 feet) to Osier is easier, averaging 1.4 percent; the scenery includes Toltec Gorge, two tunnels, and enough sharp curves that the line crosses the Colorado-New Mexico boundary eleven times.

The principal shops of the railroad are at Chama, and other cars and locomotives are on display there. Guided tours of the shops are available.

Trains leave both terminals and meet at Osier, Colo., where passengers eat lunch (snacks are available on the train) and the trains exchange engines. Passengers then reboard and return to their starting points.

Reservations are advisable; they are necessary for overnight trips. They can be made through travel agencies and AAA offices. Passengers can ride either half of the line or they can go all the way and return by van. Take a jacket or sweater — the weather can change quickly in the Rockies. Access for the handicapped is somewhat limited; persons with respiratory problems should consider the altitude.

Chama is on U. S. Routes 64 and 84, 106 miles northwest of Santa Fe; follow State Route 17 into town, and you'll find the station on your right. Antonito is 110 miles north of Santa Fe and 30 miles south of Alamosa on U. S. 285. Food and lodging are available in Chama and Antonito.

Locomotives	1 steam, 2 diesel
Cars	Coaches, gondola car
Displays	New York, Ontario & Western private car used by President Grover Cleveland
Schedule	Weekends and holidays Memorial Day weekend through October; also Wednesday in July and August, departures at 12:30, and 3 p.m. On the second and third weekends in October, trains depart at 12, 2, and 4. Charter trips available.
Fares	Adults $8, children 3-11 $4 (under 3 free). Group discounts available (reservations needed for groups).
Nearby attractions	Canal Town, Letchworth State Park
Mailing address	278 Main Street, Arcade, NY 14009
Phone	(716) 496-9877

LOCOMOTIVES

Number	Type	Former owner	Builder	Date
STEAM				
8	2-8-0	Boyne City Railroad	Alco	1920
DIESEL				
11	44 ton		GE	1947
12	65 ton	U. S. Navy	GE	1945

ARCADE & ATTICA RAILROAD

Like several other railroads in this book, the Arcade & Attica is a common-carrier freight railroad that also runs excursion trains. Passenger trains run north from Arcade to Curriers, 7 miles, and back. Art and craft events are held at Curriers. The ride takes 1½ hours.

Arcade is about 40 miles south-southeast of Buffalo, 3 miles east of Route 16. The Arcade & Attica station is on Routes 39 and 98 in downtown Arcade. Passengers should plan to be at the station a half hour before departure time. Soda, candy, and popcorn are available on the train. Restaurants and lodging can be found in Arcade.

Arcade

Locomotives	2 diesel, 1 Brill motor car (nicknamed "The Red Heifer")
Cars	Coaches, open cars
Schedule	Late May-early November, weekends and holidays; late June-Labor Day, Wednesday-Sunday; leave Arkville10:30 a.m. and 12:15, 2, and 3:45 p.m. Charter trips available.
Fares	Adults $7, children 5-11 $4 (under 5 free). Discounts available for groups of 20 or more (reservations are needed for groups). Credit cards accepted.
Special events	Railroad Festival, Ghost Train and Great Pumpkin Weekend, train robberies
Nearby attractions	Auto Memories (Arkville), Hanford Mills Museum, Farmers Museum, Baseball Hall of Fame, Catskill Park
Mailing address	P. O. Box 310, Stamford, NY 12167
Phone	Arkville depot (914) 586-3877; office (914) 652-2821; (800) 225-4132

DELAWARE & ULSTER RAIL RIDE

The Ulster & Delaware Railroad, a line from Kingston through the Catskills to Oneonta, New York, was purchased by the New York Central in 1932. It was abandoned in bits and pieces, and the last portion of the route was closed by Conrail in 1976.

The Delaware & Ulster Rail Ride is one of three portions of the U&D remaining in service as tourist railroads (the other two are the Trolley Museum of New York at Kingston and the Catskill Mountain Railroad at Mt. Pleasant). The Delaware & Ulster offers 1-hour rides from Arkville to Halcottsville, 6 miles, and return.

The station is on Route 28 in Arkville, about halfway between Kingston and Oneonta. There is a snack bar in the station and a restaurant nearby; food and lodging can be found in Margaretville 2 miles away. The station at Arkville has ramps to aid access for the handicapped.

Displays	18 subway cars, working signal tower
Dates open	Monday-Friday 10 a.m.-4 p.m., Saturday 11-4; closed major holidays
Admission	Adults $1.15; children under 17, 55 cents; age 55 and over, 55 cents
Special events	Activities for children and adults many days mid-June through August; write for leaflet. Group tours available.
Nearby attractions	Brooklyn Bridge, South Street Seaport, Brooklyn Museum
Mailing address	81 Willoughby Street, Room 802, Brooklyn, NY 11201
Phone	(718) 330-3060, 330-3063

NEW YORK CITY TRANSIT MUSEUM

The New York City Transit Authority maintains an exhibit of antique subway cars and memorabilia at its unused Court Street station, located at (or under) the corner of Boerum Place and Schermerhorn Street in Brooklyn.

The exhibit is not yet accessible to the handicapped because of steep stairs; for the same reason, the transit authority specifically cautions against wearing high heels.

The nearest subway stations are Borough Hall in Brooklyn on the IRT 2, 3, 4, and 5 lines; Jay Street on the IND A and F lines; and Lawrence Street on the BMT M and R lines.

Displays	0-6-0, box car, caboose
Dates open	June-August, Saturdays, 1-4 p.m., weather permitting; daily during Chautauqua County Fair (July 23-29, 1990) Free, except during fair
Admission	Antique Auto Show (May 18-20, 1990)
Special events	Dunkirk Historical Museum, Dunkirk
Nearby attractions	lighthouse, Chautauqua Lake, Lake Erie State Park
Mailing address	Historical Society of Dunkirk, 513 Washington Avenue, Dunkirk, NY 14048
Phone	(716) 366-3797

ALCO-BROOKS RAILROAD DISPLAY

One of the eight companies that merged in 1901 to form the American Locomotive Company (Alco) was Brooks Locomotive Works of Dunkirk, New York. On display at the Chautauqua County Fairgrounds in Dunkirk is Boston & Maine 0-6-0 No. 444, built by Alco's Brooks Works in 1916. Along with the locomotive are a Delaware & Hudson wood box car built in 1907, a New York Central

caboose built in 1905, and assorted smaller items. In the box car are historical displays and a sales counter.

Dunkirk is on the shore of Lake Erie, about halfway between Buffalo and Erie. The fairgrounds are at 1089 Central Avenue, next to I-90. There are restaurants near the fairgrounds and motels within half a mile.

Cars	Ex-Baltimore & Ohio and Lackawanna coaches, dining cars
Schedule	May 26-October 28, 1990, Saturdays, Sundays, Memorial Day, and Labor Day, leave Gowanda 1 and 3:30 p.m., leave South Dayton 2:15. Dinner trains operate May 12-December 16, 1990, Saturdays (except third Saturday of the month) at 6:30 p.m. and Sundays at 2 p.m. Charter trips available.
Fares	Adults $7.25, children 3-11 $4.25, seniors $6.50. Dinner train, $22.95-$39.95, children $11.50-$17, depending on menu selection. Reservations are required for dinner trains. Group discounts available. Checks accepted. Credit cards accepted for advance purchases.
Nearby attractions	B&B Buffalo Ranch, Allegany State Park, Salamanca Rail Museum, Arcade & Attica Railroad, Original Kazoo Factory
Mailing address	50 Commercial Street, Gowanda, NY 14070
Phone	(716) 532-5716

DIESEL LOCOMOTIVES

Number	Type	Former owner	Builder	Date
85	S-2	South Buffalo Railway	Alco	
1013	C-425	Norfolk & Western	Alco	1965
6101	C-425	Pennsylvania Railroad	Alco	

NEW YORK & LAKE ERIE RAILROAD

The New York & Lake Erie Railroad is a common carrier operating excursion and dinner trains on former Erie Railroad lines. Afternoon excursions run between Gowanda and South Dayton, 10 miles, and the round trip takes about 2 hours. Dinner trips make a round trip from Gowanda to Cherry Creek, 15 miles each way. For the first 4½ miles of the ride the train climbs a grade averaging 2.75 percent out of the valley of the Cattaraugus River.

Motive power is all Alco, and passengers ride in former Baltimore & Ohio modernized coaches, former Lackawanna electric cars, or a depressed-center flatcar reconfigured as an open excursion car.

Gowanda is south of Buffalo and east of Dunkirk on U. S. Route 62 and New York Routes 39 and 438. There are restaurants in Gowanda, and motels can be found in Hamburg, about 20 miles north.

Car	1 self-propelled railcar
Displays	9 streetcars and rapid transit cars
Schedule	Memorial Day-Columbus Day, weekends and holidays; July and August, Thursday-Monday, noon-5 p.m. Charter trips available.
Fares	Adults $1.50, children under 13 $1. Checks accepted.
Memberships	Write for information.
Special events	Christmas run
Nearby attractions	Maritime Museum, Ulster & Delaware Rail Ride, Catskill Mountain Railroad
Mailing address	89 East Strand, Kingston, NY 12401
Phone	(914) 331-3399

TROLLEY MUSEUM OF NEW YORK

The Trolley Museum of New York operates over 1½ miles of former Ulster & Delaware track at Kingston, N. Y. The scenery along the track is essentially urban: street running, waterfront industrial area, and the old U&D boat dock on the Hudson River. The only equipment in operation at the present time is an ex-New Haven Brill Model 55 gasoline-powered railcar.

Kingston is on the west shore of the Hudson River about 100 miles north of New York City and 50 miles south of Albany. To reach the museum, take Exit 19 of the New York State Thruway, then follow signs to downtown Kingston and the Urban Cultural Park on the waterfront. Food and lodging can be found in Kingston.

Locomotives	3 diesel, 2 gasoline
Cars	Flatcars
Displays	Steam locomotive, baggage car, coaches, cabooses
Schedule	Weekends and holidays Memorial Day-Columbus Day. Trains leave Mt. Pleasant hourly from 11 a.m. to 5 p.m. Charter trips available.
Fares	Adults $3 one way, $4 round trip; children 4-11 any ride $1 (under 4 free). Group discounts available. Checks accepted.
Memberships	Write for information.
Special events	Moonlight runs, hay rides, Christmas runs
earby attractions	Maritime Museum, Trolley Museum of New York, Catskills
Mailing address	P. O. Box 46, Shokan, NY 12481
Phone	(914) 688-7400; for recorded information, 657-8233

CATSKILL MOUNTAIN RAILROAD

The Catskill Mountain Railroad operates over a 3-mile portion of the former Ulster & Delaware Railroad along Esopus Creek between Mt. Pleasant and Phoenicia, New York. The round-trip ride takes about 40 minutes.

The usual motive power is a 35-ton diesel locomotive built by the Davenport Locomotive Works; passengers ride on open flatcars.

There are restaurants in Phoenicia and lodging in Mt. Pleasant. Mt. Pleasant is 20 miles west of Kingston on Route 28.

Cars	Vintage and modern coaches, dining car, open observation car
Displays	Bicycles, autos, horse-drawn vehicles, box car, railroad crane
Dates open	Museums and grounds are open whenever trains run.
Schedule	Weekends May–October, *Museum Trail* leaves Flemingville 1, 2:30, and 4 p.m., plus additional departure Sundays at 11:30 a.m. Morning Star leaves Flemingville Saturdays at 9 a.m.; *Sunset Ltd.*, Saturdays at 7 p.m.; *Red Diamond*, Sundays at 1 p.m. Charter trips available.
Fares	Museum Trail: adults $4.50, children 6–12 $2.50 (under 6 free); *Morning Star*: $10/$5 (breakfast extra); *Sunset Ltd.* and *Red Diamond*, $12/$6 (dinner extra). Group discounts available. Checks accepted for fares; credit cards accepted for meals.
Memberships	Write for information.

Special events	Owego Strawberry Festival (June 23, 1990), Newark Valley Depot Days (August 4–5, 1990), Newark Valley Apple Festival (October 6–7, 1990)
Nearby attractions	Tioga Gardens, Corning Glass Works, Watkins Glen State Park, Finger Lakes region, wineries, speedway
Mailing address	P. O. Box 490, Owego, NY 13827
Phone	(607) 687-0990 for schedule information; (607) 625-9917 for dinner reservations

DIESEL LOCOMOTIVES

Number	Type	Former owner	Builder	Date
14	S-2		Alco	1947
47	RS-1	Washington Terminal	Alco	1945
62	RS-1	Washington Terminal	Alco	1950

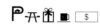

TIOGA CENTRAL RAILROAD EXCURSIONS

The Tioga Central operates *Museum Trail* excursion trains over a former Lehigh Valley line from Flemingville (5 miles north of Owego, New York, on Route 38) to Newark Valley, 5½ miles. The round trip takes 1¼ hours.

Operating from a station on West Avenue in Owego to North Harford, 25 miles, are the Saturday morning *Morning Star*, the Saturday evening *Sunset Ltd.*, and the Sunday afternoon *Red Diamond*, which offer breakfast or dinner on board. Reservations are required for dinner. Breakfast and dinner trains take 3 hours for the round trip.

Museum Trail trains stop on request at several points for passengers who want to visit parks and restaurants. The fare includes admission to the Tioga Transportation Museum at Flemingville and the Newark Valley Depot Museum. There is a snack bar at the Newark Valley depot. Food and lodging are available in Owego, just north of the Pennsylvania border 25 miles west of Binghamton.

Displays	Artifacts, photos	**Memberships**	$20 per year
Dates open	Summer weekends — call for information	**Mailing address**	P. O. Box 455, Phoenicia, NY 12464
Admission	Free	**Phone**	(914) 688-7501

EMPIRE STATE RAILWAY MUSEUM

The Empire State Railway Museum is in the process of restoring the former Ulster & Delaware (later New York Central) station at Phoenicia, New York. In addition, the museum has former Lake Superior & Ishpeming 2-8-0 No. 23 stored at Kingston, along with several passenger cars. Phoenicia is in the heart of the Catskills, about 30 miles west of Kingston on New York Route 28.

Locomotives	[1988 information] Fairmont speeder, Plymouth ML8	**Memberships** **Nearby attractions**	Write for information. Oatka Depot Railroad Museum, Darian
Cars	Open crew cars		Lake Amusement Park, Genesee Country
Displays	Interurbans, streetcars, maintenance of way equipment, automobiles, buses	**Mailing address**	Village P. O. Box 136, West Henrietta, NY 14586
Dates open	Year-round, Sundays, 11 a.m.-4 p.m. Group tours available on weekdays by reservation.	**Phone**	(716) 533-1113
Admission	Adults $1; children under 13, 50 cents. Group discounts available.		
Fares	50 cents		

NEW YORK MUSEUM OF TRANSPORTATION

The New York Museum of Transportation is located at 6393 East River Road at Town Line Road in the town of Rush, about 15 minutes south of Rochester and 2 miles south of Exit 46 of the New York State Thruway. The museum building houses streetcars and interurbans from western New York, and numerous other items are under restoration, including a gasoline-powered switching locomotive that worked in the Rochester subway. Weather permitting, the museum offers track-car rides over 1½ miles of track. The track is being extended to the Oatka Depot Railroad Museum (see next entry) to enable visitors to see both museums without having to drive the 4 miles between them. If you visit the museum in cold weather, keep in mind that the visitor center is heated but the main building is not. Food and lodging are available in Henrietta, a suburb of Rochester, and throughout Rochester.

Displays	Diesel locomotives, freight and passenger cars
Dates open	Memorial Day-Labor Day, Sundays, 1-5 p.m.
Admission	Adults $1; maximum charge per family $5. Checks accepted.
Memberships	Rochester Chapter, NRHS; write for information.
Special events	Spring Railfan Weekend
Nearby attractions	New York Museum of Transportation, George Eastman House, International Museum of Photography, Rochester Art Museum, Rochester Museum and Science Center
Mailing address	P. O. Box 664, Rochester, NY 14603
Phone	(716) 533-1431

DIESEL LOCOMOTIVES

Number	Type	Former owner	Builder	Date
6	80 ton	Eastman Kodak Co.	GE	1946
79	S-4	Nickel Plate	Alco	1953
8445	RS-3m	Pennsylvania Railroad	Alco	1953

ROCHESTER AND GENESEE VALLEY RAILROAD MUSEUM

The Rochester Chapter of the National Railway Historical Society has a museum in a former Erie Railroad station (named "Scottsville," "Pixley," "Oatka," and "Industry" at various times) 12 miles south of Rochester. It is located on Route 251 at 282 Rush-Scottsville Road. The museum's collection includes Lehigh Valley RS3m No. 211, Eastman Kodak GE 80-ton switcher No. 6, and numerous freight and passenger cars. Rochester Chapter NRHS is cooperating with the New York Transportation Museum (see previous entry) to build a line between the two museums. Rochester Chapter NRHS operates excursions Sundays during October on the Ontario Midland Railroad between Sodus and Newark. Write for schedule information. There are restaurants in nearby Scottsville; food and lodging can be found throughout Rochester.

Displays	Cabooses, passenger cars, maintenance of way equipment, photographs, artifacts
Dates open	March-September: Monday-Saturday 10 a.m.-5 p.m., Sunday 12-5; October-December Tuesday-Saturday 10 a.m.-5 p.m., Sunday 12-5. Closed in January and February.
Admission	Free; donations appreciated
Memberships	$5 per year
Special events	Citywide Falling Leaves Festival (September 29, 1990): Railroad Swap Meet and Flea Market
Nearby attractions	Allegany State Park, Seneca Iroquois National Museum, Kinzua Bridge State Park and Train Ride
Mailing address	170 Main Street, Salamanca, NY 14779
Phone	(716) 945-3133

P &. 卉 🎁

SALAMANCA RAIL MUSEUM

The former Buffalo, Rochester & Pittsburgh station in Salamanca, built in 1912, was acquired in 1980 by the Salamanca Rail Museum Association. It was restored and opened as a museum in 1984. Exhibits inside the museum emphasize the local railroads: Baltimore & Ohio (successor to the BR&P), Erie, and Pennsylvania. On display outside are various pieces of rolling stock.

The museum sponsors occasional excursion trains; contact the museum directly for fares and schedules. Salamanca is on New York Route 17 just about due south of Buffalo and a few miles north of the Pennsylvania border.

The museum is right downtown; restaurants and lodging can be found nearby.

Dates open	June-October, Sundays, 2-5 p.m. Other times by appointment.
Admission	Free
Memberships	Central New York Chapter, NRHS; write for information.
Nearby attractions	Erie Canal exhibit, fish hatchery
Mailing address	Box 229, Marcellus, NY 13108

MARTISCO STATION MUSEUM

When the Auburn & Syracuse Railroad was built in the 1830s it bypassed the village of Marcellus, 10 miles from Syracuse, but built a station about 2 miles away. The Auburn & Syracuse became part of the New York Central, and a short line was built (eventually the Marcellus & Otisco Lake Railway) to give Marcellus a rail connection. The NYC renamed its Marcellus station Martisco.

The Central New York Chapter of the National Railway Historical Society purchased the Martisco station in 1966 to save it from demolition and has created a museum in the building. A former Pennsylvania Railroad dining car is parked next to the museum and contains the chapter's library. The chapter has 3 locomotives and 7 passenger cars on display at the New York State Fairgrounds; they are open only during the fair.

The nearest restaurants are in Camillus; the nearest lodging is in Elbridge. Both are within a few minutes of the museum, and the city of Syracuse is about 10 miles away.

Displays	Adirondack RSC-2, Santa Fe dining car, Conrail caboose
Dates open	July 1-Labor Day, Tuesday-Friday 10 a.m.-4:30 p.m., Saturday and Sunday, 12:30-4:30; Labor Day-June 30, Wednesday-Sunday, 12:30-4:30
Admission	$1.50 per person (under age 3 free)
Memberships	$20 per year
Nearby attractions	Union Station, Mast's Brewery, Munson-Williams-Proctor Art Museum, Utica Zoo
Mailing address	311 Main Street, Utica, NY 13501
Phone	(315) 724-6128

P & A 🎁 $

THE CHILDREN'S MUSEUM

The Children's Museum in Utica specializes in history, natural history, and science. Of interest to rail enthusiasts are three pieces of rolling stock displayed outside: Adirondack Railway RSC-2 No. 25 (ex-Seaboard Air Line); Santa Fe dining car 1479, built by Budd in 1937; and Conrail caboose 20076, the only Pennsylvania Railroad N5 caboose to be rebuilt with four windows per side.

The equipment was acquired and restored by the Utica & Mohawk Valley Chapter of the National Railway Historical Society.

The museum is in the heart of the historic Bagg's Square District, next door to Union Station, served by Amtrak. Food and lodging can be found within a few blocks.

Utica

Cars	Open cars
Dates open	Memorial Day weekend through October, 9 a.m.-6 p.m. Full operation daily from June 13 through Labor Day; otherwise full operation weekends and limited operation Monday-Friday.
Schedule	Train runs every 30-45 minutes.
Admission	Adults $10.95, children 4-12 $8.95, age 65 and over $8.95. Admission charge includes train ride. Checks and credit cards accepted. Group discounts available (reservations needed for groups).
Special events	Old Timers' Day
Nearby attractions	Mystery Hill, The Blowing Rock, Horn in the West (outdoor drama), Grandfather Mountain
Mailing address	P. O. Box 388, Blowing Rock, NC 28605
Phone	(704) 264-9061

STEAM LOCOMOTIVES

Number	Type	Former owner	Builder	Date
12	4-6-0	East Tennessee & Western North Carolina	Baldwin	1917
190	2-8-2	White Pass & Yukon	Baldwin	1943

TWEETSIE RAILROAD

From 1918 to 1941 Boone, North Carolina, was the terminus of the 3'-gauge Linville River Railway, a subsidiary of the East Tennessee & Western North Carolina Railroad — nicknamed "Tweetsie."

Ten-Wheeler No. 12 of the ET&WNC now hauls passengers around the Tweetsie Railroad theme park at Blowing Rock, N. C., 8 miles south of Boone on U. S. Routes 221 and 321. The roster also includes ex-White Pass & Yukon 2-8-2 No. 190. The train makes a 3-mile, 30-minute run around the perimeter of the park.

The park includes a petting farm, live entertainment, kiddie rides, Indian village, gold mine, shops, and restaurants. Food and lodging can be found in Blowing Rock and Boone.

Cars	Cabooses, flatcars
Displays	Freight and passenger cars
Dates open	May-November, first Sunday of each month, noon-4 p.m.
Admission	Free; donations appreciated
Memberships	East Carolina Chapter NRHS — write for information
Radio frequency	160.425
Nearby attractions	Jordan Lake, Sherron Harris Nuclear Power Plant, state capitol
Mailing address	P. O. Box 83, New Hill, NC 27562
Phone	(919) 362-5416

DIESEL LOCOMOTIVES

Number	Type	Former owner	Builder	Date
67	45 ton	U. S. Navy	GE	1942
70	50 ton	U. S. Navy	Whitcomb	1941
71	80 ton	U. S. Marines	GE	1942

NORTH CAROLINA RAILROAD MUSEUM

In 1980 the East Carolina Chapter of the National Railway Historical Society acquired a short piece of the Durham branch of the former Norfolk Southern Railway.

Trains operate from Bonsal to New Hill, about 4 miles, and return. Bonsal is on State Route 1011, 8 miles southwest of Apex — between Raleigh and Sanford, in larger terms. The usual motive power for the train is one of two former U. S. Navy diesel switchers, General Electric No. 67 and Whitcomb No. 70. Passengers ride in cabooses or on flatcars. Occasionally motor cars are operated.

Food and lodging are available in Apex.

Bonsal

Cars	Open and closed cars
Schedule	Saturdays and Sundays in May, daily June 2-October 28, 1990: Tuckasegee River, leave Dillsboro 10 a.m. and 2 p.m. (10 a.m. only September 4-30); round trip takes about 3½ hours. Nantahala Gorge, leave Bryson City 9 a.m. and 2 p.m. (10 a.m. only, not 9, September 4-30); round trip takes about 4 hours; lunch available on 9 a.m. trains. Red Marble Gap and Valley River schedules had not been announced at press time. Reservations are required. Charter trips available.
Fares	Tuckasegee River, adults $10, children $5; Nantahala Gorge, adults $12, children $5. Credit cards and checks accepted. Group discounts available.
Nearby attractions	Great Smoky Mountains National Park, national forests
Mailing address	1 Maple Street, Sylva, NC 28779
Phone	(704) 586-8811, (800) 872-4681

DIESEL LOCOMOTIVES

Number	Type	Former owner	Builder	Date
200	GP7	Union Pacific	EMD	1954
992, 993	CF7	Texas & Northern	EMD/AT&SF	1947
1551	GP7	Burlington Northern	EMD	1953

P & 🚻 🎁 🍴

GREAT SMOKY MOUNTAINS RAILWAY

The Great Smoky Mountains Railway provides freight and passenger service on the former Murphy Branch of the Southern Railway, a scenic line in the southwestern tip of North Carolina west of Asheville. The railroad is noted for trestles, tunnels, and grades up to 4.3 percent. Four different excursions are offered: Tuckasegee River (Dillsboro-Bryson City, 16 miles), Nantahala Gorge (Bryson City-Nantahala, 36 miles), Red Marble Gap (from Andrews), and Valley River (from Murphy and Andrews). Snacks are available on board, and some trains offer a buffet lunch. Dillsboro is on U. S. Routes 23, 74, and 441; Bryson City, Andrews, and Murphy are on U. S. 19. Food and lodging are available throughout the area.

Displays	Caboose, motor car, replica of early loco-motive, HO model railroad
Dates open	Saturdays 10 a.m.-5 p.m., Sundays 1-5
Admission	Free
Nearby attractions	World Golf Hall of Fame, Sandhills Wildlife Area
Mailing address	2 Main Street, Hamlet, NC 28345

NATIONAL RAILROAD MUSEUM

The former Seaboard Air Line Railroad station at Hamlet (which still serves Amtrak) now houses the National Railroad Museum. Hamlet was an important junction on the SAL — lines to Atlanta and to Wilmington branched from the Richmond-Jacksonville main line there — and it still is for successor CSX Transportation. The building is a large two-story wood structure with a round bay facing the crossing of the lines. Displays include a Seaboard caboose, a replica of the early locomotive *Raleigh*, a motor car, and an HO scale model railroad. Hamlet is just north of the easternmost angle in the North Carolina-South Carolina state line. The museum is on Main Street south of U. S. Route 74 and between State Routes 38 and 177. There are restaurants within a block; the nearest motels are in Rockingham, 5 miles west.

		LOCOMOTIVES				
Cars	Coaches	**Number**	**Type**	**Former owner**	**Builder**	**Date**
Dates open	April-October, Monday-Saturday 9 a.m.-5 p.m., Sunday 1-5; November-March, Tuesday-Saturday 10-4, Sunday 1-4. Closed Thanksgiving, December 24, and Christmas.	STEAM				
		4	2-8-0	Buffalo Creek & Gauley	Baldwin	1926
		DIESEL				
Schedule	April 1-Labor Day, daily; Labor Day through December, weekends	620	GP9	Norfolk & Western	EMD	1958
Admission	Free; donations appreciated	6133	FP7	Southern Railway	EMD	1950

Admission

Fares Adults, steam $3, diesel $2; children 3-12 and age 65 and over, steam $2, diesel $1.50. Credit cards and checks accepted. Group discounts available; reservations required for groups.

Memberships $7.50-$1000. Write to North Carolina Transportation History Corporation Time-keepers, P. O. Box 44, Spencer, NC 28159.

Special events Automobile shows, Railfan Day, Labor Day celebration

Nearby attractions Waterworks Visual Arts Center, Grimes Mill, Hall House, Rowan Museum

Mailing address P. O. Box 165, Spencer, NC 28159

Phone (704) 636-2889

NORTH CAROLINA TRANSPORTATION MUSEUM

Spencer Shops was once the Southern Railway's primary repair facility. The railroad donated the buildings and site to the state in 1977 and 1979; they have become a transportation museum administered by the Division of Archives and History of the North Carolina Department of Cultural Resources. Exhibits range from a prehistoric Indian canoe to airplanes. The railroad exhibits include several passenger and freight cars.

Former Buffalo Creek & Gauley 2-8-0 No. 4, reborn as Southern Railway 604, pulls several coaches on a 45-minute tour of the muse-um grounds; weekdays and during off seasons the steam locomo-tive's place is taken by a green-and-white Southern FP7 or a Norfolk & Western GP9.

The museum is at 411 South Salisbury Avenue (U. S. Routes 2 and 70 and State Route 150) in Spencer, which is 2 miles east of Salisbury. Southern's busy Washington-Atlanta main line passes to the south of the museum complex. Refreshments are available in the visitor center, and there is a restaurant across the street. Additional restaurants and lodging are available in Salisbury.

Displays	Steam locomotive, caboose
Dates open	Monday-Saturday, 10 a.m.-5 p.m.; Sundays, 1-5
Admission	Suggested donation, $1 per person
Memberships	Individual $10, family $20, student $5
Special events	Azalea Festival (early April), Wilmington River Fest (first week of October)
Nearby attractions	Beaches, battleship U. S. S. *North Carolina*
Mailing address	501 Nutt Street, Wilmington, NC 28401
Phone	(919) 763-2634

WILMINGTON RAILROAD MUSEUM

The Wilmington Railroad Museum was dedicated on November 10, 1983. It is housed in the former Atlantic Coast Line freight office and warehouse, built in 1876, and oldest survivor of the group of buildings that once housed ACL's general offices. On display at the museum are ACL 4-6-0 No. 250, built in 1910; a steel caboose; and ACL artifacts. The building also houses the Cape Fear Model Railroad Club. The museum is at Red Cross and Water Streets in downtown Wilmington, about 12 blocks north of the bridge that carries U. S. Routes 17, 74, and 76 over the Cape Fear River. Food and lodging are available within a block of the museum.

Displays	Northern Pacific 4-4-0, handcar, caboose, model railroad
Dates open	Late May-late October, Monday-Friday 9 a.m.-8 p.m., Saturday and Sunday 9-5
Admission	Adults $3.25, children 6-16 $1.25. Checks and credit cards accepted ($10 minimum). Group discounts available.
Memberships	Write for information.
Special events	Pioneer Days (third weekend of August)
Nearby attractions	Comstock House, Heritage-Hjemkomst Interpretive Center, Fargo Theater, Plains Art Museum
Mailing address	P. O. Box 719, West Fargo, ND 58078
Phone	(701) 282-2822

BONANZAVILLE, USA

Bonanzaville, USA, a re-creation of a Northern Plains town, includes two Northern Pacific depots. One, the station from Embden, North Dakota, houses a railroad museum. Included in its exhibits are Northern Pacific 4-4-0 No. 684 (built in 1883), a caboose, and a steel coach. The other station is from Kathryn, N. Dak., and contains the operating model railroad of the Spud Valley Railroad Club. Among the other attractions at Bonanzaville are an airplane museum and the Red River and Northern Plains Museum, which has one of the largest and most complete American Indian collections in the Midwest.

Bonanzaville, USA, is on U. S. Highway 10 west of Exit 65 of I-29 and east of Exit 85 of I-94. Food and lodging are available nearby.

Displays	LGB model railroad, 2 steam locomotives, cars, memorabilia
Dates open	Monday-Saturday 11 a.m.-10 p.m., Sunday 10 a.m.-8 p.m. Closed Thanksgiving, Christmas, New Year's Day, and Easter.
Admission	Free; parking 50 cents per hour
Special events	Annual Train Meet (Father's Day weekend)
Nearby attractions	Blossom Music Center, All-American Soap Box Derby, Stan Hywet Hall and Gardens
Mailing address	120 East Mill Street, Akron, OH 44308
Phone	(216) 762-8434

RAILWAYS OF AMERICA

Quaker Square in Akron is a hotel, restaurant, and shopping complex located in the former Quaker Oats Co. mills and silos. In the former Railway Express Agency building is the Railways of America museum, which has an operating LGB model railroad and a collection of memorabilia such as lanterns, builder's plates, and railroad clothing. On exhibit outside are two steam locomotives and seven cars. While the museum is in the same building as the Depot Restaurant, the displays are separate from the restaurant and you needn't eat in the restaurant in order to see the museum. Quaker Square includes other eating establishments and a Hilton Hotel.

Akron

Displays	30 locomotives, freight cars, and passenger cars, including *Silver Dome*, the first dome car built in the U. S.
Dates open	Memorial Day through September, Wednesday-Sunday plus holidays, 1-5 p.m.; May and October, Sundays 1-5. Group tours available (reservations required).
Admission	Free, donations welcome
Memberships	Individual $15, family $20
Special events	Excursions and rail tours
Nearby attractions	Cedar Point, Seneca Caverns, Historic Lyme Village, Lake Erie Sorrowful Mother Shrine, Bellevue Heritage Museum
Mailing address	233 York Street, Bellevue, OH 44811-1377
Phone	(419) 483-2222

MAD RIVER & NKP RAILROAD MUSEUM

The Mad River & NKP Railroad Society founded its museum in 1976, and it was adopted as a bicentennial project by the city of Bellevue that same year. The museum has grown to encompass a diverse collection of rolling stock, one that includes all the significant types of passenger cars without a great deal of duplication. Notable in the collection is *Silver Dome*, America's first dome car, converted by the Burlington from a coach in 1945. The museum is at 253 Southwest Street, one block south of U. S. 20 (Main Street) in Bellevue. Restaurants and lodging can be found in Bellevue. The society occasionally sponsors excursion trains on mainline railroads; write for information about those trips.

Displays	Nickel Plate 2-8-4, hopper car, caboose	
Dates open	Memorial Day-Labor Day, daily noon-5 p.m.	
Admission	Free; donations appreciated	
Memberships	Write for information.	
Nearby attractions	Covered bridges	
Mailing address	P. O. Box 643, Conneaut, OH 44030	
Phone	(216) 599-7878	

CONNEAUT RAILROAD MUSEUM

The Conneaut chapter of the National Railway Historical Society operates a museum in the former New York Central depot in Conneaut. Inside are exhibits of timetables, lanterns, passes, photos, and other artifacts; there is also an operating HO scale model railroad. Outside are Nickel Plate Road locomotive No. 755, a Berkshire built in 1944; and a caboose and a hopper car from the Bessemer & Lake Erie.

The museum is at Depot and Mill Streets, north of U. S. 20 and I-90. Restaurants and lodging can be found in Conneaut.

Displays	N gauge model railroad, caboose, restored 1873 depot, railroad artifacts
Dates open	Monday-Saturday, 10 a.m.-5:30 p.m.; Sunday, 1-5:30. Closed Mondays Labor Day-Memorial Day; also closed Thanksgiving, Christmas, and New Year's Day.
Admission	Adults, $2; students and senior citizens, $1.50 (children 7 and under free). Credit cards and checks accepted. Group discounts available.
Special events	Railroad Festival (third week of May), Canteen Day (second Saturday in August), Christmas Exhibit
Nearby attractions	Warther Museum, Reeves Museum, Railway Chapel, Amish country
Mailing address	P. O. Box 11, Dennison, OH 44621
Phone	(614) 922-6776

DENNISON RAILROAD DEPOT MUSEUM

The former Pennsylvania Railroad station in Dennison, Ohio, built in 1873, has been restored with the assistance of a local vocational school and is now a railroad museum. During World War Two the building housed a servicemen's canteen that was the third busiest in the U. S.; the museum includes a re-creation of that facility.

Dennison is in eastern Ohio at the intersection of U. S. Routes 36 and 250 and State Route 800, 18 miles east of I-77 and 36 miles north of I-70. To reach the depot, take the Dennison exit off U. S. 250, turn left on Second Street, and left again on Center Street. There are restaurants in Dennison; motels can be found in Uhrichsville, New Philadelphia, and Dover.

Cars	Open-window heavyweight coaches, Pullman car
Schedule	Still tentative at press time; probably every Saturday and Sunday, June through October, plus occasional Wednesdays: leave Independence 11 a.m., arrive Hale Farm noon, Akron 12:45; leave Akron 3:45 p.m., leave Hale Farm 4:30, arrive Independence 5:45.
Fares	Not determined at press time. Reservations required. Checks and credit cards accepted. Group discounts available.
Memberships	Write for information.
Nearby attractions	Blossom Music Center, Cuyahoga Valley National Recreation Area
Mailing address	P. O. Box 158, Peninsula, OH 44264-0158
Phone	In Akron 657-2000; elsewhere (800) 468-4070

LOCOMOTIVES

Number	Type	Former owner	Builder	Date
STEAM				
4070	2-8-2	Grand Trunk Western	Alco	1918
DIESEL				
4056	RS-3	Spokane, Portland & Seattle	Alco	1951

CUYAHOGA VALLEY LINE RAILROAD

The Cuyahoga Valley Line operates excursion trains from Independence, a southern suburb of Cleveland, along the Cuyahoga River to Hale Farm, a re-creation of an early Ohio farm, and Akron. The track, now owned by the National Park Service, is a former Baltimore & Ohio line. It travels the length of the Cuyahoga Valley National Recreation Area paralleling the Ohio & Erie Canal. Usual motive power is former Grand Trunk Western 2-8-2 No. 4070; an Alco RS-3 is usually used on Wednesday trains. Snacks and souvenirs are available on board, and Pullman lounge car *Mount Baxter* can be chartered for private parties. Access for the handicapped is limited; please make your needs known when you make your reservations. The Independence station is on Old Rockside Road, .. mile west of Canal Road and 1.2 miles east of Exit 155 of I-77, a little south of I-480. There are restaurants and motels within a mile and throughout the Cleveland and Akron areas.

Displays	1872 station, caboose
Dates open	Memorial Day-Labor Day, Sundays and holidays 1-4 p.m.; other days by appointment
Admission	Free; donations welcome
Memberships	Write for information.
Special events	Strawberry Festival and Craft Bazaar (June 23, 1990); Festival At The Depot (first Saturday in October)
Nearby attractions	1848 church and barn, covered bridges
Mailing address	P. O. Box 22, Jefferson, OH 44047
Phone	(216) 293-5532

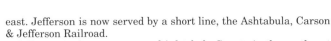

JEFFERSON DEPOT

Jefferson Depot, Inc., has restored the Lake Shore & Michigan Southern (New York Central System) station in Jefferson as a museum and community center.

The station served NYC lines from Ashtabula to Youngstown and to Oil City, Pennsylvania. Passenger service ended in 1956, and eventually traffic was consolidated on another NYC line a few miles east. Jefferson is now served by a short line, the Ashtabula, Carson & Jefferson Railroad.

Jefferson is the county seat of Ashtabula County in the northeast corner of Ohio. It is about 10 miles south of the city of Ashtabula on State Routes 46, 167, and 307. There are motels and restaurants in Jefferson.

Cars	Ex-Lackawanna coaches, gondola
Schedule	May 5-November 18, 1990, weekends and holidays; also Wednesdays May 5-June 27, and Wednesdays and Fridays September 5-November 21: leave Mason Sundays at noon and 2 p.m., other days at 11 a.m. and 1 p.m. Charter trips available.
Fares	Adults $7, children under 13 $3.50, age 65 and up $6. Checks and credit cards accepted. Group discounts available.
Nearby attractions	Kings Island, Football Hall of Fame, Jack Nicklaus Sports Center
Mailing address	P. O. Box 8150, West Chester, OH 45069
Phone	(513) 777-5777

DIESEL LOCOMOTIVE

Type	Former owner	Builder	Date
GP7	Chicago South Shore & South Bend	EMD	1950

INDIANA & OHIO SCENIC RAILWAY

The Indiana & Ohio Scenic Railway runs excursion trains between Mason and Lebanon, 8½ miles each way, on one of the lines of the freight-hauling Indiana & Ohio Railroad. The round trip takes 45 minutes and traverses low rolling hills. Snacks are available on the train. Restaurants and lodging can be found in Lebanon. Mason is about 25 miles northeast of Cincinnati on U. S 42. The station is at Forest and Western Avenues in Mason.

Displays	Depot, caboose, box car
Dates open	April-December, Wednesday-Sunday 1-4 p.m.; groups by reservation any time
Admission	Adults $2, children 5-18 $1
Nearby attractions	Toledo, Lake Erie & Western Railway & Museum
Mailing address	Maumee Valley Historical Society, 1031 River Road, Maumee, OH 43537
Phone	(419) 893-9602

P 禾 🎁

WOLCOTT MUSEUM COMPLEX

The Maumee Valley Historical Society operates the Wolcott Museum Complex in Maumee. In addition to several houses of various styles (log cabin, Federal, saltbox, and Greek Revival) the museum includes a depot from the Toledo & Grand Rapids (a predecessor of the Clover Leaf, which became part of the Nickel Plate in 1923) plus a box car and a caboose. The museum is on River Road in downtown Maumee and can be reached easily from U. S. Routes 20 and 24.

Locomotives	2 steam (2-8-0, 0-6-0), 2 diesel
Cars	Coaches
Schedule	Weekends Memorial Day through October and first three weekends of December, leave Nelsonville at noon for Diamond, at 2 p.m. for Logan. Charter trips available.
Fares	To Diamond, adults $5, children under 12 $4; to Logan, adults $9, children $6. Santa Trains are 50 cents more. Checks accepted. Group discounts available.
Memberships	Individual, $20
Special events	Santa Trains (first three weekends in December)
Nearby attractions	Wayne National Forest, Hocking State Forest, Lake Hope, Burr Oak Lake
Mailing address	P. O. Box 427, Nelsonville, OH 45764
Phone	(513) 335-0382 weekdays, (614) 753-9531 weekends

HOCKING VALLEY SCENIC RAILWAY

The Hocking Valley Scenic Railway operates over a portion of the former Hocking Valley Railroad (it ran from Toledo to Athens and Gallipolis, Ohio, and became part of the Chesapeake & Ohio in 1930) between Nelsonville and Logan, Ohio. Trips are offered to Diamond (5 miles each way, 70 minutes round trip) and to Logan (12½ miles, 3 hours). The train is usually pulled by an ex-Lake Superior & Ishpeming 2-8-0. Reservations are advised for trips in October and the Santa Trains in December.

Nelsonville is about 60 miles southeast of Columbus and 13 miles northwest of Athens on U. S. 33. The station is on Route 33 at Fulton Street. There are restaurants in Logan and Athens; lodging can be found in Nelsonville and Athens.

Locomotive	1 diesel
Cars	3 coaches, gondola, 2 cabooses
Schedule	May-October, weekends and holidays, 1 and 3 p.m. Halloween trains run evenings of the last weekend of October. Santa Claus trains operate the first two weekends of December. Charter trips available May-October.
Fares	Adults $4, children 3-11 $3 (under 3 free). Checks accepted. Discount for groups of 40 or more.
Memberships	Individual $15, family $30
Special events	Members' Day (July 4)
Nearby attractions	Heisey Glass Museum, Youth World Series Baseball, Newark Mounds (prehistoric area)
Mailing address	P. O. Box 242, Newark, OH 43055
Phone	(614) 928-3827

BUCKEYE CENTRAL SCENIC RAILROAD

One-hour train rides through fields and woods and along the Licking River are offered by the Buckeye Central. Trains operate from National Road station on U. S. 40 between Hebron and Jacktontown, Ohio, and run to Heath, 5 miles north, over a portion of a former Baltimore & Ohio branch.

The station is about 40 miles east of Columbus. From the west use Exit 129 (Route 79) from I-70; go north a mile to U. S. 40, then east. From the east use Exit 131 (Route 13); go north to U. S. 40, then west. There are restaurants and motels nearby.

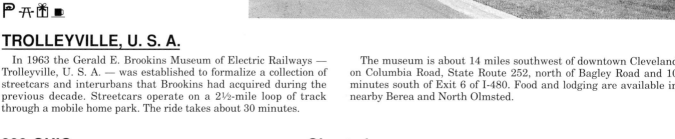

Cars	34 streetcars and interurbans
Dates open	Memorial Day through Labor Day, Sundays and holidays 1-5 p.m.; Wednesdays, Fridays, and Saturdays 10-3. Charters available mid-April through October.
Admission	Adults $2, children 4-12 $1.50. Checks accepted.
Memberships	Regular $8, family $25
Nearby attractions	Cleveland
Mailing address	7100 Columbia Road, Olmsted Township, OH 44138
Phone	(216) 235-4725

TROLLEYVILLE, U. S. A.

In 1963 the Gerald E. Brookins Museum of Electric Railways — Trolleyville, U. S. A. — was established to formalize a collection of streetcars and interurbans that Brookins had acquired during the previous decade. Streetcars operate on a 2½-mile loop of track through a mobile home park. The ride takes about 30 minutes.

The museum is about 14 miles southwest of downtown Cleveland on Columbia Road, State Route 252, north of Bagley Road and 10 minutes south of Exit 6 of I-480. Food and lodging are available in nearby Berea and North Olmsted.

Displays	Railroad artifacts, Pennsylvania Railroad N5C caboose, passenger cars
Dates open	Saturday 10 a.m.-4 p.m., except when excursions are operated.
Schedule	Write for information on excursion trains.
Admission	Free; donations appreciated
Memberships	Individual, $15 per year; family, $25
Special events	Mainline excursions; Depot Days
Nearby attractions	Orrville Historical Museum, Football Hall of Fame, Amish country
Mailing address	P. O. Box 11, Orrville, OH 44667
Phone	(216) 683-2426

P & ⛪

ORRVILLE RAILROAD HERITAGE COMMITTEE

In 1978 the Orrville Railroad Heritage Committee was formed to save the town's railroad station. The building stands at the junction of two former Pennsylvania Railroad lines: the route from Pittsburgh to Chicago via Fort Wayne now used by Amtrak's *Broadway Limited* and *Capitol Limited*, and a line from Cleveland through Akron to Columbus, now abandoned south of Orrville.

The group owns the interlocking tower that used to control the junction and a number of passenger cars and diesel locomotives. The Orrville Railroad Heritage Committee operates mainline passenger excursion trains several times a year. In recent years they have often been powered by former Nickel Plate 2-8-4 No. 765.

Orrville is southwest of Akron on State Route 57, 3 miles north of U. S. Route 30. Restaurants can be found as close as next door; there are motels along Route 30.

Cars	Coaches
Schedule	May 15-26 and September 4-October 27, 1990, Tuesday-Saturday, 11 a.m., 1 p.m., 3 p.m.; May 28-September 3, 1990, except Sundays at 10, noon, 2, and 4
Fares	Adults $6, children 3-12 $4. Checks accepted. Group discounts available.
Special events	Swiss Festival, September 28-29, 1990 (special schedules)
Nearby attractions	Amish country, Warther Museum, Roscoe Village, Dennison Railroad Depot Museum
Mailing address	P. O. Box 564, Sugar Creek, OH44681
Phone	(216) 852-4881

LOCOMOTIVES

Number	Type	Former owner	Builder	Date
STEAM				
1551	4-6-0	Grand Trunk Railway	Montreal	1912
DIESEL				
12	B-B	Timken	Alco	

OHIO CENTRAL RAILROAD

The Ohio Central is a freight railroad that also offers passenger service. Trains operate from Sugar Creek either south to Baltic or north to Dundee (6 miles for each) on former Wheeling & Lake Erie track, part of W&LE's route between Cleveland and Zanesville.

Round trip time is about an hour. Sugar Creek is on Ohio Route 39, 8 miles west of Exit 83 of I-77, about 25 south of Massillon. The station is at 111 Factory Street in Sugar Creek. There is a restaurant next to the station, and lodging is available in Sugar Creek.

Locomotives	2 diesel
Cars	Coaches, parlor car
Displays	2 steam switchers, Pullman, troop sleeper, freight cars
Schedule	Mid-May through October, weekends and holidays, leave Waterville 12:30 and 2:30 p.m., leave Grand Rapids 1:30 and 3:30; Memorial Day weekend-Labor Day, third departure from Waterville at 4:30, Grand Rapids at 5:30; July and August, Tuesday and Thursday, leave Waterville 10:30 and 1:30, leave Grand Rapids 11:30 and 2:30. Charter trips available.
Fares	Adults $4.50 one way, $6.50 round trip; children 3-15 $2.50 one way, $3.50 round trip (under 3 free); age 65 and over $4.05 one way, $5.85 round trip. Parlor car 50 cents extra each way. Checks accepted. Group discounts available.
Memberships	Write for information.
Special events	Mother's Day, Father's Day
Nearby attractions	Steamboat ride and Isaac Ludwig Mill in Providence Metropark in Grand Rapids, Wolcott Museum Complex in Maumee
Mailing address	P. O. Box 168, Waterville, OH 43566
Phone	Office/Waterville depot (419) 878-2177, Grand Rapids depot (419) 832-4671

P 木 🎁 $

TOLEDO, LAKE ERIE & WESTERN RAILWAY & MUSEUM

A few miles southwest of Toledo the Toledo, Lake Erie & Western runs excursion service over a 10-mile portion of the former Nickel Plate (before that, part of the Clover Leaf). Scenery along the way is primarily farmland. The route parallels the Maumee River and crosses it near Grand Rapids on a 900'-long bridge. The trip takes about 45 minues each way. Cars include coaches and an extra-fare parlor car with swiveling reclining seats.

To reach the depot at Waterville, take Exit 4 from the Ohio Turnpike; then U. S. 20 East (south by the compass) 2 miles to U. S. 24; then 24 southwest to Waterville. From I-475 simply take the U. S. 24 exit. In Waterville turn right on Ohio Route 64; follow it three blocks to Sixth Street and turn right again on Sixth to the station. The Grand Rapids station is at Third and Mill Streets.

Although the trains are not easily accessible to the handicapped, the staff will assist as needed. There are soda machines at the depot and restaurants in Waterville and Grand Rapids. Lodging can be found in Maumee and Toledo.

Cars	14 streetcars and interurbans
Displays	2 steam locomotives, gas-electric car, 5 passenger cars
Dates open	May 31-September 6, Sunday 1-5 p.m.
Admission	Adults $2.50, children 4-12 $1.50, age 60 and over $1.50. Checks accepted. Group discounts available.
Memberships	Write for information.
Special events	Members' Day (fall)
Nearby attractions	Ohio Historical Society, Center of Science and Industry, Columbus Zoo, Wyandot Lake Amusement Park, Park of Roses
Mailing address	Box 171, Worthington, OH 43085
Phone	(614) 885-7345

OHIO RAILWAY MUSEUM

The Ohio Railway Museum was established in 1948 with a single interurban car, Ohio Public Service No. 21. It now has more than 30 pieces of railroad equipment and operates electric cars on 1½ miles of track laid on a portion of the roadbed of the Columbus, Delaware & Marion interurban line. The ride takes about 12 minutes.

The museum is located at 990 Proprietors Road, just north of Ohio Route 161, in Worthington, a northern suburb of Columbus. From I-71, take the Worthington-New Albany exit, turn west, then north at the third traffic light. From U. S. 23 turn east on Route 161, then north at the second traffic light.

The museum has only a soda machine, but food and lodging can be found in Worthington.

Displays	Caboose, tank car, box car, small diesel locomotive, large collection of lanterns	Nearby attractions	Pawnee Bill Museum, Lincoln County Historical Museum, historic Victorian town of Guthrie
Dates open	By appointment	Mailing address	P. O. Box 844, Cushing, OK 74023
Admission	Free, donations welcome	Phone	(918) 225-1657

CIMARRON VALLEY RAILROAD MUSEUM

In 1969 the Santa Fe closed its station at Yale, Oklahoma. The Read family purchased the building and moved it to a new site in nearby Cushing. It now houses a large collection of railroad artifacts and an extensive library. In 1974 the Oklahoma Heritage Association gave the museum an award for its role in preserving Oklahoma's history. The museum is a family operation and is open only by appointment. It is located on South Kings Highway, 1½ miles south of State Soute 33 in Cushing, which is approximately equidistant from Tulsa and Oklahoma City. Food and lodging are available in Cushing.

Locomotives	AT&L diesels	Fares	Excursion train, adults $5; dinner train, adults $27.50. Reservations are necessary. Checks and credit cards accepted. Group discount available.
Cars	Rock Island, Burlington, and Great Northern cabooses; Union Pacific observation car; Santa Fe dining car; Great Northern coach		
Schedule	January-May and September-December, trains to the river operate Saturday at 10 and 11 a.m. and 1 and 2 p.m.; dinner trains depart Sunday at 1 p.m. No summer operations. Charter trips available.	Memberships	$15 per year
		Special events	Watonga Cheese Festival (first weekend in November)
		Nearby attractions	Roman Nose State Park
		Mailing address	2936 Bella Vista, Midwest City, OK 73110
		Phone	(405) 732-0566

WATONGA CHIEF

Central Oklahoma Chapter of the National Railway Historical Society operates Watonga Chief excursion and dinner trains on the AT&L Railroad (formerly a Rock Island branch line). Excursion trains make a 1-hour round trip to Greenfield, 8 miles south of Watonga; dinner trains take 2½ hours and go to the Canadian River, 8 miles farther.

The chapter's museum project is the Oklahoma Transportation Museum. Equipment is on display in Watonga.

Watonga is about 70 miles west-northwest of Oklahoma City on U. S. Routes 270 and 281 and State Highways 3, 8, and 33. The boarding location is at the intersection of Main Street and Nash Boulevard. Restaurants and motels can be found in Watonga.

Locomotives	Woodburning Heisler locomotive, Plymouth diesel
Cars	Open excursion cars, caboose
Displays	Two 2-8-2s undergoing restoration, freight cars
Schedule	Memorial Day weekend through September, weekends and holidays, 10 a.m., noon, 2 p.m., and 4 p.m.
Fares	$4 per person, children 6 and under free. Checks accepted. Group discounts available.
Memberships	Write for information.
Special events	Moonlight rides July 7 and September 2, 1990; Founder's Day (August 18, 1990)
Radio frequency	160.365
Nearby attractions	Oregon Trail Regional Museum, Union Creek Campground, Phillips Lake, historic town of Sumpter
Mailing address	Sumpter Valley Railroad Restoration, Inc., P. O. Box 389, Baker, OR 97814
Phone	(503) 894-2268

SUMPTER VALLEY RAILROAD

The Sumpter Valley Railway was a 3'-gauge lumber-carrying railroad that ran from Baker to Prairie City, Oregon — 80 miles through the Blue Mountains of eastern Oregon. The railroad was abandoned in 1948, except for a 2-mile portion at Baker that remained in operation until the end of 1961.

A group of local residents began a restoration effort in 1970. In 1971 they acquired a Heisler locomotive that had belonged to the W. H. Eccles Lumber Co. and had run years earlier on the Sumpter Valley. In 1977 the group got two 2-8-2s that had been built in 1920 as Sumpter Valley 101 and 102, renumbered 20 and 19, then sold to the White Pass & Yukon in 1940 to become Nos. 80 and 81. They are now being restored along with several freight cars.

Trains operate on more than 3 miles of track just off State Highway 7; the round trip takes about an hour.

The station is about 25 miles from Baker, west of Phillips Lake. The elevation is over 4,000 feet, and the weather can be cool during the early and late parts of the season. There are motels in Baker and restaurants in the historic mining town of Sumpter, about 5 miles from the station.

Displays	More than 20 streetcars and interurbans			
Dates open	May-October, weekends and holidays 11 a.m.-5 p.m. Charters are available.	**Memberships**	Write for information.	
Admission	Adults $3, children 5-17 $2, age 65 and over $2. Admission includes unlimited rides. Checks and credit cards accepted. Group discounts	**Nearby attractions**	Wineries	
		Mailing address	17744 S. W. Ivy Glenn Drive, Beaverton, OR 97007	
		Phone	(503) 642-5097 evenings only	

available; reservations required for groups.

TROLLEY PARK

The Oregon Electric Railway Historical Society operates a museum on roadbed that once served a logging railroad at Glenwood, Oregon, 38 miles west of Portland.

The museum includes a 1¾-mile track on which trolleys operate, a carbarn and shops, a gift shop and bookstore, and picnic, swimming, and overnight camping areas. To reach Trolley Park, follow U. S. 26, the Sunset Highway, west from Portland to the junction with Oregon Route 6, the Wilson River Highway. Follow Route 6 west 12 miles; the museum is near milepost 38.

There are restaurants in Glenwood and lodging in Hillsboro, about 20 miles back toward Portland. Children visiting the museum must be accompanied by adults.

Displays	Model locomotives, HO and O model railroads	**Nearby attractions**	Oregon Caves, Crater Lake, national forests
Dates open	Monday-Friday 10 a.m.-6 p.m, Saturdays 10-4	**Mailing address**	1951 Redwood Avenue, Grants Pass, OR 97527
Admission	Free	**Phone**	(503) 476-1951

THE TRAIN GALLERY

The Train Gallery has on display more than a thousand brass model locomotives and cars along with O and HO scale layouts that are still under construction. Grants Pass is on I-5 in southwest Oregon. Restaurants and motels can be found in Grants Pass about 4 miles from the Train Gallery.

Cars	Streamlined coaches, combine
Schedule	April 7-June 3 and September 5-30, 1990, leave Hood River 10 a.m. Wednesday-Sunday, 3 p.m. Saturdays and Sundays. June 5-September 2, leave Hood River 10 and 3 daily except Mondays. October 6-November 25, leave Hood River 10 and 3 Saturdays and Sundays only. December 1, 2, 8, and 9, leave Hood River 10 a.m. Train at 10 goes to Parkdale, returns to Hood River at 2:15 p.m. Train at 3 goes to Odell, returns at 5.
Fares	Odell: Adults $10, chldren 2-11 $6, age 60 and over $8; Parkdale: $17/$10/$15. Credit cards and checks accepted. Group discounts available.
Special events	Blossom Festival (April)
Nearby attractions	Columbia River Gorge, wind surfing, sternwheeler
Mailing address	110 Railroad Avenue, Hood River, OR 97031
Phone	(503) 386-3556

DIESEL LOCOMOTIVES

Number	Type	Former owner	Builder	Date
88	GP9	Southern Pacific	EMD	1959
89	GP9	Milwaukee Road	EMD	1959

MT. HOOD RAILROAD

The Mt. Hood Railroad is a freight railroad which also offers excursion service. The railroad was built by the Oregon Lumber Company in 1906. The Union Pacific, with which it connected at Hood River, bought the line in 1968, then sold it to local interests in 1987. Excursion trains run to either Odell, 8 miles, or Parkdale, 22 miles, and return. Total trip time is 2 hours or 4 hours. The route includes a stretch of 3 percent grade, a switchback, and views of Mt.

Hood and Mt. Adams. Hood River is on the Columbia River abou 60 miles east of Portland and 25 miles west of The Dalles. Use Ex 64 from I-84 to reach the Hood River station. Amtrak's *Pionee* stops in Hood River and the Portland section of the *Empire Builde* stops at Bingen-White Salmon, Washington, directly across th Columbia River (there is a bridge).

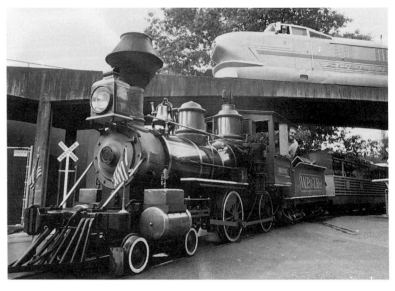

Cars	Semi-enclosed cars			
Dates open	Daily except Christmas, opens at 9:30 a.m. Closing time depends on the season.			
Schedule	Daily during spring and summer, weekends during the winter. Off-season operation subject to weather and demand. Charter trips available.			
Admission	Adults $3.50, children 5 and under $2, age 65 and over $1.50.			
Fares	Adults $2.50, children 3 and under $1.50, age 65 and over $1.50. Short trips, adults $1, children 50 cents. Group discounts available.			
Nearby attractions	Forestry Center, Rose Gardens, Japanese Garden, Oregon Museum of Science & Industry			
Mailing address	4001 S. W. Canyon Road, Portland, OR 97221			
Phone	(503) 226-1561 ext. 314			

LOCOMOTIVES

Number	Type	Former owner	Builder	Date
STEAM				
	4-4-0		Oregon Locomotive Works	1959
DIESEL AND GASOLINE				
	Aerotrain replica		Northwest Marine Iron Works	1958
	Industrial	Weyerhaueser	Baldwin	1935
	Switcher		Portland Zoo RR	1962
	Switcher	Weyerhaeuser	Whitcomb	1938

WASHINGTON PARK & ZOO RAILROAD

Portland's Metro Washington Park Zoo has a 30"-gauge railroad on which trains powered by steam, diesel, and gasoline locomotives operate. Most of the year trains run to a station overlooking the city. There passengers can walk through the International Rose Test Gardens and the Japanese Gardens. Total time for the 4-mile round trip is about 35 minutes. During winter trains make a shorter loop on the zoo grounds. The line includes a stretch of 6 percent grade, and the railroad has a railway post office. Restaurants and lodging can be found throughout the Portland metropolitan area.

Portland

Cars	Streamlined coaches
Schedule	Memorial Day weekend through September, Saturdays and Sundays, leave Prineville 11 a.m. and 2 p.m. Charter trips operated.
Fares	Adults $15, children 3-12 $7.50. Checks and credit cards accepted. Tickets are also available at Tour Time Travel in Bend, Redmond, and Prineville and at Norwester Tours in Portland. Group discounts available.
Nearby attractions	Bowman Museum, Smith Rock State Park, Prineville Reservoir
Mailing address	408 S. W. 2nd Avenue, Suite 230, Portland, OR 97204
Phone	(503) 223-9197; (503) 447-4838

DIESEL LOCOMOTIVES

Number	Type	Former owner	Builder	Date
985, 989	GP9	Milwaukee Road	EMD	1954

RIMROCK SCENIC RAIL TOURS

Rimrock Scenic Rail Tours operates an excursion train on the City of Prineville Railway, one of the few municipally owned railroads in the U. S. The train makes a round trip from Prineville west to Prineville Junction, 2 miles north of Redmond, where the railway connects with Burlington Northern's former Oregon Trunk route.

The round trip totals 32 miles and takes 2½ hours. Snacks and light meals are available on board. The station is in Ochoco Creek Park at the Juniper Street Crossing in Prineville. Prineville is in central Oregon on U. S. Route 26 and State Route 126. There are restaurants and motels in Prineville.

Cars	Rebuilt Southern Pacific gallery cars, ex-Burlington Northern cabooses
Schedule	Starting May 1, 1990, leave Tillamook for Wheeler Sunday-Friday at 8 a.m. and 1 p.m., Saturdays at 10 a.m. and 5:30 p.m. Round trip takes about 4 hours. Caboose train leaves Tillamook daily for the blimp hangar at 10:30 a.m. and 12:30 p.m.
Fares	Adults $15, children 3-12 $8, seniors $12. In-state checks accepted. Reservations are suggested.
Nearby attractions	Blimp hangar, wineries, Tillamook Creamery
Mailing address	4000 Hangar Road, Tillamook, OR 97141
Phone	(503) 842-9344, 842-2768

DIESEL LOCOMOTIVES

Number	Type	Former owner	Builder	Date
701	C-415	Columbia & Cowlitz	Alco	1968
702	C-415	Southern Pacific	Alco	1968
701B	Slug	Columbia & Cowlitz	MK	1973

OREGON COASTLINE EXPRESS

The Oregon Coastline Express runs on the rails of the Port of Tillamook Bay Railroad — the former Tillamook Branch of the Southern Pacific. Trains run from Tillamook north 22 miles along the coast to Wheeler, stopping in both directions at Garibaldi and Rockaway Beach. Passengers may ride round trip from any of the four stations. Passengers ride in extensively rebuilt bilevel commuter coaches or a caboose. Snacks, coffee, and soft drinks are available on board. A caboose train operates between Tillamook and the blimp hangar 4 miles south. The hangar is the largest wood building in the world. Plannning is in progress for a dinner train to operate between Tillamook and Hillsboro.

Tillamook is about 75 miles west of Portland on the Pacific coast. The Tillamook station is directly south of 3rd Street. Food and lodging can be found in the four towns where the train stops.

Locomotive Displays	K4s steam locomotive No.1361 Pennsylvania Railroad GG1 electric locomotive, passenger cars, caboose, HO scale model railroad
Dates open	Year-round Tuesday-Saturday 10 a.m.-5 p.m., Sunday 12:30-5; Memorial Day through September Monday 10-5
Admission	Adults $2.50, children under 12 $1.50, age 60 and over $2. Group discounts available.
Memberships	Write for information.
Nearby attractions	Horse Shoe Curve, Fort Roberdeau, Bedford Village, Baker Mansion, Glendale Lake
Mailing address Phone	1300 Ninth Avenue, Altoona, PA 16602 (814) 946-0834

RAILROADERS MEMORIAL MUSEUM

Altoona, Pennsylvania, was where the Pennsylvania Railroad began its climb over the Alleghenies — a few miles west of the city is Horse Shoe Curve, where the line doubled back on itself to gain altitude — and Altoona was the site of the Pennsy's principal shops. (Under Conrail's ownership the line is the busiest mountain railroad in the U. S. and the shops are still repairing diesels and freight cars.) The history of the Pennsylvania Railroad in Altoona is the central theme of the Railroaders Memorial Museum. Displays include numerous pieces of PRR rolling stock, artifacts, and memorabilia. The museum's K4s, No. 1361, has had its status changed from display to active and is the official steam locomotive of the commonwealth of Pennsylvania. The museum is located at the end of Station Mall, on Ninth Avenue three blocks northeast of 17th Street. To get to the museum, follow U. S. 220 into Altoona from the north or south, then turn northwest onto 17th Street. Follow 17th to Ninth Avenue, and turn right on Ninth. There are restaurants in the adjacent mall; lodging can be found in Altoona. To reach Horse Shoe Curve from the museum, follow 17th Street northwest to Broad Avenue, Broad southwest to 40th Street, then 40th west several miles.

Locomotives	2 steam
Cars	Rebuilt mine cars, caboose
Dates open	Memorial Day-Labor Day: daily 10 a.m.-6 p.m. May, September, and October: weekends 10-6; Monday-Friday, mine tour at 11 and 2
Admission	Mine: Adults $4, children $2
Fares	Train: adults $1.75, children under 12 $1. Group discounts available. Reservations required for groups.
Nearby attractions	Ashland Anthracite Museum, Knobles Grove
Mailing address	19th and Oak Street, Ashland, PA 17921
Phone	(717) 875-3850

ASHLAND COMMUNITY ENTERPRISES

The Pioneer Tunnel Coal Mine at Ashland is a museum of anthracite mining. Tours of the mine are conducted with battery locomotives and open mine cars, and a steam-powered 42"-gauge train takes visitors through a strip-mining area. The ¾-mile train ride takes about 30 minutes; the mine tour takes 35 minutes (jackets or sweaters are recommended). Ashland is about halfway between Harrisburg and Wilkes-Barre on Route 61 about 8 miles west of the Frackville exit of I-81. There are motels and restaurants in Ashland.

Car	RDC-1
Displays	Snowplow, 2 cabooses, N scale model railroad
Schedule	Memorial Day through October, weekends and holidays — write for details. Charter trips operated.
Fares	Adults $4, children under 13 $2. Checks accepted.
Memberships	Write for information.
Special events	Victorian Christmas Special (December), Pennsy Railfan Special (September)
Nearby attractions	Pennsylvania State University, Curtin Village Museum, Horseshoe Curve
Mailing address	The Train Station, Bellefonte, PA 16823
Phone	(815) 355-0311

BELLEFONTE HISTORICAL RAILROAD SOCIETY

The Bellefonte Railroad Historical Society was organized in 1984 to operate excursion trains over the Nittany & Bald Eagle Railroad, which had just taken over several former Pennsylvania Railroad branch lines from Conrail. The society borrowed a former New Haven RDC-1 (Rail Diesel Car, a self-propelled, air-conditioned coach) from the Pennsylvania Historical & Museum Commission. The train makes a 1-hour round trip from Bellefonte totaling about 30 miles to Curtin and Unionville or a shorter trip to Lemont. Bellefonte is about 40 miles northeast of Altoona and about the same distance southwest of Williamsport, near Exit 23 of I-80. Soft drinks are available on the train. Food and lodging are available in Bellefonte; advance motel reservations are advised on weekends of Penn State home football games.

Locomotives	2 steam, 2 diesel
Cars	Coaches, double-deck open car; plus food service car on the Mt. Holly Springs trains
Schedule	To Biglerville: June-October, weekends 1 and 3 p.m.; also May and June, Thursday and Friday at 11 a.m. and 1 p.m., and July and August, Monday-Friday at 11 and 1
	To Mt. Holly Springs: dinner trips May 5, 1990, 2 p.m.; June 23, 2 p.m.; and August 24, 2 p.m. Non-dinner trips July 14, September 8, October 6, 7, 13, 14, and 20, 10 a.m., return to Gettysburg at 3 p.m. Reservations required. Charter trips available.
Fares	Biglerville: Adults $5.50, children 3-12 $3.50 (under 3 free); Mt. Holly Springs: adults $14, children $8 (price does not include dinner). Credit cards accepted. Group discounts available.
Special events	Raid by Confederate soldiers July 4 and September 15, 1990
Nearby attractions	Gettysburg National Military Park
Mailing address	P. O. Box 3722, Gettysburg, PA 17325
Phone	(717) 334-6932

GETTYSBURG RAILROAD

The Gettysburg Railroad operates freight and excursion service on a former Reading branch line between Gettysburg and Mt. Holly Springs, Pennsylvania. Two excursions are offered: a 75-minute round trip from Gettysburg to Biglerville, 8 miles each way, and from Gettysburg to Mt. Holly Springs, 25 miles each way. Reservations are required for the Mt. Holly Springs trips; some of those trips include dinner at the destination. The Gettysburg depot is on Constitution Avenue just off North Washington Street, one block north and one block west of Lincoln Square at the center of Gettysburg. Food and lodging are available in Gettysburg.

Displays	Union Railroad 0-10-2, Bessemer & Lake Erie ore jenny and caboose
Dates open	May-Labor Day, noon-6 p.m.; September and October, noon-5
Admission	Free; donations welcome
Memberships	Write for information.
Nearby attractions	Lakeland Festival (third week of July) Pymatuning, Shenango, Conneaut, and Wilhelm Lakes
Mailing address	314 Main Street, Greenville, PA 16125
Phone	(412) 588-4917, 588-9479

GREENVILLE AREA RAILROAD MUSEUM

Greenville Area Railroad Museum is dedicated to local residents who worked on railroads in the area and at Greenville Steel Car Co. Centerpiece of the display is Union Railroad 304, later Duluth, Missabe & Iron Range 604, the only survivor of eight 0-10-2s built by Baldwin in 1936 — largest switchers in the world. The museum is located in a park on Main Street, State Route 358, across Conrail's ex-Erie line from the junction with State Routes 18 and 58. Restaurants can be found nearby. The museum and park are maintained by the Shenango-Pymatuning Railway Historical Society, a chapter of the National Railway Historical Society.

Cars	RDCs, ex-Lackawanna coaches
Displays	Reading GP30 5513 and C-630 5308 (owned by Reading Company Technical & Historical Society, which also has a display at Leesport); Canadian Pacific 4-6-4 2839
Schedule	May-October, Friday-Sunday; July and August, daily: leave South Hamburg at noon, 2, and 4 p.m.; leave Temple 1 and 3 p.m. Charter trips available.
Fares	Adults $6, children 3-12 $4 (under 3 free), senior citizens $4. Checks accepted; credit cards accepted in gift shop for purchases over $20. Group discounts available.
Radio frequency	161.310
Memberships	Annual passes are available; write for information.
Special events	Children's Clown Weekend, Hobo Weekend, Steam Weekend, Fall Foliage Weekends, Santa Claus Specials, Easter Bunny Express
Nearby attractions	Wanamaker, Kempton & Southern; Roadside America; Crystal Cave; outlet shopping malls; Hawk Mountain Sanctuary
Mailing address	P. O. Box 425, Hamburg, PA 19526
Phone	(215) 562-4083

LOCOMOTIVES

Number	Type	Former owner	Builder	Date
STEAM				
425	4-6-2	Gulf, Mobile & Northern	Baldwin	1928
2102	4-8-4	Reading	Reading	1945
DIESEL				
5308	C-630	Reading	Alco	1967
5513	GP30	Reading	EMD	1962
5706, 5859	E8A	Pennsylvania Railroad	EMD	1952
9166	RDC-3	Boston & Maine	Budd	1958
9168	RDC-3	New York Central	Budd	1950
9169	RDC-1	Chicago & North Western	Budd	1951

BLUE MOUNTAIN & READING RAILROAD

The Blue Mountain & Reading began operating freight service over a former Pennsylvania Railroad line between Temple and South Hamburg, Pa., 13 miles, in September 1983. On July 13, 1985, steam-powered passenger trains returned to the line. Trains make the 26-mile round trip in 1½ hours. The station in Temple, just north of Reading, is on Tuckerton Road between Routes 61 and U. S. 222. The Hamburg station is on Route 61 at Station Road, 1 mile south of exit 9A of I-78. Refreshments are available on the train. Food and lodging can be found in Temple, Reading, and Hamburg.

Locomotive	1 diesel (ex-Bangor & Aroostook BL2)
Cars	Coaches
Displays	Replicas of Stourbridge Lion and gravity coach
Schedule	Trains operate in May, July through October, and December. Write for specific dates and times. Reservations are required. Charter trips available.
Fares	Adults $15, children under 12 $6.50, age 60 and over $14. Group discounts available. Checks and credit cards accepted.
Special events	Dinner-Theater trains, Bavarian Festival (August), Rail & Sail
Nearby attractions	Pocono Mountains, Delaware State Forest
Mailing address	742 Main Street, Honesdale, PA 18431
Phone	(717) 253-1960

STOURBRIDGE LINE RAIL EXCURSIONS

The Wayne County Chamber of Commerce operates excursions between Honesdale and Lackawaxen, Pennsylvania, 25 miles, over the rails of the Lackawaxen & Stourbridge, a former Erie Railroad branch that is now part of the Delaware Otsego System.

The usual power for the train is a rare and unusual diesel, a BL2, designed for branchline service by Electro-Motive. The route follows the Lackawaxen River, and the round trip takes 4½ hours. Sightseeing and food are available during the layover at Lackawaxen, and refreshments are available on board the train. Children under 12 must be accompanied by adults. Restaurants and lodging can be found in Honesdale, about 30 miles northeast of Scranton on U. S. Route 6.

Cars	10 steel coaches
Displays	Several restored cabooses
Schedule	Memorial Day weekend-Labor Day, weekends and holidays, also weekends in September, leave Jim Thorpe at noon, 1, 2, and 3 p.m. October Saturdays, leave 1:30; October Sundays, leave 10 a.m. and 1:30 p.m. Reservations are required for trips in October. Charter trips available.
Fares	May-September (8-mile round trips): adults $3.75, children 3-11 $3 (under 3 free). October (foliage specials): adults $11, children $6. Checks accepted for mail orders. Group discounts available.
Special events	Autumn Leaf Specials, Santa Claus Specials
Nearby attractions	Asa Packer Mansion, Flagstaff Park
Mailing address	P. O. Box 285, Jim Thorpe, PA 18229
Phone	(717) 325-4606

LOCOMOTIVES

Number	Type	Former owner	Builder	Date
STEAM				
2	4-6-0	Canadian Pacific	Montreal	1912
98	4-6-0	Canadian Pacific	Canadian Loco. Co.	1913
DIESEL				
	F3A	Bangor & Aroostook	EMD	1948

RAIL TOURS, INC.

Rail Tours, Inc., operates excursions out of Jim Thorpe (formerly Mauch Chunk), Pennsylvania, on a former Central Railroad of New Jersey branch. From the end of May through September trains operate to Nesquehoning, 4 miles; the round trip takes 40 minutes. Foliage specials in October run to Haucks, 17 miles, and return; trips take 2½ hours. The trains are usually pulled by a former Canadian Pacific D10-class 4-6-0 or by a restored Bangor & Aroostook F3 now painted and lettered for the Central Railroad of New Jersey. Trains leave from the former Jersey Central station on U. S. 209 opposite the Carbon County courthouse. Food and lodging are available in Jim Thorpe, which is about halfway between Allentown and Wilkes-Barre.

Jim Thorpe

Cars	Coaches, gondola
Displays	Cabooses, business car, HO scale model railroad
Schedule	April: Sundays except Easter, 1, 2, 3, and 4 p.m. (motor car). May-October: Saturdays, 1, 2, 3, and 4 (motor car in May, September, and October); Sundays, 1, 2, 3, 4, and 5. Memorial Day and Labor Day (but not July 4), steam train at 1, 2, 3, and 4. November, first two Sundays, 1, 2, and 3 (motor car). Charter trips operated; individual cars can be chartered also.
Fares	Adults $3, children 2-12 $1.50. Group discounts available.
Special events	Antique Car Show, Harvest Moon, Christmas Specials
Nearby attractions	Blue Mountain & Reading Railroad, Crystal Cave, Hawk Mountain Bird Sanctuary, Roadside America, Kempton Farm Museum
Mailing address	P. O. Box 24, Kempton, PA 19529
Phone	(215) 756-6469

LOCOMOTIVES

Number	Type	Former owner	Builder	Date
STEAM				
2	0-4-0T	Colorado Fuel & Iron	Porter	1920
65	0-6-0T	Safe Harbor Power & Light	Porter	1930
DIESEL AND GASOLINE				
35	Gas-electric	Mack Trucks	Mack	1929
602		Gulf Oil	Whitcomb	1944

WANAMAKER, KEMPTON & SOUTHERN RAILROAD

The Wanamaker, Kempton & Southern operates excursion trains over a portion of a former Reading Company branch from Kempton to Wanamaker. Steam-powered trips take about 40 minutes and cover 6 miles in all, 3 each way; on Saturdays except during June, July, and August a self-propelled car named "Berksy Trolley" makes a 35-minute round trip covering 9 miles of track. Passengers have the option of detraining at Furhrman's Grove for a picnic an boarding a later train. Trains leave from the Kempton station Kempton is about 5 miles north of Krumsville and Lenhartsvill exits from U. S. 22 and I-78; it's about 30 miles north of Readin Food and lodging can be found in Reading and in the towns locate along I-78.

Cars	Ex-Lackawanna coaches; dining and lounge cars
Schedule	Saturdays and Sundays in April, 2 p.m.; Saturdays May-October, 1 and 3 p.m.; Sundays May-October, 1* and 4 p.m.; Monday-Friday June 11, 1990-Labor Day, 11:30 a.m. and 2* p.m.; Wednesday evenings June-October, dinner train at 6:30 p.m. (* indicates train to Mifflinburg; other trains go to Winfield). Charter trips available.
Fares	To Winfield: Adults $5, children 3-12 $3, seniors $4. To Mifflinburg: $6.50/$4/$5.50. Dinner train, $20. Checks and credit cards accepted.
Special events	Easter Bunny Express, Mother's Day and Father's Day Expresses, Fall Foliage Tours, Santa Claus Express
Nearby attractions	Little League Baseball Museum, Lycoming County Historical Museum, Mifflinburg Buggy Museum, Packwood House Museum, Slifer House Museum
Mailing address	196 North 3rd Street, Mifflinburg, PA 17844
Phone	(717) 966-9390

DIESEL LOCOMOTIVES

Number	Type	Former owner	Builder	Date
2233	GP30	Pennsylvania Railroad	EMD	1963
425	SW1	Pennsylvania Railroad	EMD	1950

WEST SHORE RAIL EXCURSIONS

The West Shore Railroad operates freight service over a former Pennsylvania branch from Montandon, Pa., through Lewisburg and Vicksburg to Mifflinburg, almost 12 miles, and south from Lewisburg to Winfield, about 7 miles, on a former Reading line. West Shore Rail Excursions operates passenger service on the same routes: Susquehanna Special trains to Winfield (1½ hours for the round trip) and Buffalo Valley Limited trains to Mifflinburg (3 hours). Trains load at the Delta Place station on Route 15, 2 miles north of Lewisburg. Passengers should be there at least 20 minutes before train time. Lewisburg is on the Susquehanna River about 55 miles north of Harrisburg and 7 miles south of I-80. Restaurants and lodging are available in Lewisburg.

Cars	Ex-Lackawanna coaches
Schedule	June and September, Friday-Sunday; July and August, Tuesday-Sunday; October, first two weeks, Wednesday-Sunday; second two weeks, Saturdays and Sundays: leave Marienville 8:30 a.m., leave Kane 10:45; return to Kane 2:15 p.m., to Marienville, 4:30
Fares	From Marienville: adults $20, children 3-12 $13. From Kane: $12.50/$8. Reservations are required. Checks accepted. Group discounts available.
Nearby attractions	Allegheny National Forest
Mailing address	P. O. Box 422, Marienville, PA 16239
Phone	(814) 927-6621, (717) 334-2411

LOCOMOTIVES

Number	Type	Former owner	Builder	Date
STEAM				
38	2-8-0	Huntingdon & Broad Top Mountain	Baldwin	1927
1658M	2-8-2	New	Tang-Shan	1989
DIESEL				
1	Switcher	Union Switch & Signal	Porter	1945
14	GP9	Western Maryland	EMD	1957
44	S-6	South Buffalo	Alco	1957

KNOX, KANE & KINZUA RAILROAD

In 1982 the Knox & Kane Railroad purchased a line between Knox and Mt. Jewett from the Baltimore & Ohio Railroad; it was built as a narrow-gauge line in the early 1880s and became part of the Pittsburgh & Western Railroad. In 1986 the company purchased the right of way of an abandoned Erie branch between Mt. Jewett and the Kinzua Bridge and relaid track on it. The Kinzua Bridge was built in 1882 to span the valley of Kinzua Creek. It is 2053 feet long and 301 feet high, fourth highest in the U. S. It has been placed on the National Register of Historic Places and is a national Historic Civil Engineering Landmark.

Trains operate from Marienville through Kane to the bridge an return. From Marienville it's a 96-mile, 8-hour round trip, largel through the Allegheny National Forest. The round trip from Kan totals 32 miles and takes 3½ hours. Snacks are available on boar and box lunches can be ordered when you make your reservations.

Kane is on U. S. Route 6 and State Route 66 in northwester Pennsylvania, about halfway between Pittsburgh, Pa., an Rochester, New York. Marienville is about 25 miles southwest o Kane on State Route 66. There are restaurants and motels i Marienville and Kane.

Cars	Ex-Lackawanna coaches
Schedule	Saturdays, June-August and October,
Admission	Sundays June-October, 1, 2:30, and
	4 p.m.
Fares	Adults $4.75, children 4-11 $2.50.
	Checks accepted. Group discounts avail-
	able. Reservations required for Santa
	trains; fares slightly higher.
Special events	Craft Fair (June 9-10, 1990), Ride With
	Uncle Sam, Halloween Special (October
	27, 1990), Ride With Santa (December 8,
	9, 15, 16, 22, 23, 1990)
Nearby attractions	Three Mile Island, Indian Echo Caverns,
	Hershey Park, Chocolate World
Mailing address	P. O. Box 242, Hummelstown, PA 17036
Phone	(717) 944-4435

LOCOMOTIVES

Number	Type	Former owner	Builder	Date
STEAM				
1	2-6-0	Grand Trunk	Canadian Locomotive Co.	1910
DIESEL				
	65 ton	U. S. Army	General Electric	1941
	65 ton	Standard Slag	General Electric	1955

MIDDLETOWN & HUMMELSTOWN RAILROAD

The Middletown & Hummelstown operates a former Reading Company route between the towns of its name. The railroad follows the banks of Swatara Creek and the towpath of the old Union Canal. Caves, lime kilns, and canal locks are visible from the train. The 11-mile round trip takes about 75 minutes. The steam locomotive is usually used on Sunday trains, except during very hot weather; Saturday trains are diesel-powered. Middletown is 10 miles southeast of Harrisburg on the Susquehanna River. The station is on Brown Street at Race, east of State Route 441. It is 3 blocks from Amtrak's Middletown station and 2 miles from Harrisburg International Airport. There are restaurants in Middletown; motels can be found in Harrisburg and Hershey.

Displays	[1988 information] Heisler fireless steam locomotive, passenger and freight cars, railroadiana
Dates open	Memorial Day weekend, 1-5 p.m.; June-August, Wednesday-Sunday 1-5; September, weekends and Labor Day, 1-5. Other times by appointment.
Admission	Free, donation appreciated
Memberships	Write for information.
Special events	Wine Country Harvest Festival (last weekend of September), Christmas at the Station (first weekend of December)
Nearby attractions	Lake Erie beaches, Fort LeBoeuf Museum, Firefighters Museum, wineries
Mailing address	P. O. Box 571, North East, PA 16428-0571
Phone	(814) 725-1911 when museum is open; (814) 825-2724 for recorded information and to leave messages

P ♿ 🎋 🎁

LAKE SHORE RAILWAY MUSEUM

The Lake Shore Railway Historical Society, a chapter of the National Railway Historical Society, operates a museum at the former New York Central passenger and freight stations in North East, Pennsylvania. The museum is at Robinson and Wall Streets on the north side of Conrail's main line three blocks south of U. S. 20 and two blocks west of Pennsylvania Route 89. Food and lodging are available in North East, which is on Lake Erie just west of the New York border. The society also maintains a small fleet of passenger cars used for mainline excursion service; write for information on those trips.

Locomotive	1 diesel
Cars	Coaches, Pullman, concession car
Schedule	Friday, Saturday, and Sunday: leave Perry Street Station 11:40 a.m. and 3:10 p.m.; leave Drake Well Park noon and 3:30; leave Rynd Farm 1:30. Charter trips available.
Fares	Adults $7, children 3-12 $4, age 60 and over $6. Checks accepted. Discounts available for groups of more than 20.
Memberships	Write for information.
Nearby attractions	Drake Well, Music Museum
Mailing address	P. O. Box 68, Oil City, PA 16301
Phone	(814) 676-1733

OIL CREEK & TITUSVILLE RAILROAD

The Oil Creek & Titusville operates excursion trains through northwestern Pennsylvania's oil country — where in 1859 oil was first extracted from the ground by drilling — over a former Pennsylvania Railroad line. Passengers may board at any of three points: Rynd Farm on Route 8 about 3 miles north of Oil City, Drake Well Park on the south side of Titusville east of Route 8, and a station at 409 South Perry Street — Truck Route 8 — in Titusville.

The train ride is 13½ miles each way, and the round trip takes 2½ to 3 hours. Snacks are available on board the train. Reservations may be made and tickets may be purchased 10 days before your trip (enclose a stamped, self-addressed envelope with your ticket request). Be at the boarding area 30 minutes before departure. Tickets are available at the stations before departure.

Food and lodging can be found in Titusville and Oil City.

	[1988 information]
Cars	Wooden coaches, caboose
Displays	Roundhouse and shop
Schedule	June-October, weekends, on the hour, 11 a.m.-4 p.m. Charter trips available.
Fares	Adults $5, children 5-12 $2.50. Checks accepted. Group discounts available (reservations required).
Special events	Fall Spectacular (call for information)
Nearby attractions	Rockhill Trolley Museum (see next entry), Raystown Lake, Lincoln Caverns
Mailing address	Rockhill Furnace, PA 17249
Phone	(814) 447-3011

LOCOMOTIVES

Number	Type	Former owner	Builder	Date
STEAM				
12	2-8-2	EBT	Baldwin	1911
15	2-8-2	EBT	Baldwin	1914
17	2-8-2	EBT	Baldwin	1918
GAS AND DIESEL				
M-1	Baggage-coach	EBT	Westinghouse-Brill-EBT	1927
M-3	Dinky	EBT	Nash-EBT	1928
M-4	14 ton	Warner Corp.	Plymouth	1948

EAST BROAD TOP RAILROAD

The East Broad Top Railroad was the last 3'-gauge common carrier in the U. S. east of the Mississippi River. Its principal business was carrying coal. It ceased operation in April 1956, and the locomotives and cars were stored on the property.

In 1960 the railroad's owner, a scrap dealer, was asked if the line could be reactivated to help celebrate the bicentennial of the town of Orbisonia. The East Broad Top reopened in August 1960 as a tourist railroad — doing business in its original location with the same locomotives, cars, and shop and roundhouse facilities. Staff are on the premises year-round. The EBT offers a 50-minute round trip ride over 5 miles of track north from Orbisonia.

Food is available within 2 blocks of the station in Orbisonia; lodging can be found 15 miles north in Mt. Union. Orbisonia is on U. S. 522 about 15 miles north of Exit 13 of the Pennsylvania Turnpike (from the east use Exit 14) and about 50 miles southeast of Altoona.

Schedule	Memorial Day weekend through October, weekends and holidays, every half hour from 11:30 a.m. to 4 p.m. Charter trips available.
Fares	$2 per person; family rate $7. Group discounts available.
Memberships	Sustaining $25, associate $15
Radio frequency	151.625
Special events	Fall Spectacular, Santa's Trolley
Nearby attractions	East Broad Top Railroad, Raystown Lake, Lincoln Caverns
Mailing address	Railways to Yesterday, Inc., P. O. Box 1601, Allentown, PA 18105
Phone	(814) 447-9576; (215) 965-9028 and (717) 367-6754 year-round

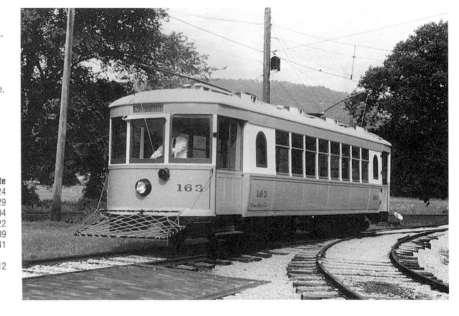

ELECTRIC CARS

Number	Type	Original city or railroad	Builder	Date
163	City car	York, Pa.	Brill	1924
72	Single-truck	Oporto, Portugal		1929
249	Double-truck	Oporto, Portugal	Brill	1904
311	City car	Johnstown, Pa.	Wason	1922
315	Interurban	Chicago Aurora & Elgin	Kuhlman	1909
803-804	Electroliner	Chicago North Shore & Milwaukee	St. Louis	1941
1875	Open car	Rio de Janeiro	St. Louis	1912

 $

ROCKHILL TROLLEY MUSEUM

In 1963 a mile of standard gauge track was laid on the roadbed of the East Broad Top's Shade Gap Branch (see previous entry) by Railways to Yesterday. Trolleys run every half hour from a station across the tracks from the East Broad Top Railroad's Orbisonia station; the ride takes about 20 minutes.

The museum has an exhibit of photographs depicting the history of Pennsylvania's electric railways. The trolley ride is not readily accessible to the handicapped, but the staff will assist as necessary. Children must be accompanied by adults. For notes on food and lodging, see the previous entry (East Broad Top Railroad).

Displays	Baldwin 4-10-2 No. 60,000
Dates open	Monday-Friday, 9:30 a.m.-4:30 p.m.; Saturdays and Sundays, 10-5
Admission	Adults $6, children 4-11 $5 (under 4 free), age 65 and over $5. Group discounts available (reservations required).
Memberships	Write for information.
Nearby attractions	Independence Hall, Philadelphia Museum of Art
Mailing address	20th Street and The Parkway, Philadelphia, PA 19103
Phone	(215) 448-1200

FRANKLIN INSTITUTE SCIENCE MUSEUM AND PLANETARIUM

On October 6, 1989, the Franklin Institute, with the financial assistance of Conrail, opened its new Railroad Hall. The centerpiece of the exhibit is Baldwin Locomotive Works No. 60,000, a 3-cylinder 4-10-2 built in 1926 and moved to the Franklin Institute in 1933. Two other locomotives share the room: Reading's *Rocket* of 1838 and a Reading 4-4-0 built in 1842. New to the exhibit is a G gauge model railroad which viewers can operate; it includes full-size sig-nals actuated by the trains and a video hookup between the locomotive and a monitor in a half-size cab.

The remainder of the museum collection covers the larger subject of U. S. industrial technology and science. There are models, film and quizzes on videodiscs, and a giant walk-through heart. The Franklin Institute is at 20th Street and The Parkway in downtown Philadelphia, within walking distance of Suburban Station.

Cars	4 streetcars (1 from Philadelphia Rapid Transit, 3 from Red Arrow Lines)
Schedule	April through November 25, 1990, weekends 11 a.m. till dusk; July-Labor Day, Thursday-Sunday, 11-dusk; Santa Claus Special December 8, 9, 15, and 16, 1990. Charter trips available.
Fares	Adults $1.50; children under 12, 75 cents. Checks accepted. Group discounts available.
Memberships	Buckingham Valley Trolley Association; write for information.
Nearby attractions	Independence Hall, U. S. S. *Olympia*
Mailing address	P. O. Box 7285, Philadelphia, PA 19101
Phone	(215) 627-0807

PENN'S LANDING TROLLEY

The Buckingham Valley Trolley Association, the Fidelity Bank, and the city of Philadelphia have teamed up to operate historic streetcars on a mile of track along the city's Delaware River waterfront. The 20-minute round trip passes historic neighborhoods such as Society Hill and Queen Village and offers views of a number of historic ships. The cars run on Delaware Avenue, five blocks east of Independence Hall. The north end of the run is at Race Street near the Ben Franklin Bridge; the south end is at Catherine Street. To reach the area from I-95, take the Tasker Street exit northbound or the Center City exit southbound. The 2nd Street station of the Market Street Subway is two blocks west of Delaware Avenue.

Philadelphia

PENNSYLVANIA-229

Cars	Ex-Lackawanna and Central of New Jersey coaches
Displays	8 steam locomotives, maintenance of way equipment
Dates open	May 25-October 28, 1990, 9 a.m.-6 p.m.
Schedule	May 25-October 28, 1990, Friday-Sunday, 1 p.m.
Admission	Free
Fares	Adults $7.50, children 12 and under $5. Group discounts available.
Nearby attractions	Anthracite Museum, Everhart Museum, Marine Corps Museum, Pocono Mountains, Lackawanna coal mine tour
Mailing address	150 South Washington Avenue, Scranton, PA 185013
Phone	(717) 961-2033

STEAM LOCOMOTIVES

Number	Type	Former owner	Builder	Date
3	0-6-0	Baldwin Locomotive Works	Baldwin	1925
2317	4-6-2	Canadian Pacific	Montreal	1926

STEAMTOWN NATIONAL HISTORIC SITE

Steamtown was established in 1963 by F. Nelson Blount, who had been acquiring steam locomotives for nearly a decade. By 1966 his collection was consolidated in Bellows Falls, Vermont, and excursion trains were operating over a portion of the defunct Rutland Railway. Blount was killed in a plane crash in 1967 but Steamtown continued to operate.

In 1984 the collection was moved from Vermont to the former Lackawanna freight yards in downtown Scranton, Pennsylvania. In October 1986 Congress approved legislation adding Steamtown to the National Park System. Excursion trains run over a 29-mile portion of the ex-Lackawanna main line from Scranton north to Kingsley, Pa. The train crosses the Nicholson Viaduct, largest reinforced concrete structure of its time. Steamtown is at 150 South Washington Avenue in Scranton. Use Exit 52 of I-81. Restaurants and lodging can be found in Scranton.

230-PENNSYLVANIA   Scranton

Dates open	Daily except Christmas, weekends 10-6; weekdays 10-5
Admission	Adults $3.25, children 6-11 $1 (under 6 free). Group discount available.
Nearby attractions	Blue Mountain & Reading; Wanamaker, Kempton & Southern; Crystal Cave; Christmas Village
Mailing address	Box 2, Shartlesville, PA 19554
Phone	(215) 488-6241

ROADSIDE AMERICA

Roadside America is one of the largest miniature villages in the U. S. Six O gauge trains and four trolleys run on 2,250 feet of track through the village.

Shartlesville is at Exit 8 of I-78 about halfway between Allentown and Harrisburg. Food and lodging are available within 1,500 feet of Roadside America.

Shartlesville

PENNSYLVANIA-231

Locomotives	2 diesel, 1 gasoline
Cars	Ex-Reading coaches
Schedule	Memorial Day weekend through November 4, 1990, Sundays and holidays, leave Stewartstown 1 and 3 p.m. Charter trips available.
Fares	Adults $5, children 4-11 $3 (under 4 free). Checks and credit cards accepted. Discount of 10 percent for groups of 20 or more.
Special events	Easter Bunny Hop (April 13-14, 1990), Photo Special (August 11, 1990), Santa Claus Specials, dinner and breakfast excursions to various restaurants
Mailing address	P. O. Box 155, Stewartstown, PA 17363
Phone	(717) 993-2936

STEWARTSTOWN RAILROAD

The Stewartstown Railroad was opened in 1885 from Stewartstown, Pennsylvania, west 7½ miles to a connection at New Freedom with the Northern Central (later Pennsylvania, then Penn Central) line between Baltimore and Harrisburg. In 1972 floods damaged the PC line, and the Stewartstown ceased operations because its connection with the world was cut off. Eventually the commonwealth of Pennsylvania acquired the PC line and repaired it, and in January 1985 the Stewartstown resumed freight operations not only to New Freedom but all the way into York.

Excursion trains began operating in July of that year. Trains operate from Stewartstown to New Freedom; Santa Claus Specials go only as far as Shrewsbury, 4 miles; the Photo Special and the dinner excursions go to Hyde, just south of York. There are restaurants in Stewartstown and Shrewsbury. Stewartstown is on Pennsylvania Route 851 4 miles east of Exit 1 of I-83, just north of the Maryland border. York is less than 20 miles away, and Harrisburg and Baltimore are each about 45 miles.

Strasburg, Pennsylvania, has more railroad museums and tourist railroads per square mile than any other place in North America. Within a mile or two of the intersection of Routes 741 and 896 are the Strasburg Rail Road, the Railroad Museum of Pennsylvania (across the road from each other), the Choo-Choo Barn (a large operating Lionel layout), the Strasburg Train Shop (both just west of the Railroad Museum), the Toy Train Museum, and the Red Caboose Motel (sleep in cabooses, eat in dining cars). Strasburg is about 8 miles southeast of Lancaster in the heart of the Amish country. There are restaurants and motels throughout the area, some within a mile of the Strasburg Railroad station. Advance reservations for lodging are advised during the tourist season.

Displays	65 cars and locomotives, interpretive exhibits
Dates open	Monday-Saturday 9 a.m.-5 p.m., Sunday 12-5. Closed Mondays November-April and some holidays.
Admission	Adults $3, children 6-17 $1.50; age 65 and over $2. Checks accepted. Group discounts available.
Memberships	Friends of the Railroad Museum, P. O. Box 125, Strasburg, PA 17579
Mailing address	P. O. Box 15, Strasburg, PA 17579
Phone	(717) 687-8628

RAILROAD MUSEUM OF PENNSYLVANIA

The Railroad Museum of Pennsylvania, operated by the Pennsylvania Historical and Museum Commission, is directly across the road from the Strasburg station. It has one of the largest collections of locomotives and cars in North America, with emphasis on rolling stock of the Pennsylvania Railroad. Many cars and locomotives are inside the building, and many more are stored outside (the outdoor exhibit is open on weekends May through November). The museum houses an entire train of Pennsylvania Railroad wood passenger cars of a century ago, and an observation pit allows inspection of the running gear of an 1888 2-8-0. Two of the museum's Pennsylvania Railroad steam locomotives, 4-4-0 No. 1223 and 4-4-2 No. 7002, make occasional mainline appearances. A third steam locomotive, a replica of Camden & Amboy's *John Bull*, operates at the museum on special occasions.

Cars	Wood and steel coaches and open cars	
Schedule	Third Saturday in March through April, weekends plus Good Friday and Easter Monday; May-November, daily (Closed Thanksgiving Day); first two weekends in December: noon, 1, 2, and 3 p.m. As spring and summer advance, trains are added at 11 a.m. and 10 a.m. except Sundays and at 4, 5, and 7 p.m., with extra trains on the half hour as needed; fall brings a tapering back to the noon, 1, 2, and 3 p.m. departures.	
Fares	Adults $5, children 3-11 $3. Group discounts available.	
Mailing address	P. O. Box 96, Strasburg, PA 17579-0096	
Phone	(717) 687-7522	

LOCOMOTIVES

Number	Type	Former owner	Builder	Date
STEAM				
4	0-4-0	Reading	Burnham-Williams	1903
31	0-6-0	Canadian National	Baldwin	1913
89	2-6-0	Canadian National	Canadian Locomotive Co.	1910
90	2-10-0	Great Western	Baldwin	1924
DIESEL, GASOLINE, AND PROPANE				
1	29 ton	Strasburg	Plymouth	1926
	10 ton		Plymouth	1910
21	Railbus	Buffalo Creek & Gauley	Mack-Brill	1920
33	44 ton	Pennsylvania Railroad	GE	1948
	Railcar	Lancaster, Oxford & Southern	Sanders	1915

STRASBURG RAIL ROAD

The Strasburg Rail Road is the oldest railroad in the U. S. operating under its original charter, and it was one of the first railroads to go after the tourist business in modern times. It was chartered in 1832 and operated until 1957, when storm damage caused a suspension of service.

The line was purchased by a group of railroad enthusiasts who restored freight service and began running excursion trains in 1959. Trains make a 45-minute round trip from the station at Strasburg 4½ miles through lush farmland and woods to a junction with Amtrak's Philadelphia-Harrisburg line (formerly Pennsylvania Railroad's main line) at Paradise (the railroads call it Leaman Place).

Displays	Toy trains, both static and operating
Dates open	April and November, weekends; also Good Friday, Easter Monday, Thanksgiving Friday, first two weekends of December, and Christmas week; May-October, daily, 10 a.m.-5 p.m.
Admission	Adults $2.50, children 7-12 $1, age 65 and over $2.25. Credit cards accepted. Group discounts available.
Memberships	Train Collectors Association; write for information.
Mailing address	P. O. Box 248, Strasburg, PA 17579
Phone	(717) 687-8976

TOY TRAIN MUSEUM

The Train Collectors Association opened its national headquarters and museum building at Strasburg in 1977. The building contains displays of old toy trains bearing such famous brand names as Lionel and Ives and three large operating layouts. The museum is on Paradise Lane — from the Strasburg station drive east on Route 741 a short way, then turn left (north) onto Paradise Lane and go past the Red Caboose Motel.

Cars	More than 30 streetcars
Dates open	May-September, weekends and holidays, noon-5 p.m.; July 4-Labor Day, daily, noon-5; October, Sundays, noon-5. Charters available.
Fares	Adults $3, children under 12 $1.50, family $7. Checks accepted; credit cards accepted in bookstore. Group discounts available.
Memberships	Write for information.
Special events	Trolley Fair (last weekend of June), County Fair (grounds adjacent to museum — second week of August), Santa Trolley (first and second weekends of December)
Nearby attractions	Meadowcroft Village, covered bridges, harness racing
Mailing address	Pennsylvania Railway Museum Association, P. O. Box 832, Pittsburgh, PA 15230
Phone	(412) 734-5780

ARDEN TROLLEY MUSEUM

The Arden Trolley Museum, established in 1954, operates streetcars on 1½ miles of the former Pittsburgh Railways right of way between Pittsburgh and Washington, Pennsylvania (the line still has regular trolley service from downtown Pittsburgh to Drake). The cars operated and displayed at the museum are primarily from streetcar and interurban lines of Pennsylvania, and the museum's unusual track gauge, 5'2½", was used extensively in Pennsylvania.

The streetcar ride takes about 20 minutes. The museum is on the northern outskirts of Washington, about 25 miles southwest of Pittsburgh. Take Exit 8 (Meadowlands) from I-79 and follow the blue signs to the Arden Trolley Museum. Food and lodging are available in Washington and Meadowlands, each about 2 miles from the museum.

Mailing address	33 Wilkes-Barre Boulevard, Wilkes-Barre, PA 18702
Phone	(717) 829-0000; in Pennsyvlania (800) 242-1077; rest of U. S. (800) 441-1354

℗ ⑪ ♿

MARKET STREET SQUARE

The long-abandoned Central Railroad of New Jersey station in Wilkes-Barre has been restored as a restaurant, nightclub, and hotel complex. A number of freight and passenger cars were included in the project, and it is possible to spend the night or have a drink in a railroad car. Guided tours are available, and there are plans to include an operating train in the complex. Market Street Square is right in downtown Wilkes-Barre, about a block southeast of Public Square

Displays	O and standard gauge trains, operating O and HO model railroads	Nearby attractions	Little League Birthplace, World Series Stadium and Museum; Paddle-wheel Scenic Riverboat Ride, Bald Eagle Mountain
Dates open	Tuesday-Saturday 9:30 a.m.-4 p.m., Sunday 1:30-4, closed Mondays and holidays		
Admission	Adults $3, children under 12 $1, age 65 and over $2.50. Checks and credit cards accepted.	Mailing address	858 West Fourth Street, Williamsport, PA 17701
Memberships	Write for information.	Phone	(717) 326-3326, 326-3673

℗ ♿ 🎁

LYCOMING COUNTY HISTORICAL MUSEUM

In 1983 the Lycoming County Historical Museum acquired the LaRue Shempp toy train collection. It includes many standard gauge and O gauge trains. In addition the museum has operating O and HO scale model railroads. Another exhibit of possible interest to railroad enthusiasts is the museum's lumbering gallery. The museum is at the corner of Fourth and Maynard Streets, 3 blocks south of the Maynard Street exit of I-80. There are restaurants and motels within a few blocks of the museum.

Cars	Coach, parlor car, caboose
Schedule	May and June, Sundays; July 1-Labor Day, Wednesdays, Thursdays, Saturdays, and Sundays, leave Newport daily 12:30 p.m. Charter trips available.
Fares	Adults $6, children under 14 $3, age 60 and over $5, family $15. Parlor car supplement $9 per person. Group discounts available. Checks accepted.
Special events	Easter Bunny Special, Santa Claus Special
Nearby attractions	Historic Newport, International Tennis Hall of Fame
Mailing address	P. O. Box 343, Newport, RI 02840
Phone	(401) 849-0546, year-round (401) 624-6951

DIESEL LOCOMOTIVES

Number	Type	Former owner	Builder	Date
84	45 ton	General Electric	General Electric	1942
4764	45 ton	U. S. Navy	General Electric	1941

OLD COLONY & NEWPORT RAILWAY

The Old Colony & Newport was chartered in 1863 to build a railroad from Newport, Rhode Island, to a connection with the Old Colony Railroad. Soon both names disappeared into the New Haven — but the Old Colony & Newport name reappeared on a tourist railroad in 1978. It carries excursionists north from Newport along the east shore of Narragansett Bay to Melville Marina and the Green Animals Topiary Gardens at Portsmouth, 9 miles. (Admission to Green Animals is $3 for adults, $1.50 for children 6-11 with train ticket.) After a 50-minute layover the train returns to Newport. The Newport station is downtown at 19 America's Cup Avenue, next to the Newport Tourist Center. There are restaurants within a block of the station; lodging is available in Newport.

Locomotives	Diesels
Cars	Coaches, diner, lounge
Schedule	Weekends spring and fall, daily during summer — call for schedules. Charter trips available.
Fares	Depend on trip — call for information
Nearby attractions	Golf, beaches
Mailing address	P. O. Box 2022, Conway, SC 29526
Phone	(803) 248-4531

WACCAMAW COAST LINE RAILROAD

The Waccamaw Coast Line is a short line operating freight and passenger service between Conway and Myrtle Beach, about 15 miles, using a variety of diesels and cars, some restored to their original paint and some in Waccamaw Coast Line's silver and purple. Sights along the way include two drawbridges and several miles of river scenery. Depending on the distance, round trips take 45 minutes to 3 hours. Schedules and fares had not been established at press time; call for details. The station in Conway is on 4th Avenue North Extension. Conway is in the eastern tip of South Carolina on U. S. Routes 378, 501, and 701. Food and lodging are available there and in Myrtle Beach.

Cars	Open coaches
Schedule	June 1-September 1, daily; weekends in September
Fares	Not set at press time. Checks accepted. Group discounts available.
Special events	Days of 76 (first week in August)
Nearby attractions	Black Hills Central Railroad, Mount Rushmore
Mailing address	P. O. Box 48, Deadwood, SD 57732
Phone	(605) 578-2255, year-round 578-3408 or (605) 342-4937

LOCOMOTIVES

Number	Type	Former owner	Builder	Date
STEAM				
11	2-4-0	North Michigan Iron Mine	Alco	1924
DIESEL				
4	0-4-0	A&K Railroad Salvage	Whitcomb	1939
	Railbus	Lonesome Pine Railroad	LPRR	1979

P ⊼ 🎁 ▣ $

DEADWOOD CENTRAL RAILROAD

The Deadwood Central offers a 75-minute round trip through the scenic Black Hills on 4½ miles of standard gauge track. The line includes bridges and steep grades. Snacks are available on the train. Deadwood is northwest of Rapid City, a few miles south of I-90 on U. S. Routes 85, 385, and Alternate 14. Food and lodging can be found in Deadwood.

Locomotives	3 steam
Cars	Coaches, open cars
Schedule	Mid-June to late August, Monday-Saturday leave Hill City 8:1 5 and 10:30 a.m., leave Keystone Junction 9 and 11:30; daily leave Hill City 1 and 3:15 p.m., leave Keystone Junction 2 and 4 (no return trip from Hill City with the 4 o'clock departure).
Fares	Adults $12.50, children 6-12 $8 (under 6 free). Persons in wheelchairs and blind persons free. Checks accepted. Group discount available.
Special events	Gold Spike Day (mid-June)
Nearby attractions	Deadwood Central Railroad, Mount Rushmore, Black Hills, Badlands
Mailing address	P. O. Box 1880, Hill City, SD 57745
Phone	(605) 574-2222

P ♿ ⊼ 🎁 ▣

BLACK HILLS CENTRAL RAILROAD

The Black Hills Central offers a 2-hour, 20-mile round trip on its 1880 Train between Hill City and Keystone Junction, South Dakota, over a former Burlington line. More than half the route is on a 4 percent grade; the scenery includes mountain forests and meadows. Hill City is 27 miles from Rapid City in the Black Hills National Forest. Food and lodging are available in Hill City; motel reservations are advised in late July and early August. Reservations are recommended for the train ride — as is preparation for changeable weather.

Displays	Freight cars; maintenance-of-way equipment; American Baptist Publication Society chapel car No. 2, *Emmanuel*
Dates open	Memorial Day-Labor Day, daily 9 a.m.-5 p.m.
Schedule	Motor cars operate daily. Narrow gauge steam is available by appointment in May and June. Both steam locomotives operate on the last weekend of August. Charter trips available.
Admission	Adults $4, children 6 and under free.
Fares	Adults $3, children 6 and under $1 Group rates available. Checks accepted.
Special events	Annual show (last weekend of August)
Nearby attractions	County Museum, Lake Herman State Park
Mailing address	Box 256, Madison, SD 57042
Phone	(605) 256-3644, year-round 256-6141 or 256-4845

P & ⛩ 🎁

STEAM LOCOMOTIVES

Number	Type	Former owner	Builder	Date
	0-4-0T		Orenstein & Koppel	1927
9	0-6-0	Duluth & Northeastern	Lima	1944

MOTOR CARS

	Former owner	Builder	Date
	U. S. Army	Kalamazoo	1952
	Soo Line	Fairmont	1975

PRAIRIE VILLAGE, HERMAN & MILWAUKEE RAILROAD

The Prairie Historical Society operates Prairie Village on a 160-acre plot of land near Madison. It includes 4 square blocks of antique buildings moved in from as far as 175 miles away. Accompanying the village are two railroads, one standard gauge and one 60-centimeter-gauge (23⅝").

The train operates on a circular track which includes a 3 percent grade and passes through agricultural land and the village of Herman, then returns to the starting point next to a former Milwaukee Road line.

Prairie Village is 2 miles west of Madison on U. S. Route 81 and South Dakota Route 34. Madison is in southeast South Dakota, about 30 miles northwest of Sioux Falls.

Madison

Cars	Air-conditioned and open-window coaches			
Displays	2 station buildings; mail, dining, sleeping, and business cars; artifacts			
Dates open	Last weekend of March to Thanksgiving weekend, Saturdays and Sundays; May-Labor Day, daily. Open for groups of 40 or more at other times by appointment.			
Schedule	Trains leave East Chattanooga hourly from 10:40 a.m. to 4:40 p.m. except Sundays, 12:40-4:40 Sundays; leave Grand Junction hourly 11:05-5:05 except Sundays; 1:05-5:05 Sundays. Charter trips available. Downtown Arrow: Saturdays and Sundays, leave Grand Junction 1:05 and 5 p.m.; leave Chattanooga Choo-Choo Holiday Inn 3:10 and 6:10 p.m.			
Fares	Adults $6.50, children 6-11 $3 (under 6 free), age 65 and up $6. Downtown Arrow, adults $11, children $7.50. Tickets are also sold at the Chattanooga Choo-Choo front desk. Checks and credit cards accepted. Group discounts available (reservations required).			
Memberships	$25 annually			
Radio frequency	160.425			
Special events	Mainline excursions			

Nearby attractions Lookout Mountain, Rock City, Ruby Falls, Chickamauga Battlefield, Chattanooga Choo-Choo, National Model Railroad Association headquarters

Mailing address 4119 Cromwell Road, Chattanooga, TN 37421-2119

Phone (615) 894-8028

LOCOMOTIVES

Number	Type	Former owner	Builder	Date
STEAM				
610	2-8-0	U. S. Army	Baldwin	1950
630	2-8-0	Southern Railway	Alco	1904
4501	2-8-2	Southern Railway	Baldwin	1911
DIESEL				
8669, 8677	RSD1	U. S. Army	Alco	1945

TENNESSEE VALLEY RAILROAD

The Tennessee Valley Railroad has two display sites connected by 3 miles of track. Trains shuttle hourly between Grand Junction at 4119 Cromwell Road and East Chattanooga at 2200 North Chamberlain Avenue; the ride takes 14 minutes each way. Parking is available at both locations. To reach Grand Junction, take Exit 4 (Route 153-Chickamauga Dam) from I-75, then the fourth exit, Jersey Pike, from 153. Turn left (south) on Jersey, then right almost immediately onto Cromwell Road.

To reach East Chattanooga station from downtown, follow Broad Street north, Riverside Drive east, and Wilcox Boulevard east. A the fourth traffic light on Wilcox turn north on Chamberlain and g approximately half a mile to the depot. On weekends the railroa also operates the *Downtown Arrow* between Grand Junction, Eas Chattanooga, and the Chattanooga Choo-Choo Holiday Inn. Th 7.3-mile ride takes 55-65 minutes each way.

The Tennessee Valley Railroad also sponsors mainline excursio trains in October — write for information on these trips.

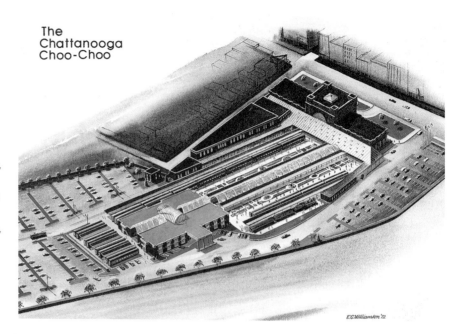

The
Chattanooga
Choo-Choo

Displays	24 coaches converted to sleeping rooms, HO gauge model railroad
Dates open	Year-round, daily
Admission	Model railroad: adults $1.95, children 95 cents
Fares	Trolley: 50 cents per person
earby attractions	Lookout Mountain, Rock City, Ruby Falls, Chickamauga Battlefield, Tennessee Valley Railroad Museum
Mailing address	1400 Market Street, Chattanooga, TN 37402
Phone	(615) 266-5000

CHATTANOOGA CHOO-CHOO HOLIDAY INN

Chattanooga's Terminal Station was opened in 1909 and closed in 1970. It reopened in 1973 not as a station but as a hotel, the Chattanooga Choo-Choo. The lobby of the hotel is under the dome of the station, and the guest rooms are in remodeled passenger cars on tracks along the platforms. The hotel and restaurant complex includes a railroad-theme gift shop and a large HO scale model railroad, built and operated by the Chattanooga Area Model Railroad Club. On weekends the Tennessee Valley Railroad operates the *Downtown Arrow* between the Chattanooga Choo-Choo and its museum sites at East Chattanooga and Grand Junction (see the next entry). To reach the Chattanooga Choo-Choo from I-24 in downtown Chattanooga, westbound take Exit 179B and follow Market Street north to 14th. Eastbound on I-24, take Exit 178 and follow the signs to the Chattanooga Choo-Choo.

Chattanooga

Displays	Steam locomotive, flat car, caboose
Dates open	May-October, Thursday, Friday, and Saturday 10 a.m.-4 p.m., Sunday 1-4
Admission	Free; donations appreciated
Memberships	Write for information.

Nearby attractions	Falls Mill, Hundred Oaks Castle, Old Jail Museum
Mailing address	P. O. Box 53, Cowan, TN 37318
Phone	(615) 967-7365 for recorded information

COWAN RAILROAD MUSEUM

The CSX line from Nashville to Chattanooga (once Nashville, Chattanooga & St. Louis, later Louisville & Nashville) climbs over Cumberland Mountain south of Cowan, Tennessee. The grades are steep enough to require helpers in each direction; they are added to southbound trains at Cowan. The former station is now a museum housing a re-creation of a turn-of-the-century telegraph operator's office, various artifacts, and an HO scale model of the Cowan Pusher District. Cowan is on U. S. 41A and 64 12 miles west of Exit 1? of I-24 and about 15 miles north of the Alabama border. Food available in Cowan; lodging can be found in Winchester, 7 mil: west.

Displays	Steam locomotive, mail car, dining car, artifacts
Dates open	Summer, daily 8 a.m.-8 p.m.; winter, daily 10-4
Admission	Adults $3, children under 13 $2, senior

	citizens $2.25. Checks and credit cards accepted. Group discounts available.
Mailing address	Casey Jones Village, Jackson, TN 38305
Phone	(901) 668-1222

CASEY JONES HOME AND RAILROAD MUSEUM

On April 30, 1900, an Illinois Central passenger train ran into the rear of a freight at Vaughan, Mississippi. At the throttle was John Luther Jones, originally from Cayce, Kentucky. He was killed in the wreck. An engine-wiper named Wallace Saunders wrote a song about the incident, and a legend was born. The house Jones was living in has been moved to a park in Jackson, Tennessee, ar has become a museum containing memorabilia and artifacts. Th museum is located at Exit 80A (U. S. 45 bypass) of I-40 on th northwest side of Jackson. Casey Jones Village includes a resta rant; lodging is available nearby.

Cars	Stainless steel dining, lounge, and dome cars
Schedule	April-December, Thursdays, Fridays, and Saturdays; January-March, Saturday only. Train departs at 7 p.m.
Fares	$39.50 per person. Credit cards and checks accepted. Group discount available. There is a parking fee.
Radio frequency	160.365
Special events	New Year's Eve, Valentine's Day
Nearby attractions	Opryland, Grand Ole Opry, Music Row, Fort Nashboro
Mailing address	P. O. Box 25085, Nashville, TN 37202-5085
Phone	(615) 254-8010

DIESEL LOCOMOTIVES

Number	Type	Former owner	Builder	Date
4254, 4264	E8A	Pennsylvania	EMD	1952

BROADWAY DINNER TRAIN

The Broadway Dinner train operates over the rails of the Nashville & Eastern Railroad (ex-Tennessee Central) from a station at First and Broadway in downtown Nashville, next to Riverfront Park. The train goes to Old Hickory, 17½ miles, then returns to Nashville. The trip takes 2½ hours.

Train equipment includes former Santa Fe dining cars and dome lounge, Seaboard coaches converted to dining cars, a Florida East Coast tavern-observation car, and a Rock Island mail car converted to a power car.

Lodging can be found throughout the Nashville area.

Locomotives	2 steam
Cars	Open cars
Dates open	April 28-October 28, 1990, daily 9 a.m.-6 p.m.
Admission	Adults $16.95, children 4-11 $11.95, age 60 and over $13.50. Checks and credit cards accepted. Group discount available. Parking $2.
Fares	Included with park admission
Nearby attractions	Great Smoky Mountains National Park
Mailing address	700 Dollywood Lane, Pigeon Forge, TN 37863-4101
Phone	(615) 428-9400

DOLLYWOOD EXPRESS

One of the rides at Dollywood, a rustic theme park in the Smoky Mountains, is the Dollywood Express, running on 5 miles of 3'-gauge track. The two steam locomotives were built by Baldwin in 1939 and 1943 for the U. S. Army; passengers ride in open coaches.

There are restaurants in Dollywood and motels in Pigeon Forge. Pigeon Forge is on U. S. Routes 321 and 441 about 30 miles south east of Knoxville.

Locomotives	2 steam
Cars	Open excursion cars
Dates open	Mid-March to Memorial Day, weekends; Memorial Day through August, daily; September to mid-November, weekends. Opening time is usually 10 a.m.; closing time is 6 p.m. to midnight, depending on season.

Admission	Adults $19.95, children under 48" tall $9.98, age 55 and over $13.95. Group discounts available. Admission includes all rides.
Mailing address	P. O. Box 191, Arlington, TX 76004
Phone	(817) 640-8900

IX FLAGS RAILROAD

Circling the perimeter of Six Flags Over Texas, a theme park, is the 36"-gauge Six Flags Railroad. The two locomotives used on the railroad are from the Patout Plantation: One was built by Porter in 1897 and the other by American in 1901. The passenger cars are flatcars rebuilt with benches and roofs. The 1-mile train ride takes about 15 minutes. Six Flags Over Texas is on I-30 at State Highway 360, about halfway between Dallas and Fort Worth. Food is available at Six Flags Over Texas, and lodging can be found nearby.

Displays	Steam, diesel, and electric locomotives; passenger and freight cars of Texas railroads
Dates open	Year-round, Saturdays and Sundays 11 a.m.-5 p.m., Thursdays and Fridays 9-1; daily during State Fair in October
Admission	Adults $2, children under 17 $1
Memberships	Write for information.
Nearby attractions	Natural History Museum, Science Museum, Texas Hall of State, Civic Garden Center, Aquarium, Cotton Bowl, Six Flags Over Texas, Texas State Railroad
Mailing address	P. O. Box 26369, Dallas, TX 75226-0369
Phone	(214) 428-0101

LOCOMOTIVES ON DISPLAY

Railroad and Number	Type	Builder	Date
STEAM			
St. Louis-San Francisco 4501	4-8-4	Baldwin	1942
Union Pacific 4018	4-8-8-4	Alco	1942
Eagle Picher 1625 (ex-Frisco)	2-10-0	Alco	1918
Union Terminal Co. (Dallas) 7	0-6-0	Baldwin	1923
ELECTRIC			
Pennsylvania 4903	GG1	PRR	1940
DIESEL			
Atchison, Topeka & Santa Fe M.160	motor car	Brill	1931
Union Pacific 6913	DDA40X	EMD	1969

AGE OF STEAM RAILROAD MUSEUM

The Southwest Railroad Historical Society maintains a large collection of rolling stock at a site at Washington and Parry Streets in the northwest corner of the Texas State Fair Park. The collection includes a complete passenger train of the 1920s and several steam locomotives. State Fair Park is just off the I-30-U. S. 67-80 freeway at Exit 47A about 3 miles east of downtown Dallas.

Locomotives	1 steam, 2 diesel, 1 RDC
Cars	Coaches
Displays	More than three dozen passenger and freight cars and locomotives
Dates open	Daily 10 a.m.-5 p.m.
Schedule	Summer Saturday afternoons — inquire at the museum.
	A one-day Texas Limited round trip from Galveston to Houston is possible on Saturdays: leave Galveston 1 p.m., get back to Galveston at 6:30. See the entry for the Texas Limited on the next page.
Admission	Adults $4, children 4-12 $2 (under 4 free), age 65 and over $3. Checks and credit cards accepted. Group discounts available.
Memberships	Write for information.
Special events	Annual model train exhibit, visiting locomotives and cars
Nearby attractions	The Strand Historic District, historic ships
Mailing address	123 Rosenberg Avenue, Galveston, TX 77550
Phone	(409) 765-5700

LOCOMOTIVES

Number	Type	Former owner	Builder	Date
STEAM				
5	2-8-0	Magma Arizona	Alco	1922
DIESEL				
410	H20-44	Southwest Portland Cement	FM	1954
1303	NW2E	Southern Pacific	EMD	1949

GALVESTON RAILROAD MUSEUM

The former Santa Fe station in Galveston, Texas, is now the Galveston Railroad Museum. The displays include a large collection of cars and locomotives, an HO gauge model railroad, an orientation theater, and in The People's Gallery an exhibit titled "A Moment Frozen in Time": a waiting room populated with 39 life-size figures and equipped with a sound system for the conversations these people might have been having.

On summer Saturday afternoons the museum operates steam powered train rides that take about 20 minutes. A restaurant, "Dinner … On the Diner," is housed in two dining cars (reservations are suggested, (409) 763-4759). The museum is the Galveston station of Texas Limited excursion trains to and from Houston.

The museum is at The Strand and 25th Street in Galveston. Food and lodging are available nearby.

Locomotives	2 diesel
Cars	Converted ore cars
Dates open	Spring, summer, and fall, weekends, open 10 a.m.; summer, also Monday-Friday, open 11 a.m.
Admission	Adults $18.50 plus tax, children under 48" tall $9.25, age 65 and over $10.15. Parking $3. Checks and credit cards accepted. Group discounts available.
Nearby attractions	WaterWorld, AstroDome, AstroDomain
Mailing address	9001 Kirby, Houston, TX 77054
Phone	(713) 799-8404; 799-1234 for recorded information

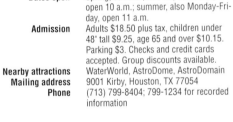

ASTROWORLD

A 36"-gauge railroad winds through AstroWorld and WaterWorld, theme parks in Houston. A complete 2-mile trip takes about 20 minutes; the train stops in several different areas of AstroWorld and WaterWorld. The trains, which consist of converted ore cars, are pulled by two diesel locomotives, one a diesel-electric and the other a diesel-hydraulic.

AstroWorld is on I-610 southwest of downtown. There are restaurants and snack bars in the park, and lodging is available nearby.

Locomotives	2 diesel
Cars	5 stainless steel passenger cars
Schedule	Leave Houston Thursdays and Sundays at 9:30 a.m., Fridays at 4:15 p.m., and Saturdays at 8:30 a.m. and 4:15 p.m. Leave Galveston Thursdays and Sundays at 3 p.m., Fridays at 9:30 p.m., and Saturdays at 1 and 9:30 p.m. Charter trips available
Fares	Adult round trip: $27.50 tourist, $37.50 first class, $42.50 dome. One-way: $18.75, $25.75, and 29.25. Children's fares (2-12) are approximately 70 percent of the adult fares. Credit cards accepted. Tickets may be purchased through Ticketron. Group discounts available.
Nearby attractions	Tall Ship *Elissa*, Galveston beaches, Grand Theater, Strand Avenue
Mailing address	3131 West Alabama, Suite 100, Houston, TX 77098
Phone	(713) 522-0574 (offices); (713) 522-9090 for reservations

TEXAS LIMITED

The *Texas Limited* operates between the Amtrak station at 902 Washington Street in Houston and the Galveston Railroad Museum in Galveston, 50 miles to the southeast. Travel time is 2 hours 15 minutes each way. A highlight of the trip is the mile-long causeway across Galveston Bay.

The train comprises five stainless-steel passenger cars: Santa Fe *Chimayo*, Rock Island *Hawkeye*, Burlington *Silver Stirrup* and *Silver Queen* (originally a Minneapolis & St. Louis coach), and New York Central 61. Beverage service is available on board. Scenery visible from the windows of the train includes Houston's skyline, the Lyndon Baines Johnson Space Center, and Galveston Bay. The train runs on the rails of the Galveston, Houston & Henderson Railroad, now part of the Union Pacific but for many years jointly owned by the Missouri Pacific and the Missouri-Kansas-Texas.

Locomotives	2 steam
Cars	Open cars, heated and air-conditioned cars
Schedule	March 27-October 28, 1990, Saturdays at 11 a.m., 2:30, 4, and 5:30 p.m., Sundays at 11 and 2:30; additional runs May 28-August 19: Mondays and Thursdays at 2:30 and 4 and Fridays at 2:30, 4, and 5:30. Charter trips operated.
Fares	Adults $4.50, children 12 and under $2, age 55 and over $3.50. Group discounts available.
Special events	Jefferson Pilgrimage (first weekend of May), Founders Day (third weekend of October), Candlelight Tour (first weekend of December)
Nearby attractions	Lake o' the Pines, Caddo Lake
Mailing address	P. O. Drawer A, Jefferson, TX 75657
Phone	(214) 665-8400, year-round 665-3933 or 665-3934

JEFFERSON & CYPRESS BAYOU RAILROAD

Jefferson, 60 miles west of Shreveport, Louisiana, was once the largest inland port and the fifth largest city in Texas. Efforts to improve navigation in 1873 went awry and lowered the water level in Cypress Bayou so that navigation was no longer possible; by then railroads were replacing river boats. Jefferson has become a historic town with restored homes, antique shops, restaurants, and bed-and-breakfasts. The Jefferson & Cypress Bayou, which began operation in 1987, is a 3'-gauge steam-powered railroad that offers a 5-mile, 45-minute ride along Big Cypress Bayou past the sites of lumber mills and iron works. The station is at the east end of Austin Street. Jefferson is in the northeast corner of Texas on U. S. 59, 15 miles north of Marshall and 55 miles south of Texarkana.

Jefferson

		Cars	Coaches (mostly former Rock Island suburban cars)

Cars — Coaches (mostly former Rock Island suburban cars)

Schedule — March 24, 1990-May 27, Saturdays and Sundays; May 28-August 19, Thursday-Monday; August 25-October 28, Saturdays and Sundays. Trains leave Rusk and Palestine 11 a.m., get back at 3 p.m. Charter trips available.

Fares — Adults $8 round trip, $6 one way; children 3-12 $6 round trip $4 one way. Checks accepted.

Special events — Moonlight trips once a month in May, September, and October

Nearby attractions — Jim Hogg State Park, Caddoan Mounds State Park, Tyler Rose Gardens, Tyler State Park, Mission Tejas State Park

Mailing address — P. O. Box 39, Rusk, TX 75785

Phone — (214) 683-2561; in Texas (800) 442-8951

LOCOMOTIVES

Number	Type	Former identity	Builder	Date
STEAM				
200	4-6-0	SP 2248	Cooke	1896*
201	4-6-0	T&P 316	Cooke	1901
300	2-8-0	Tremont & Gulf 28	Baldwin	1917*
400	2-8-2	Tremont & Gulf 30	Baldwin	1917
500	4-6-2	Santa Fe 1316	Baldwin	1911
610	2-10-4	Texas & Pacific 610	Lima	1927*
DIESEL				
1	45 ton	Temple Industries	GE	1944
7	RS-2	Point Comfort & Northern	Alco	1947
8	MRS-1		Alco	1953

* not in service

P ♿ ⛱ 🎁 ◼

TEXAS STATE RAILROAD HISTORICAL PARK

Construction of the Texas State Railroad was begun in 1896 to furnish transportation to an iron furnace that was part of a state prison at North Rusk. The iron plant closed in 1913 and the railroad was leased to the Texas & New Orleans (Southern Pacific) in 1921. For a period in the 1960s the line was leased to the Texas South-Eastern; then in 1972 the property was transferred to the Texas Parks & Wildlife Department to form a state historical park.

The railroad offers a ride over 25 miles of track through rolling hills and pine woods. A one-way ride takes 90 minutes, and there is a 1-hour layover before the return trip — total, 4 hours. Reservations are recommended and can be booked well in advance; a tour of the locomotive cab is available during the hour before departure. The coaches are neither heated nor air-conditioned, so dress appropriately for the weather.

Sandwiches, snacks, and ice cream are available on board; restaurants and lodging can be found in Rusk and Palestine. The Rusk station is on U. S. 84, 2½ miles west of Rusk; the Palestine station is 3½ miles east of Palestine on U. S. 84. Rusk and Palestine are north of Houston, southeast of Dallas, and southwest of Shreveport, Louisiana.

Locomotives	F units
Cars	Lounge, dining, dome lounge and dome dining cars, all air conditioned
Schedule	Wednesday-Saturday, depart 7 p.m.; Sundays, depart 5 p.m. $50 including dinner; $65 for dome seating. Reservations required. Checks and
	credit cards accepted. Group discounts available.
Special events	New Year's Eve, Valentine Day
Nearby attractions	San Antonio Riverwalk, The Alamo, Seaworld
Mailing address	P. O. Box 5752, San Antonio, TX 78201
Phone	(512) 225-2337, year-round 225-1080

  $

TEXAS SOUTHERN RAILROAD

   Texas Southern Railroad operates *The Texan*, an elegant dinner train. It operates from the Amtrak (Southern Pacific) station at St. Paul Square in San Antonio. The train is ready for boarding an hour before departure. The train runs west 50 miles along SP's main line, then returns. Trip time is 3½ hours. The fare includes hors d'oeuvres and a four-course dinner. Children under 14 are not allowed; men are requested to wear sport coats. Reservations are required.

Locomotives	1 diesel
Cars	Missouri Pacific and Union Pacific cabooses
Displays	Pullman car *McKeever*, Santa Fe business car 404, HO gauge model railroad, automobiles and trucks
Dates open	Year-round, Thursday-Sunday 10 a.m.-3 p.m.,
	weather permitting
Schedule	Trains run Sundays 1-3 p.m.
Admission	Suggested donation, adults $2, children $1. Checks accepted.
Memberships	$25 per year
Nearby attractions	The Alamo, Sea World
Mailing address	Longhorn Station, 11731 Wetmore Road, San Antonio, TX 78247
Phone	(512) 490-3554

TEXAS TRANSPORTATION MUSEUM

   The Texas Transportation Museum maintains an operating museum with a mile of track on Wetmore Road near the San Antonio airport. Operations are carried on with an ex-U. S. Air Force General Electric 45-ton diesel; passengers ride in cabooses. Also on hand are a 1911 2-8-0, Moscow, Camden & San Augustine No. 6, and a Baldwin-built 0-4-0T from the Comal Power Co. Operation is subject to weather conditions. The displays include an open trolley car from Veracruz, Mexico; a 12 section-1 drawing room Pullman sleeping car; and a collection of vintage automobiles and trucks. Restaurants and lodging can be found nearby.

Displays	Santa Fe 4-6-2, caboose, station
Dates open	Tuesday-Friday, 1-4 p.m.; Saturdays, 10 a.m.-4 p.m. Closed major holidays.
Admission	Adults $2, children 6-12 $1, age 60 and over $1. Checks accepted. Group discounts available.
Memberships	Individual, $15; family, $25
Special events	Texas Train Festival (third weekend of September)
Nearby attractions	Czech Heritage Museum, Texas Ranger Museum (Waco), 1st Cavalry and 2d Armored Division Museums (Fort Hood)
Mailing address	P. O. Box 5126, Temple, TX 76505
Phone	(817) 778-6873

RAILROAD & PIONEER MUSEUM

The city of Temple operates the Railroad & Pioneer Museum, which is housed in the Gulf, Colorado & Santa Fe depot that was formerly located in Moody, a few miles north. The exhibits cover Texas pioneer life (blacksmithing, woodworking, farming, ranching, and town life) as well as railroading. Outside are Santa Fe 4-6-2 No. 3423 and a steel caboose.

The museum is at 710 Jack Baskin Street (the corner of 31st Street and Avenue H). Temple, where Santa Fe's line to west Texas and California diverges from the Houston-Oklahoma City-Kansas City route, is on I-35 about halfway between Waco and Austin. Food and lodging can be found within a mile of the museum.

Locomotives	2 steam, 1 diesel
Cars	Coaches, open cars, dining car
Displays	7 steam locomotives, 2 diesels, 1880 western village, working blacksmith shop
Schedule	Weekends and holidays May through Columbus Day, and daily mid-June to Labor Day, departures at 10 a.m. and 2:30 p.m.; additional train Memorial Day to mid-June, daily at 11:45. Charter trips available.
Fares	Adults $11, children 3-12 $6.75. Credit cards and checks accepted (check guarantee card necessary). Reservations required. Discounts available for groups of 25 or more.
Special events	Doubleheaded steam on Labor Day
Nearby attractions	Wasatch Mountain State Park, Park City, Deer Creek and Strawberry Reservoirs
Mailing address	P. O. Box 103, Heber City, UT 84032
Phone	Heber, (801) 654-2900; Salt Lake City, (801) 531-6022

HEBER CREEPER

The Utah Eastern Railroad opened its line from Heber City to Provo, Utah, in 1899. A year later it was acquired by the Rio Grande Western, which in turn became part of the Denver & Rio Grande Western. About 1970 the D&RGW abandoned the branch and it became a tourist railroad, the Wasatch Mountain Railway, nicknamed the Heber Creeper.

The line offers a 3-hour round trip covering 16 miles of track from Heber City to Vivian Park. The scenery along the route includes meadows, mountains, streams, and canyons. The railroad is notable for having a large collection of "Harriman" locomotives and cars — equipment built to a standard design for the railroads that were controlled by E. H. Harriman, among them Union Pacific and Southern Pacific.

Food is available on the train and in Heber City, 46 miles southeast of Salt Lake City and 28 miles northeast of Provo on U. S. 40 and 189. Staff is on the premises year round.

Dates open	Year round, Monday-Saturday 10 a.m.-6 p.m.; also Sunday 1-5 from June 1 through Labor Day
Admission	Adults $2, children 12 and under $1, age 65 and over $1.50. Checks and credit cards accepted. Group discounts available.
Memberships	Write for information.
Special events	Autumnfest, Christmas Tree Express, Gem and Mineral Show, Railroad Festival
Nearby attractions	Golden Spike National Historic Site, Historic 25th Street, Eccles Community Art Center, Hill Air Force Museum
Mailing address	Union Station, Room 212, 2501 Wall Avenue, Ogden, UT 84401
Phone	(801) 399-8582, 399-8585

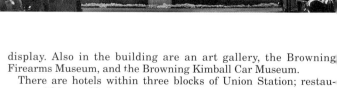

ROLLING STOCK ON DISPLAY

Former owner	Number	Type	Builder	Date
Southern Pacific	1555	Caboose		
Southern Pacific	3769	GP9	EMD	1957
Union Pacific	26	Gas-turbine	GE	1961
Union Pacific	6916	DDA40X	EMD	1969
Union Pacific	25176	Cupola caboose	Pullman Standard	1944
Union Pacific	25766	Wood caboose		1921
Union Pacific	25880	Bay-window caboose	International Car Co.	1979

UNION STATION

Ogden, Utah's Union Station, once the hub of Union Pacific's passenger train network, is now an exhibition hall, civic center, and museum. The Wattis-Dumke Railroad Museum in the building contains an HO scale model railroad depicting Ogden's role in railroading; the museum's collection of full-size rolling stock will soon be on display. Also in the building are an art gallery, the Browning Firearms Museum, and the Browning Kimball Car Museum.

There are hotels within three blocks of Union Station; restaurants within one block.

Displays	2 operating steam locomotives, films, slide shows, 30 miles of roadbed
Dates open	Memorial Day-Labor Day, daily 8 a.m.-6 p.m.; rest of the year 8-4:30. Closed Thanksgiving, Christmas, and New Year's Day. Steam locomotives on display 9-4 in May and September, 10:30-5:50 June-Labor Day.
Admission	$3 per car; $1 per bus passenger; senior citizens free with Golden Age Passport. Checks accepted.
Special events	Anniversary Celebration (May 10), Railroaders' Festival (first Saturday in August)
Nearby attractions	Bear River Migratory Bird Refuge, Great Salt Lake, Ogden Union Station
Mailing address	P. O. Box W, Brigham City, UT 84032
Phone	(801) 471-2209

GOLDEN SPIKE NATIONAL HISTORIC SITE

As the Union Pacific and the Central Pacific built toward each other in 1869, Congress chose Promontory Summit, Utah, north of the Great Salt Lake, as their meeting point. The rails were joined on May 10, 1869, with a symbolic golden spike — it was the first North American rail line to connect the Atlantic and Pacific.

In 1903 the Southern Pacific, which had absorbed the Central Pacific, began constructing a cutoff directly across the Great Salt Lake. It opened in 1904 and relegated the original route through Promontory to secondary status. The rails were lifted in 1942 and contributed to a wartime scrap drive.

In recent years the monument marking the site of the Golden Spike ceremony has been augmented by a visitor center and colorful working replicas of the two locomotives that participated: Central Pacific *Jupiter* and Union Pacific No. 119. The 2700-acre site is operated by the National Park Service, U. S. Department of the Interior; park ranger talks are offered in summer.

The Golden Spike National Historic Site is 32 miles west of Brigham City, Utah — follow Route 83 west to Promontory Junction, turn left and go 2 miles to the next junction, then right and another 5 miles.

Food is not available at the site; motels and restaurants can be found in Brigham City and Tremonton.

Locomotives	5 first-generation diesels
Cars	Ex-Central of New Jersey steel coaches, ex-Rutland wood coach and combine
Schedule	Weekend of June 23-24, then daily June 30-September 3 and September 15-October 14, 1990: leave Bellows Falls 11 a.m. and 2 p.m., leave Chester 12:10 p.m. Charter trips available.
Fares	Adults $9, children 3-12 $5. Discounts available for groups of 20 or more.
Special events	Fall Foliage Specials, Bellows Falls to Ludlow, 54 miles round trip, weekends of September 29-30 and October 6-7, 1990
Nearby attractions	Santa's Land, Fort No. 4, Green Mountains, MG Museum
Mailing address	P. O. Box 498, Bellows Falls, VT 05101-0498
Phone	(802) 463-3069

GREEN MOUNTAIN RAILROAD

Green Mountain Railroad Corporation operates freight service on the former Rutland Railway between Bellows Falls and Rutland, 50 miles. It also operates the *Green Mountain Flyer*, now in its fifth season of passenger service between Bellows Falls and Chester, 13 miles.

Equipment includes two former Rutland cars, a combination baggage-coach and a coach; and a lunch coach offering food service. Green Mountain's roster includes the last Rutland locomotive still in New England, RS1 No. 405. The train leaves Bellows Falls sta-

tion and follows the west bank of the Connecticut River for 2 miles then follows the Williams River to Chester. The ride takes 1 hour and 40 minutes. A round trip originating in Chester or Chester South is also possible. From I-91 take Exit 5 or Exit 6, then U. S. 5 to downtown Bellows Falls. Take Canal Street to Depot Street or Bridge Street to Island Street. Vermont's signage law forbids all but the most modest signs, so it's helpful to know the station in Bellows Falls is on an island formed by the Connecticut River and a power canal. Food and lodging are available in Bellows Falls and Chester.

Cars	Coaches
Displays	Snowplow, caboose
Schedule	May 28-October 7, 1990, 2-hour excursion trains depart Morrisville at 9 a.m. and 1:30 p.m.; 1-hour trips leave at noon and 4:30 p.m. Charter trips available.
Fares	Adults $15 for the 2-hour trip; $10 for the 1-hour trip; children under 5 free. Checks and credit cards accepted. Group discounts available.
Nearby attractions	Ice cream factory, cider mill, Stowe, Mt. Mansfield, St. J. & L.C. Railroad
Mailing address	RD 1, Box 790, Morrisville, VT 05661
Phone	(802) 888-4255, (800) 332-2068

DIESEL LOCOMOTIVES

Number	Type	Former owner	Builder	Date
7801, 7805	RS-3	Delaware & Hudson	Alco	1952
3608, 3612	RS-11	Duluth, Winnipeg & Pacific	Alco	1956

LAMOILLE VALLEY RAILROAD

The Lamoille Valley operates freight service over a portion of the former St. Johnsbury & Lake Champlain and offers excursions from Morrisville, Vermont. The line includes one of the last railroad covered bridges in the U. S. The railroad offers 1-hour and 2-hour excursions; the longer trips go to Greensboro, 20 miles from Morrisville. Snacks are available on board.

Morrisville is north of Montpelier and about halfway between Burlington and St. Johnsbury on Routes 12, 15, and 100. Restaurants and lodging can be found there; Stowe, a major resort town, is 10 miles to the south. The station in Morrisville is at the end of Stafford Avenue.

Morrisville

Displays	Central Vermont 4-6-0, private car *Grand Isle*, station, memorabilia
Dates open	Mid-May through mid-October, 9 a.m.-5 p.m.
Admission	Adults $12.50, children 6-16 $4.50. Group discounts available (reservations required).
Memberships	Write for information.
Nearby attractions	Lake Champlain
Mailing address	Shelburne, Vermont 05482
Phone	(802) 985-3346; 985-3344 for recorded information

SHELBURNE MUSEUM

The Shelburne Museum grew from the Americana collection of Electra Havemeyer Webb, wife of a descendant of Cornelius Vanderbilt. After World War Two the collection became a museum, and the 45-acre site has grown to resemble a good-size village.

The village includes a railroad station — the Shelburne Station of the Rutland Railway — with a short train on the track in front. Nearby is Delaware & Hudson's Lake Champlain steamer *Ticonderoga*.

Food is available at the museum, and restaurants and lodging can be found in Shelburne and in Burlington, 7 miles north.

Displays	Locomotives, cars, and equipment that illustrate and interpret the history of U. S. Army transportation from the Civil War to the present
Dates open	Daily 9 a.m.-4:30 p.m.; closed New Year's Day, Martin Luther King Day, Presidents' Day, Easter Sunday, Columbus Day, Veterans' Day, Thanksgiving, and Christmas
Admission	Free
Memberships	Write for information.
Nearby attractions	Colonial Williamsburg, Busch Gardens, Colonial National Historical Park, War Memorial Museum, Mariners Museum
Mailing address	Building 300, Attn: ATZF-PTM, Fort Eustis, VA 23604-5260
Phone	(804) 878-1115, -1182, -1183

P & ⛩ 🎁

U. S. ARMY TRANSPORTATION MUSEUM

In the mid-1950s the U. S. Army Transportation School at Fort Eustis was a focus of rail enthusiast interest because of its steam locomotives — the Army thought its soldiers should be ready to handle the locomotives they would encounter overseas. One of the 2-8-0s used then, No. 607, built in 1945 by Lima Locomotive Works, is among the rolling stock exhibited at the U. S. Army Transportation Museum. Also on display are a crane, a track motor car, and a Jordan spreader.

Fort Eustis is between Newport News and Williamsburg, about 2 miles west of I-64 at the Fort Eustis Boulevard exit. The museum is on Washington Boulevard. Food and lodging are available within half a mile of the museum.

Displays	50 locomotives and cars, including Virginian rectifier electric and 0-8-0 steam switcher, Pennsylvania GG1, Wabash E8 No. 1009, Electro-Motive's 10,000th diesel unit
Dates open	Monday-Saturday 10 a.m.-5 p.m., Sunday 12-5; closed Thanksgiving, Christmas, and New Year's Day
Admission	Adults $3, children 13-18 $2, children 3-12 $1.75 (under 3 free), age 60 and over $2.50. Checks accepted. Group discounts available.
Memberships	Write for information.
Nearby attractions	Fine Arts Museum, outdoor market, Science Museum
Mailing address	303 Norfolk Avenue, Roanoke, VA 24011
Phone	(703) 342-5670

VIRGINIA MUSEUM OF TRANSPORTATION

The Roanoke Transportation Museum was owned and operated by the city of Roanoke from 1963 to 1976. It came under the direction of a nonprofit corporation in 1977. In 1983 it was designated as the official transportation museum of the commonwealth of Virginia, and in 1985 it received its present name.

The collection includes two Norfolk & Western locomotives, 4-8-4 No. 611 and 2-6-6-4 No. 1218, that are in active excursion service.

The museum is three blocks west of the city market in downtown Roanoke. To get there, leave I-581 at Exit 6, Elm Avenue. Go west on Elm, north (right) on Jefferson, west (left) on Salem, and north (right) on Third to the museum.

Food and lodging are available in Roanoke.

Locomotive	1 steam (0-4-4T)
Cars	1 open car, 1 parlor-observation car, 1 baggage-parlor car
Displays	Railroad artifacts and photographs in station
Schedule	June 16, 1990-Labor Day, Saturday and Sunday, frequent departures from 11:30 a.m. to 4:30 p.m.
Fares	$1.00. Checks accepted.
Special events	Taste of Skagit Tulip Festival (April 20-22, 1990), Anacortes Arts & Crafts Festival (first weekend of August)
Nearby attractions	Ferry to San Juan Islands, Maritime Museum, Lake Whatcom Railway
Mailing address	387 Campbell Lake Road, Anacortes, WA 98221
Phone	(206) 293-2634

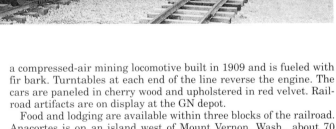

ANACORTES RAILWAY

The Anacortes Railway is an 18"-gauge railroad in downtown Anacortes, Washington. It is one of the world's smallest narrow-gauge passenger railroads (as distinguished from a miniature railway). It offers a .8-mile ride from the former Great Northern depot at 7th and R Avenue to 9th and Commercial Avenue. The ride takes 20-25 minutes.

The line's Forney-type steam locomotive was rebuilt in 1969 from a compressed-air mining locomotive built in 1909 and is fueled with fir bark. Turntables at each end of the line reverse the engine. The cars are paneled in cherry wood and upholstered in red velvet. Railroad artifacts are on display at the GN depot.

Food and lodging are available within three blocks of the railroad. Anacortes is on an island west of Mount Vernon, Wash., about 70 miles north of Seattle.

Cars	Coaches, open cars, caboose
Schedule	Year-round, Saturdays and Sundays, 1:30 p.m. Additional trains: April 3-October 30, 1990, Tuesdays and Saturdays, 10 a.m.; June 16-September 30, Tuesday-Friday, 10 and 1:30, Saturdays at 6:30 p.m., and Sundays, 10 and 2:30; also Memorial Day and Labor Day at 10 and 1:30 Charter trips available.
Fares	Moulton Falls: adults $9 children $5; Chelatchie: $14/$7; higher for special trains. Credit cards and checks accepted.
Special events	Rib Trains (dinner), Christmas Tree Trains Fridays, Saturdays, and Sundays December 1-23, 1990, 10:30 a.m.
Mailing address	P. O. Box 604, Battle Ground, WA 98604
Phone	(206) 687-2626

DIESEL LOCOMOTIVES

Number	Type	Former identity	Builder	Date
80	SW8	SP 1105	EMD	1953
81	SW8	SP 1127	EMD	1953
82	SW8	SP 1120	EMD	1954

LEWIS & CLARK RAILWAY

The Lewis & Clark Railway operates freight and excursion service from Battle Ground to Moulton Falls (10 miles) and Chelatchie (19 miles) on a former Northern Pacific branch (later Longview, Portland & Northern). Passengers have a choice of open cars or coaches, and the snack caboose offers cupola seating.

The engine is one of three ex-Southern Pacific SW8s, two of which are unusual in that they are equipped with dynamic brakes (they were originally assigned to the Northwestern Pacific Railroad).

Battle Ground is in southwest Washington, a few miles northwest of Vancouver. From Exit 30 of I-205, follow Washington Route 503 north; from Exits 9 and 14 of I-5, follow Route 502 east. The station is on Main Street in Battle Ground. There are restaurants nearby; lodging can be found along I-5 and throughout the Portland, Oregon-Vancouver, Wash., area.

Cars	Coaches, open car with benches
Displays	Steam locomotives, logging equipment
Schedule	Memorial Day weekend through September, weekends; June 15-Labor Day, daily: leave 11 a.m. and 1:15 and 3:30 p.m.
Fares	Adults $6.75, children 12 and under
Special events	$3.75, age 60 and over $5.75. Checks and credit cards accepted. Group discounts available. Spring and fall railfan excursions
Nearby attractions	Mount Rainier, Mount St. Helens
Mailing address	P. O. Box 921, Elbe, WA 98330
Phone	(206) 569-2588, 569-2507 year-round

LOCOMOTIVES

Number	Type	Former owner	Builder	Date
STEAM				
5	2-8-2	Carlton & Coast	Porter	1924
10	3-truck	Hillcrest Lumber	Climax	1928
91	3-truck	Kinzua Pine Mills	Heisler	1930
DIESEL				
30	S1	Northern Pacific Term.	Alco	1940
41	RSD1	Rock Island	Alco	1941
7012A	F9	Northern Pacific	EMD	1956

MOUNT RAINIER SCENIC RAILROAD

The Mount Rainier Scenic Railroad operates over a 7-mile portion of a former Milwaukee Road branch (originally the Tacoma Eastern) from Elbe, Washington, to a logging display and picnic area at Mineral. The line includes an 800'-long trestle over the Nisqually River and stretches of 3 percent grade, and affords a view of Mount Rainier. The round trip takes 1½ hours. Live music and entertainment are featured during the ride. Train operation is subject to cancellation in bad weather. Elbe is about 40 miles south-southeast of Tacoma on Route 7; from the south, take U. S. 12 east from I-5 to Morton, then follow Route 7 north to Elbe. Snacks are available at Elbe and Mineral. There is a railroad-theme restaurant next to the Elbe station; the nearest lodging is 6 miles away in Ashford.

Cars	4 streetcars
Schedule	Weekdays 7:15 a.m.-6:30 p.m., week-ends and holidays 8:45 a.m.-11 p.m. Cars run every 20-30 minutes.
Fares	Age 5-64, 55 cents off-peak, 75 cents peak periods; age 65 and over, 25 cents; or valid Metro pass or transfer. All-day pass: weekdays $2.50, weekends $1.
Nearby attractions	Underground Seattle, Pike Place Public Market, Seattle Aquarium, Waterfront Park, ferries, Seattle Center, Space Needle
Mailing address	Metro, 821 Second Avenue, Seattle, WA 98104
Phone	(206) 684-4800

WATERFRONT STREETCAR

Seattle's transit system, Metro, includes a streetcar line along the waterfront between South Main Street and Broad Street, about 1 mile. The streetcars on the line are from Melbourne, Australia, and were built in 1927. At each station there are ticket-vending and bill-changing machines.

The north terminal at Broad Street is six blocks southwest of the Seattle Center, site of the 1962 World's Fair. The south terminal of the line, Pioneer Square, is about four blocks west of the Amtrak station, but a half-mile extension is under construction and should be in service by summer 1990.

Locomotives	2 steam, 3 diesel
Cars	Steel coaches and combine, observation car, open car
Displays	Steam, gasoline, diesel, and electric locomotives, interurbans, trolleys, passenger and freight cars, logging and mining railroad equipment
Schedule	April-October, Sundays; also Saturdays and holidays May-September; also Friday, June-Labor Day weekend: leave Snoqualmie 11 a.m. and 12:30, 2, and 3:30 p.m., also 5 p.m. Memorial Day weekend-Labor Day weekend; leave North Bend 30 minutes later. Charter trips available.
Fares	Adults $6, children 3-13 $4 (under 3 free), age 62 and over $5. Local checks accepted. Group discounts available.
Memberships	$20 per year
Nearby attractions	Snoqualmie Falls, state fish hatchery, hiking trails
Mailing address	P. O. Box 459, Snoqualmie, WA 98065
Phone	(206) 888-3030; (206) 746-4025 year-round and for recorded information

PUGET SOUND & SNOQUALMIE VALLEY RAILROAD

The Puget Sound Railway Historical Association operates 5 miles of a former Northern Pacific branch between North Bend and Snoqualmie as the Puget Sound & Snoqualmie Valley Railroad. The train takes 70 minutes to make the 10-mile round trip along a scenic valley; on the way it passes a 268-foot-high waterfall. On display are more than 100 locomotives and cars. Passengers may board at either North Bend or Snoqualmie. Both stations are just off I-90 about 30 miles east of Seattle; the Snoqualmie station is at 109 King Street. Food and drink are not allowed on the train, but there is a snack bar next to the Snoqualmie depot and restaurants in Snoqualmie and North Bend. Lodging can be found in North Bend; reservations are advised in summer.

Locomotives	1 steam, 1 gas-mechanical, 1 locomotive crane, 2 speeders
Cars	Covered flat cars with benches, cabooses
Displays	Logging and logging railroad equipment
Dates open	January-October, Wednesday-Sunday and holidays, 10 a.m.-4 p.m.; April and May and summer weekdays, open till 5; summer weekends, open till 6.
Schedule	Speeders operate weekends and holidays in April and May, noon-4 p.m; and Memorial Day through September, Wednesday-Friday, 11-4. Steam trains operate Memorial Day through September weekends and holidays, 11-6. Charter trips available.
Fares	Adults $2, children 3-11 $1, age 65 and over $1, speeder rides $1. Local checks accepted. Group discounts available by prior arrangement.
Memberships	Write for information.
Special events	Steam Logging Spectacular (April, biennial), School Days, Speeder Festival, Santa Train (December 8, 9, 15, and 16, 1990, 10-4)
Nearby attractions	Fort Nisqually, Point Defiance Zoo, Old Steilacoom, Mount Rainier, Mount St. Helens, Seattle
Mailing address	Tacoma Chapter, NRHS, P. O. Box 340, Tacoma, WA 98401
Phone	(206) 752-0047

P & 두

CAMP SIX LOGGING EXHIBIT

The Tacoma Chapter of the National Railway Historical Society operates the Point Defiance, Quinault & Klickitat Railroad on the property of the Camp Six Logging Exhibit of the Western Forest Industries Museum.

The museum is in Point Defiance Park in the city of Tacoma, at the tip of the peninsula that separates Commencement Bay from The Narrows. Food is available within the park, and there are restaurants in Ruston, 5 minutes away.

Locomotives	1 steam, 1 gasoline
Cars	Coaches, coffee-shop car
Schedule	July and August, Saturdays, leave Wickersham 11 a.m. and 1 p.m. Charter trips and charter cars operated.
Fares	Adults $8, children under 18 $4. Checks accepted. Group discounts available.
Special events	Valentine Train (February 9, 1991), Easter Bunny Train, Autumn Train, Santa Claus Christmas Trains (December 1, 8, 15, and 22), all at 11 a.m. and 1 p.m. Reservations required for Autumn and Santa Claus trains.
Nearby attractions	Puget Sound, Anacortes Railway, North Cascades National Park, Mt. Baker National Forest
Mailing address	P. O. Box 91, Acme, WA 98220
Phone	(206) 595-2218

LOCOMOTIVES

Number	Type	Former owner	Builder	Date
STEAM				
1070	0-6-0	Northern Pacific	Alco (Manchester)	1907
GASOLINE				
3		Mt. Vernon Terminal	Plymouth	1944

LAKE WHATCOM RAILWAY

The Lake Whatcom Railway operates over a 4-mile portion of the former Northern Pacific branch from Wickersham to Bellingham, Washington. The usual motive power is Northern Pacific 0-6-0 No. 1070; the coaches are also former Northern Pacific equipment.

Wickersham is on State Route 9 southeast of Bellingham and about 30 miles south of the Canadian border. Take the Route 20 ex from I-5 and drive 7 miles east to Sedro Woolley, then 11 mile north to Wickersham. Refreshments are available on the trair There are restaurants in Acme, 5 miles north of Wickersham, an motels in Sedro Woolley.

Locomotive	1 diesel
Cars	Former Santa Fe coaches and dome lounge, former Reading Crusader observation car
Schedule	Dinner train, April-September, leaves Kennewick 6 p.m. Fridays, leaves Yakima 6 p.m. Saturdays. Brunch train, year-round, leaves Yakima 10 a.m. Sundays. Charter trips and charter cars available.
Fares	Friday and Saturday dinner, $45 ($50 in the dome); Sunday brunch $35 ($40 in the dome). Group discounts available.
Special events	Mother's Day and Father's Day dinner trains (in addition to brunch trains those days)
Nearby attractions	Antique shops, Historic Front Street, Track 29
Mailing address	32 North Front Street, Yakima, WA 98901
Phone	(509) 452-2336, (800) 876-RAIL

SPIRIT OF WASHINGTON DINNER TRAIN

The Washington Central Railroad operates a dinner train on two segments of its line, the former Northern Pacific main line: from Yakima to Ellensburg, 37 miles, and from Kennewick to Prosser, also 37 miles. Round trips take 3 hours.

Dinner trains operate during the spring and summer, Friday nights from Kennewick and Saturday nights from Yakima. A Sunday brunch train operates from Yakima year-round. The equipment comprises four cars built by Budd in 1937 and a Santa Fe dome lounge built by Pullman in 1947. The Yakima station is at 32 North Front Street; the Kennewick station is the former Northern Pacific depot. Scenery visible from the train includes the Columbia River Gorge and the Yakima River Canyon.

Cars	4 streetcars
Schedule	May 1 to mid-October, Saturdays, Sundays, and holidays, hourly noon-3 p.m.; July and August, Monday-Friday at 6:30 and 7:30 p.m. Charters available.
Fares	Adults $3, children 6-12 $1.50 (under 6 free if they do not occupy a seat), age 60 and over $1.50, family fare $9. Charters, $90 for a 1-hour trip boarding at carbarn. Checks accepted.
Memberships	Write for information.
Nearby attractions	Yakima Valley Museum, Yakima Indian Nation Cultural Center
Mailing address	Yakima Interurban Lines Association, P. O. Box 649, Yakima, WA 98907
Phone	(509) 575-1700

P & 🎁

YAKIMA INTERURBAN LINES ASSOCIATION

In 1985 Union Pacific abandoned its electrically operated subsidiary, the Yakima Valley Transportation Company, and donated its right of way and rolling stock to the city of Yakima. Included were two 1906-design streetcars from Oporto, Portugal, which had been running in excursion service since 1974. Two 1930 Brill Master Unit cars which originally ran in Yakima were returned to the system in 1989. The Yakima Interurban Lines Association was established to operate the streetcar excursions. The cars make a 1 hour round trip over 6 miles of track between the corner of 3r Avenue and Pine in Yakima and the town of Selah. The streetcar locomotive, and line car are all available for charter. The carbarn a South 3rd Avenue and West Pine in Yakima is open to view.

Food and lodging can be found in Yakima, Selah, and Wapato Yakima is on I-82 about 145 miles southeast of Seattle.

Locomotives	10 steam, 7 diesel
Cars	Open excursion cars
Displays	Logging equipment, passenger cars, cabooses, steam and diesel locomotives
Schedule	To Bald Knob (4 hours): Memorial Day-Labor Day, daily except Mondays; Labor Day through October, weekends; first two weeks of October, Wednesday-Sunday; leave Cass at noon. To Whittaker (2 hours): Saturday before Memorial Day-Labor Day, daily; Labor Day through October, weekends; leave Cass 11 a.m., 1 p.m., 3 p.m. (11 a.m. runs begin mid-June); first two weeks of October, Wednesday-Friday, leave Cass 1 and 3; weekends leave Cass 11, 1, and 3. Charter trips available.
Fares	Adults $11 to Bald Knob, $8 to Whittaker; children 6-11 $5 to Bald Knob, $4 to Whittaker (under 6 free); $1 discount for West Virginia seniors. Checks and credit cards accepted. Group discounts available.
Special events	Railfan Weekend (May), Saturday night dinner trains (June-August)
Nearby attractions	National Radio Astronomy Observatory, Seneca Caverns, Smoke Hole Caverns, Monongahela National Forest, Pearl Buck birthplace
Mailing address	P. O. Box 107, Cass, WV 24927
Phone	(304) 456-4300

CASS SCENIC RAILROAD

The Cass Scenic Railroad was established in 1961 by the state of West Virginia to operate excursion trains over a former logging railroad out of the town of Cass. It has become one of the most successful and interesting tourist railroads in North America. The line to the summit of Bald Knob climbs 2390 feet in 11 miles and includes stretches of 10 percent grade — up 10 feet for every 100 feet forward. Passengers may also choose a ride to Whittaker, 4 miles from Cass. Pets are not allowed on the train. Food and lodging are available in Cass; former lumber company houses have been refurbished for use as vacation lodging (reservations are necessary and can be made through the railroad). Cass is near the Virginia border about halfway between Covington, Va., and Elkins, W. Va.

Displays	1,200-square-foot Lionel layout
Dates open	Daily, 11 a.m.-5 p.m.; extended hours during summer and Christmas
Schedule	Trains operate daily on demand May-August; weekends only during spring and fall.
Admission	Zoo: adults $3.75, children and senior citizens $2.75. Checks and credit cards accepted. Group discounts available.
Fares	85 cents per person
Memberships	Write for information.
Nearby attractions	Victorian Wheeling, glass outlets, dog racing, historic National Road suspension bridge
Mailing address	Oglebay, Wheeling, WV 26003
Phone	(304) 242-3000

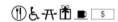

OGLEBAY

Oglebay is a 1,600-acre municipal park with gardens, a golf course, tennis courts, a museum, and a children's zoo. Within the zoo is a large, fully scenicked model railroad. Five Lionel trains run simultaneously, and scenic features include two operating boats in a river of real water and a working drive-in theater. Push buttons let visitors control items on the layout. There is also a miniature railroad with 1½ miles of track circling through the zoo; its locomotive is a replica of Southern Pacific's *C. P. Huntington*. The park is on State Route 88 about 3 miles northeast of downtown Wheeling. Food and lodging are available in the park as well as in Wheeling.

Cars	3 interurbans, 1 rapid transit car, 1 streetcar
Displays	Artifacts, cars under restoration
Schedule	Weekends May through October, cars leave East Troy at noon, 1:20, 2:40, and 4 p.m. Charter trips available.
Fares	Adults $5, children 6-12 $2.50. Checks accepted. Group discounts available.
Memberships	Write for information.
Special events	Railfan weekend, usually last weekend in April; Christmas Parade Train, first Saturday of December, leaves Mukwonago 6 p.m.
Nearby attractions	Lake Geneva, Old World Wisconsin, Kettle Moraine State Forest, Kettle Moraine Railway
Mailing address	222 North Charles Street, Waukesha, WI 53186
Phone	(414) 642-3263 during operations; year-round 542-5573

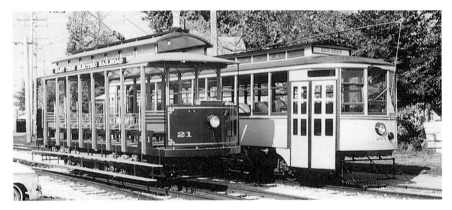

EAST TROY ELECTRIC RAILROAD

In 1939 the Milwaukee Electric Railway & Light Company abandoned its interurban line to East Troy, Wisconsin. The village of East Troy purchased the outermost 6 miles of the line to connect the industries in the village with the Soo Line at Mukwonago. The East Troy Electric Railroad operates on 5 miles of that track between East Troy and the intersection of County Highways ES and J at The Elegant Farmer, near Mukwonago.

The round trip takes an hour. East Troy is about 35 miles southwest of Milwaukee on Route 15. To reach the museum, take Exit 42 (Route 20) from Route 15 and go west on 20 a short distance to County Highway ES. Turn left on ES and follow it into East Troy, then turn right on Church Street and go two blocks to the museum.

There are restaurants in East Troy; lodging can be found in Lake Geneva, about 15 miles south.

East Troy

Displays	Approximately 80 locomotives and cars	**Special events**	Railroad Days (June 30-July 4, 1990)
Dates open	May 1-October 1, daily, 9 a.m.-5 p.m.	**Nearby attractions**	Green Bay Packer Hall of Fame, Heritage
Schedule	Trains run at 10 and 11:30 a.m. and 1, 2:30, and 4 p.m.		Hill State Park
		Mailing address	2285 South Broadway, Green Bay, WI
Admission	Adults $5.50, children 15 and under $2.75, age 62 and over $4.75. Checks and credit cards accepted. Group discounts available.		54304
		Phone	(414) 435-7245 (museum);
			(414) 437-7623 (offices)
Memberships	Write for information.		

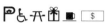

NATIONAL RAILROAD MUSEUM

The National Railroad Museum's extensive collection of locomotives and cars includes large, modern steam locomotives such as a Santa Fe 2-10-4, a Milwaukee Road 4-8-4, and a Union Pacific Big Boy.

The museum also has a number of diesel locomotives, including a Milwaukee Road E9 No. 38A and Green Bay & Western C430 No. 315, plus exotic items: a General Motors *Aerotrain* of 1955 (a lightweight streamliner with cars based on GM's intercity bus body and a locomotive styled along the lines of a 1955 Oldsmobile) and the London & North Eastern locomotive and cars that served a wartime staff headquarters for Dwight Eisenhower. Admission to the museum includes a train ride on a 1-mile loop of track.

The museum is located on the bank of the Fox River on the south side of Green Bay. Food and lodging are available in Green Bay.

Displays	2500 railroad models, operating layouts		Mid-Continent Railway Museum, River-
Dates open	Mid-May to mid-September, daily 10 a.m.-6 p.m.	**Nearby attractions**	side & Great Northern Railway, Circus World Museum, Wisconsin Dells
Admission	Adults $3.50, children 6-12 $1.75 (under 6 free). Credit cards accepted. Group discounts available.	**Mailing address**	S-2083 Herwig Road, Reedsburg, WI 53959
			(608) 254-8050

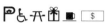

PARK LANE MODEL RAILROAD MUSEUM

The Park Lane Model Railroad Museum has a large collection of railroad models of all scales and ages plus several operating layouts and layouts under construction, among them the Z scale Western Pacific featured in MODEL RAILROADER Magazine in 1986. The museum is a few minutes southwest of Exit 89 (Route 23) of I-90 and I-94 at Lake Delton, near Wisconsin Dells. Follow Route 23 west; the museum is at the intersection of 23 and Herwig Road. Food and lodging can be found in Lake Delton and Wisconsin Dells.

Locomotive	1 steam
Cars	Coaches, cabooses
Dates open	June 16-August 25 (closed Sundays)
Schedule	Trains leave Laona hourly from 11 a.m. to 2 p.m.; trains leave Camp 5 Farm at 11:20, 12:20, 1:20, 3, and 4. Charter trips available for groups of 200 or more.
Admission	Adults $9.50, children 3-12 $4, tax additional. Checks and Elan Card are accepted. Discounts available for groups of 30 or more (reservations required).
Nearby attractions	Nicolet National Forest
Mailing address	Camp 5 Museum Foundation, Route 1, Laona, WI 54541 (summer); 1011 Eighth Street, Wausau, WI 54401 (winter)
Phone	(715) 674-3414 (summer), (715) 845-5544 (winter)

LAONA & NORTHERN RAILWAY

One of the attractions at Camp 5, a logging museum at Laona, Wisconsin, is the Laona & Northern's "Lumberjack Special" steam train ride to Camp 5 Farm. The train makes a 2½-mile, 15-minute run through forests and fields. The steam locomotive is a 2-6-2 built by Vulcan Iron Works, Wilkes-Barre, Pennsylvania, in 1916.

Other attractions at Camp 5 include the logging museum, a forest tour, an ecology walk, a nature center, and a domestic animal corral. Guided tours are available.

Snacks are available at Camp 5. Restaurants and lodging can be found in Laona, Crandon (12 miles west), and Rhinelander (40 miles west). Laona is on U. S. 8 and State Route 32 in northeast Wisconsin, about 90 miles north-northwest of Green Bay.

Displays	Soo Line 0-6-0, depot
Dates open	Memorial Day-Labor Day, daily; Labor Day-October 14, weekends: 10 a.m.-5 p.m.
Admission	Adults $3.50, students $1.50 (age 5 and under free), family (parents plus children through age 17) $10
Memberships	Write for information.
Nearby attractions	Manitowoc Maritime Museum, Rahr-West Art Museum, Zunkers Auto Museum, Rogers Street Fishing Village, Point Beach State Forest
Mailing address	Manitowoc County Historical Society, P. O. Box 574, Manitowoc, WI 54221-0574
Phone	(414) 684-5110; 684-4445 year-round

PINECREST HISTORICAL VILLAGE

Five miles west of the city of Manitowoc, the Manitowoc County Historical Society has gathered 17 historic structures from nearby towns to depict a typical rural village in Manitowoc County at the turn of the century. One of the buildings is the 1896 Soo Line depot from Collins, Wisconsin. Part of the station exhibit is Soo Line 0-6-0

No. 321, built in 1887. Special events are scheduled during the season and also in December.

Pinecrest Historical Village is about 3 miles west of Exit 79 of I-43 — follow highway JJ, then turn left on Pine Crest Lane. Food and lodging can be found in Manitowoc.

Locomotive	1 diesel (E9, ex-Milwaukee Road 32A, built 1956)
Cars	2 dome dining cars, 1 dome lounge-observation car, 1 kitchen car
Schedule	February 14-December 31, 1990: Tuesdays, train leaves at noon; Wednesdays and Fridays, 6:30 p.m.; Sundays, 1 p.m.; Thursdays and Saturdays, departure varies with season
Fares	Tuesday-Friday, $52; Saturdays and Sundays, $62 (including the meal). Checks and credit cards accepted. Group discount available.
Radio frequencies	160.575, 161.145
Nearby attractions	Milwaukee County Zoo, Summerfest, Horicon Marsh Wildlife Area, Kettle Moraine State Forest, Kettle Moraine Railway
Mailing address	11340 West Brown Deer Road, Milwaukee, WI 53224
Phone	(414) 354-5544

SCENIC RAIL DINING

Scenic Rail Dining operates dinner trains over the rails of the Wisconsin & Southern Railroad from a station in the extreme northwest corner of Milwaukee to Horicon, 38 miles, and back. Power for the train is an E9; the cars are elegantly rebuilt, immaculately maintained former Union Pacific equipment. [The service is equally elegant; the food, which is superb, combines cosmopolitan sophistication in its choice and preparation and Milwaukee's own ideas on large portion sizes. — G.H.D.]

The round trip takes 4 hours. To reach the station at 11340 West Brown Deer Road, take the Brown Deer Road (Route 100) exit from I-43 north of downtown Milwaukee and drive west 7 miles. Brown Deer Road becomes Route 74 just east of the station. From the west and northwest, use the Main Street (Route 74) exit of U. S. 41-45 in Menomonee Falls and go east about 2 miles.

Lodging is available at the intersection of U. S. 41-45 and Route 74 and throughout metropolitan Milwaukee.

	Cars	Steel, open-vestibule coaches
	Displays	Turn-of-the-century locomotives, freight and passenger cars, and work equipment
	Dates open	May 14-Labor Day, 1990, daily; Labor Day-October 21, weekends: 9:30 a.m.-5 p.m.
	Schedule	Trains leave at 10:30, 12:30, 2, and 3:30. Charter trips available.
	Fares	Adults $6, children 5-15 $3, family $18, age 62 and over $5. Checks and credit cards accepted. Group discounts available.
	Memberships	Mid-Continent Railway Historical Society — write for information.
	Special events	Autumn Color Weekends (first two weekends of October), Snow Train (third weekend of February)
	Nearby attractions	Circus World Museum, Park Lane Model Railroad Museum, Wisconsin Dells, Devils Lake State Park
	Mailing address	P. O. Box 55, North Freedom, WI 53951
	Phone	(608) 522-4261

LOCOMOTIVES

Number	Type	Former owner	Builder	Date
STEAM				
1	4-6-0	Western Coal & Coke	Montreal	1913
2	2-8-2	Saginaw Timber	Baldwin	1912
1385	4-6-0	Chicago & North Western	Alco	1907
GAS-ELECTRIC				
31		Montana Western	EMD	1925

P & 🚹 🎁

MID-CONTINENT RAILWAY MUSEUM

The Mid-Continent Railway Museum was founded in 1959 and moved from its original location at Hillsboro, Wisconsin, to North Freedom in 1963. It operates 4½ miles of a former Chicago & North Western branch line originally built to serve iron mines in the area.

The museum specializes in equipment and operation of the 1885-1915 era and offers a 45- to 60-minute train ride through woods and farmland. The museum's Chicago & North Western 4-6-0 No. 1385 has been operated and exhibited system-wide by the C&NW in recent years. North Freedom is about 45 miles northwest of Madison.

To reach the museum from the south and east take the Route 33 exit from I-90 and I-94 west of Portage; follow 33 west to West Baraboo. From the north, leave the interstate on U. S. 12 south of Wisconsin Dells and go south to West Baraboo; from there follow Route 136 and County Highway PF to North Freedom. There are restaurants in North Freedom and motels in Baraboo.

Cars	Steel coaches and combine, cabooses, open car
Schedule	June through third Sunday of October plus Labor Day, Sundays at 1, 2:30, and 4 p.m.; also 11 a.m. on the first three Sundays of October. Charter trips available.
Fares	Adults $5.50, children 3-11 $2.750 (under 3 free), age 60 and over 10
Special events	Ice Cream Social
Nearby attractions	Kettle Moraine State Forest, East Troy Electric Railroad, Holy Hill, Mapleton Cheese Factory, Honey Acres
Mailing address	Box 247, North Lake, WI 53064
Phone	(414) 782-8074, 966-2866

percent discount. Checks accepted. Group discounts available.

LOCOMOTIVES

Number	Type	Former owner	Builder	Date
STEAM				
9	2-6-2	McCloud River	Baldwin	1901
3	2-truck	Craig Mountain Railway	Heisler	1917
GASOLINE AND GAS-ELECTRIC				
M-3	0-4-0	U. S. Air Force	Davenport	
M-1000		Chicago Great Western	McKeen	1914

KETTLE MORAINE RAILWAY

The Kettle Moraine Railway operates a 4½-mile portion of the former North Lake branch of the Milwaukee Road. The train ride through the rolling countryside includes several steep grades and lakes and takes approximately an hour. The usual locomotive is ex-McCloud River 2-6-2 No. 9. North Lake is on the northwest fringes of suburban Milwaukee.

To reach the station at North Lake, take State Route 83 north from either I-94 or U. S. 16 about 23 miles west of downtown Milwaukee. North Lake is 9 miles north of I-94 and 7 miles south of Holy Hill.

There are restaurants in North Lake; motels can be found along I-94 toward Milwaukee.

Locomotives	1 gasoline (5-ton Whitcomb)
Cars	Modified ore cars
Displays	Ore railroad equipment
Dates open	May-October, daily 9 a.m.-4 p.m. Group tours year-round by appointment.
Admission	Adults $3.50, children 5-15 $1.50 (under 5 free), age 65 and over $3.
Fares	Admission includes train ride; train ride alone, 50 cents
Memberships	Write for information.
Special events	Mine Day
Nearby attractions	Mitchell-Rountree Stone Cottage,

Checks accepted. Discount available for groups of 20 or more.

| Mailing address | Wisconsin's first capital, Wisconsin Shakespeare Festival, Chicago Bears training camp, City of Platteville — Museum Department, P. O. Box 52, Platteville, WI 53818 |
| Phone | (608) 348-3301 |

THE MINING MUSEUM & ROLLO JAMISON MUSEUM

The Mining Museum traces the development of lead and zinc mining in the upper Mississippi Valley. Along with photos, artifacts, and dioramas there is a tour of an 1845 lead mine and a ride around the grounds on a 24"-gauge mine train.

The Rollo Jamison Museum has a large collection depicting turn-of-the-century residential and commercial life. On the second floor of the mining museum is an art gallery featuring work by local artists. There are 90 steps down into the mine, and the temperature there is 52 degrees year-round — comfortable shoes and a jacket are suggested.

Platteville is on U. S. Highway 151 in the southwest corner of Wisconsin. Food and lodging can be found there.

Locomotives	2 steam
Cars	Open-window coaches
Dates open	Memorial Day-Labor Day, daily; Labor Day through October, weekends: 10 a.m.-6 p.m. Open for groups at other times by advance arrangement. Charter trips available.
Fares	Adults $3, children 12 and under $2
Memberships	Riverside & Great Northern Preservation Society — write for information
Special events	Opening Day, May 15, 1990
Nearby attractions	Mid-Continent Railway Museum, Park Lane Model Railroad Museum, Circus World Museum
Mailing address	P. O. Box 842, Wisconsin Dells, WI 53965
Phone	(608) 254-6367

STEAM LOCOMOTIVES

Number	Type	Former owner	Builder	Date
82	4-4-0	Milwaukee County Zoo	Sandley	1957
Tom Thumb	0-4-0	Riverside & Great Northern	Sandley	1961

RIVERSIDE & GREAT NORTHERN RAILWAY

The Riverside & Great Northern Railway was opened in 1954, a project of the Sandley Light Railway Equipment Works. It is a 15"-gauge line on a short stretch of the old right of way of the La Crosse & Milwaukee Railroad (replaced in 1902 by the double-track main line of the Milwaukee Road, now Soo Line).

The railway has lain dormant for the past eight years but has been revived and will again carry passengers in 1990. The Riverside & Great Northern station is on Stand Rock Road, County Highway A, a mile north of the Wisconsin Dells business district.

Wisconsin Dells is on I-90 and I-94 about 110 miles from Milwaukee and 85 miles from La Crosse. Food and lodging are available in Wisconsin Dells, a tourist area.

Mailing address   P. O. Box 1653, Laramie, WY 82070
Phone   (307) 742-9162

DIESEL LOCOMOTIVES

Number	Type	Former owner	Builder	Date
510, 1512	FP7	Alaska Railroad	EMD	1952
511	F7B	Alaska Railroad	EMD	1953

WYOMING & COLORADO RAILROAD

The Wyoming & Colorado offers occasional excursion trains on its line from Laramie south to Fox Park, Wyoming, and Walden, Colorado, 94 miles. Motive power is a set of F units; passengers ride in Budd-built cars of the early 1950s, including domes. The round trip takes 6 to 8 hours. The route is the former Laramie, North Park & Western Railroad. At press time, schedules and fares had not been established; call for information.

Food and lodging are available in Laramie.

Cars	Wood and steel coaches
Displays	4 locomotives; business, passenger, freight, and work cars
Dates open	May 19-September 3, 1990, daily 10 a.m.-6 p.m. (until 4 weekdays in May and June); September 8-October 8, 1990, weekends and holidays 10-5
Admission	Adults $5.50, youths 12-17 $4, children 11 and under $2.75, age 65 and over $4.50. Credit cards accepted. Group discounts available.
Fares	$1 per person
Memberships	Write for information.
Special events	Railway Days (July 21-22, 1990)
Nearby attractions	Glenbow Museum, Calgary Tower, Calgary Zoo and Prehistoric Park, Calgary Stampede, Banff National Park
Mailing address	1900 Heritage Drive S. W., Calgary, AB T2V 2X3
Phone	(403) 255-1182; for recorded information (403) 252-1858

STEAM LOCOMOTIVES

Number	Type	Former owner	Builder	Date
4	0-6-0	Canmore Mines	CPR	1905
2023	0-6-0	Pacific Coast Terminals	Alco	1942
2024	0-6-0	Pacific Coast Terminals	Lima	1944

HERITAGE PARK HISTORICAL VILLAGE

Heritage Park Historical Village presents a re-creation of life in western Canada before 1915. More than 100 antique buildings have been acquired and moved to the 66-acre park to portray a town; only a few structures are reproductions.

Circling the park is a ⅞-mile loop of track; every 20 minutes a steam-powered train makes a circuit of the loop, stopping at three stations. Passengers may get off at any station to see the exhibits nearby, then reboard the train. A roundhouse and turntable are open to view. Two streetcars, replicas of cars that ran in Calgary, carry visitors from the parking lot to the main gate.

There are restaurants and snack bars in the park; food and lodging can be found in Calgary. The park is in southwest Calgary on the east shore of Glenmore Reservoir. Take Glenmore Trail (the South-West Bypass) to 14th Street S. W., then 14th Street south to Heritage Drive.

Cars	Coaches, cabooses
Displays	60 locomotives and cars
Dates open	May 17-September 3, 1990, Thursday-Monday, 10 a.m.-6 p.m.
Admission	Adults $3, children 18 and uner $2, age 60 and over $2. There is a fee for parking.
Fares	Free
Memberships	Write for information.
Nearby attractions	Alberta Wildlife Park, Elk Island National Park
Mailing address	Box 6102, Station C, Edmonton, AB T5B 4K5
Phone	(403) 472-6229; (403) 486-0234 year-round

LOCOMOTIVES

Number	Type	Former owner	Builder	Date
STEAM				
3	2-8-0	Northern Alberta Railways	Canadian Locomotive Co.	1927
392	4-6-0	Canadian National	Montreal	1913
DIESEL				
619	S-11	Canadian Pacific	Montreal	1959
944	NW2	Canadian National	EMD	1946
000	F3A	Canadian National	EMD	1948

ALBERTA RAILROAD MUSEUM

The Alberta Railroad Museum was established in 1964 by the Alberta Pioneer Railway Association. Its extensive collection of rolling stock is the largest in western Canada and encompasses steam and diesel locomotives and a full variety of passenger, freight, and work cars.

The museum offers a 15-minute ride on a half-mile of track. Steam locomotives operate on Canadian holiday weekends: In 1990 they are May 19-21, June 30-July 2, August 4-6, and September 1-3.

The museum is located at 24215 34 Street in the northeast corner of Edmonton. To reach the museum, follow Route 28 (97 Street) north to Namao, Route 37 east to 34 Street, and 34 Street south to the museum. There are motels and restaurants within 3 miles of the museum.

Displays	Completely restored Trans-Canada Limited train, 1900 station		
Dates open	June-August, daily 9 a.m.-8 p.m.; rest of the year daily noon-5		
Admission	Art gallery: free; viewing corridor: family $4, adults $2, seniors and students $1 (children under 5 free); guided tour of interior of train:		

	adults $1.50 extra, seniors and students 75 cents extra, children under 5 50 cents extra. Credit cards accepted. Group discounts available.
Memberships	Write for information.
Special events	Great Train dinners, Labor Day Railroad Caper

Nearby attractions	Fort Steele Historic Park and Steam Railway, Wildlife Museum, Kimberley Bavarian City
Mailing address	Box 400, Cranbrook, BC V1C 4H9
Phone	(604) 489-3918

CRANBROOK RAILWAY MUSEUM

The Cranbrook Railway Museum, operated by the Cranbrook Archives, Museum, and Landmark Foundation, features a restored Trans-Canada Limited train, one of ten luxurious train sets built in 1929 for the Canadian Pacific Railway. The train includes a baggage-sleeper that was used as a crew dormitory, a dining car, three sleepers, and a solarium-lounge. The cars are notable for the wood paneling and inlay work of their interiors. A 1928 business car and a station built in 1900 are also on exhibit. A steam locomotive will be added to the display in the future.

The museum is at 1 Van Horne Street North, downtown. Cranbrook is in southeast British Columbia on Routes 3 and 95; food and lodging can be found within two blocks of the museum.

Cars	Flatcar, 1955 British Railways coach
Displays	Coach, caboose, snowplow, private car of the Duke of Sutherland
Dates open	May-October, daily 10 a.m.-5 p.m.; June 16-September 3, 1990, 9:30-5:30
Schedule	June 29-September 3 — times not determined at press time. Charter trips available.
Admission	[1989 rates] Adults $5, children 6-12 $1, ages 13-18 and 65 and over $3
Fares	[1989 fares] Adults $3.50, children under 13 $1.50, ages 13-18 and 65 and over $2.50
Memberships	Write for information.

Nearby attractions	Cranbrook Railway Museum, Kootenay Trout Hatchery, Kimberley Bavarian City, provincial parks
Mailing address	Fort Steele, BC V0B 1N0
Phone	(602) 489-3351; (604) 426-6923 for recorded information

STEAM LOCOMOTIVES

Number	Type	Former owner	Builder	Date
115	Shay	Merrill, Ring & Wilson Timber	Lima	1934
1077			Montreal	1923
Dunrobin		Duke of Sutherland	Sharp, Stewart & Co.	1895

FORT STEELE HERITAGE TOWN

The town of Fort Steele was the commercial center of the East Kootenays until a railroad was constructed into the area — through nearby Cranbrook instead of Fort Steele. Fort Steele's population dwindled and its buildings fell into disrepair. It has been restored as a turn-of-the-century village, complete with a steam railroad. Fort Steele is in southeast British Columbia, about 10 miles northeast of Cranbrook on Routes 93 and 95. Food and lodging are available in Cranbrook.

Locomotives	3 steam (two 0-4-0T, one Shay)
Cars	Roofed excursion cars
Displays	Logging industry exhibits
Dates open	May-late September, daily 9:30 a.m.-6 p.m.
Schedule	Train runs every half hour
Admission	Adults $4.50, age 13-18 $3.50, children 6-12 $2 (under 6 free), age 65 and over $3.50.

Admission includes train ride. Credit cards accepted. Group discounts available.

Nearby attractions	Chemainus, Victoria
Mailing address	RR 4, Trans-Canada Highway, Duncan, BC V9L 3W8
Phone	(604) 746-1251

P & ⛟ 🎁 ▣

BRITISH COLUMBIA FOREST MUSEUM

The British Columbia Forest Museum, established in 1957, displays and interprets the lumber industry of British Columbia. It includes the Cowichan Valley Railway, 1½ miles of 3'-gauge track, on which three steam locomotives, a Shay and two Vulcan-built 0-4-0Ts, pull excursion trains. Access to the train is possible for the handicapped; it may be difficult elsewhere in the museum, but the staff will assist. The museum is about a mile north of Duncan on Highway 1. Duncan is on Vancouver Island about 40 miles north of Victoria and 30 miles south of Nanaimo. There are restaurants and motels in Duncan.

Cars	Ex-Canadian Pacific coach, crew car
Schedule	Weekends and holidays July 1-Labor Day, 11 a.m.-4 p.m., on the hour
Fares	Adults $2, children 6-16 $1 (5 and under free), age 65 and over $1. Checks accepted.
Memberships	Write for information.
Special events	Christmas Eve Santa Run
Nearby attractions	Lady Rose Alberni Inlet trips, Harbor Quay
Mailing address	4608 Tenth Avenue, Port Alberni, BC V9Y 4Y2
Phone	(604) 724-3441

LOCOMOTIVES

Number	Type	Former owner	Builder	Date
STEAM				
2	Shay	Alberni Pacific Lumber	Lima	1912
GASOLINE AND DIESEL				
7	Buda	McLean Lumber	Westminster Iron Works	1928
11	45 ton	MacMillan Bloedel	GE	1942

P & ⛟ 🎁

WESTERN VANCOUVER ISLAND INDUSTRIAL HERITAGE SOCIETY

The Western Vancouver Island Industrial Heritage Society offers train rides along 1½ miles of waterfront industrial track in Port Alberni. Trains depart from the former Canadian Pacific station; the ride takes 25 minutes round trip. Port Alberni is on Vancouver Island, about 50 miles west of Nanaimo and 115 miles from Victoria, at the head of Alberni Inlet. Food and lodging are available within ¼ mile of the railway.

Locomotive	1 steam (Canadian Pacific 4-6-4 No. 2860)
Cars	Air-conditioned coaches, snack car
Schedule	May 20-September 30, 1990, Wednesday-Sunday (daily July 1-Labor Day), boat leaves Vancouver 9:30 a.m., train leaves North Vancouver 10:30. Train returns to North Vancouver 4 p.m., shuttle bus arrives Vancouver 4:30; boat arrives Vancouver 4:30, shuttle bus arrives North Vancouver 5 p.m.
Fares	Train round trip: Adults $24, youth (age 12-18) $20, children 5-11 $14 (under 5 free), age 65 and over $20. Train and boat: Adults $42, youths and seniors $38, children $25 (under 5 free). Credit cards accepted. Group discounts available. Tickets are available through travel agents, the Vancouver Travel Information Centre, and Harbour Ferries.
Mailing address	Harbour Ferries Ltd., No. 202, 1810 Alberni, Vancouver, BC V6G 1B3
Phone	(604) 688-7246 (or 68-TRAIN); Western Canada and U. S., (800) 663-1500

ROYAL HUDSON STEAM TRAIN

The Royal Hudson Steam Train Society and Harbour Ferries Ltd. team up to offer a boat-and-train excursion between Vancouver and Squamish, about 40 miles — boat in one direction and train in the other, and there is also the option of riding the train both ways.

The train uses BC Rail tracks along the shore of Howe Sound. The line was opened in 1956 by the Pacific Great Eastern (BC Rail's original name), extending PGE's line south from its long-time terminal at Squamish to Vancouver. BC Rail operates regular passenger trains on its scenic line to Lillooet and Prince George.

Motive power is Royal Hudson No. 2860, built by Montreal Locomotive Works in 1940 for Canadian Pacific. The train that carried King George VI and Queen Elizabeth from Quebec to Vancouver in 1939 was pulled by Hudson No. 2850, which was adorned with cast metal replicas of crowns on its running board skirting. After the trip, with Royal assent, CPR applied crowns to all 45 of its semistreamlined Hudsons and designated them "Royal Hudsons."

The boat departs from the north foot of Denman Street in Vancouver, between the Westin Bayshore Hotel and Stanley Park. The train departs from 1311 West 1st Street in North Vancouver, across the harbor from Vancouver. At the end of the trip shuttle buses return you to your starting point.

There is a snack bar on the train, and a salmon dinner is available on the boat. There are picnic facilities in Squamish.

Locomotive	1 steam
Cars	5 wood coaches, 1 steel coach
Schedule	June-September, Sundays, leave Winnipeg 11 a.m. and 3 p.m. Charter trips available.
Fares	Adults $10, youths 12-17 $8, children 2-11 $5 (under 2 free if not occupying a seat), age 65 and over $8
Memberships	Write for information.
Special events	Fall foliage trips (last Saturday of September and first Saturday of October)
Nearby attractions	Manitoba Museum of Man and Nature, Western Canada Aviation Museum, Winnipeg Mint
Mailing address	Vintage Locomotive Society, Box 217, St. James P. O., Winnipeg, MB R3J 3R4
Phone	(204) 832-5259

PRAIRIE DOG CENTRAL

   Using the name Prairie Dog Central, the Vintage Locomotive Society operates excursion trains from Winnipeg northwest to Grosse Isle, Manitoba, over 18 miles of Canadian National Railways' Oakpoint Subdivision. The locomotive, an ex-Canadian Pacific 4-4-0 built in 1882 by Dübs & Company of Glasgow, Scotland, is the oldest locomotive operating on a Class 1 railroad in Canada.

   The train departs from Canadian National's St. James station on Portage Avenue west of St. James Street, west of downtown Winnipeg and southeast of the airport. The 36-mile round trip takes 2 hours.

   Refreshments and souvenirs are available on the train; souvenirs can also be purchased at the station.

Winnipeg

Displays	Mail car, coach, sleeper	**Mailing address**	Government of Newfoundland and
Dates open	Late June through August, daily, 9 a.m.-8 p.m.		Labrador, Department of Development and
Admission	Free		Tourism, St. John's, NF A1C 5T7
Memberships	Write for information.	**Phone**	(800) 563-6353 (Department of Develop-
Nearby attractions	Signal Hill National Historic Park		ment and Tourism)

NEWFOUNDLAND AND LABRADOR MUSEUM OF TRANSPORTATION

The Newfoundland Transportation Society has a museum on a 4-acre site in Pippy Park in St. John's. The collection includes a mail car, a coach, and a sleeping car from Canadian National Railway's 3'6"-gauge Newfoundland lines. The park is on Mount Scio Road in St. John's. There is a restaurant in Pippy Park; food and lodging can be found in the city of St. John's.

Displays	Caboose, several passenger and freight cars
Dates open	June-September, daily 9 a.m-5 p.m. (until 7 p.m. during July and August)
Admission	Free
Memberships	Write for information.
Special events	Annual Reunion (second Sunday of September)
Nearby attractions	Fortress of Louisbourg National Historic Park
Mailing address	P. O. Box 225, Louisbourg, NS B0A 1M0
Phone	(902) 733-2720, 733-2767 year-round

SYDNEY & LOUISBURG RAILWAY MUSEUM

The Sydney & Louisburg Railway Historical Society operates a museum in the former S&L station in Louisbourg, Nova Scotia. The station was built in 1895, and several pieces of rolling stock are on display there. In addition to the railroad items, there are exhibits of marine items, including a collection of watercolors, and displays depicting life in Louisbourg. Louisbourg is about 22 miles from Sydney, near the eastern tip of Cape Breton Island.

There is a restaurant next door; lodging options include a motel and numerous bed-and-breakfasts.

	[1988 information]
Displays	School car
Dates open	May 24-June 30 and Labor Day-September 30, weekends and holidays 2-5 p.m.; July and August, weekends and holidays 11 a.m.-7 p.m., weekdays, 2-7
Admission	Free
Memberships	$5 per year
Nearby attractions	Town Hall, Piano Factory, Benmiller Inn, Blyth Festival, Lake Huron beaches
Mailing address	Box 400, Clinton, ON N0M 1L0
Phone	(519) 482-9583

P&A

ORIGINAL CNR SCHOOL ON WHEELS 15089

In 1926 the province of Ontario put into service a school car — a coach rebuilt to contain a classroom and living quarters for a teacher. It was an experiment in educating children in remote areas. It was a success, and soon seven such cars were traveling through northern Ontario. In 1982 one of the cars, No. 15089 was discovered in derelict condition. The town of Clinton, home of Fred Sloman, who had taught on that car for 38 years, recognized the value of the car, purchased it, and placed it in the Sloman Memorial Park in Clinton to be restored by volunteers. The park is on Victoria Terrace, off Victoria Street (Route 4) two blocks south of the Canadian National crossing in Clinton. Clinton is 33 miles northwest of Stratford; food and lodging are available in Clinton.

Displays	Steam locomotive, passenger cars, caboose	Nearby attractions	Polar Bear Express, Drury Park
Dates open	June 22-September 3, 1990, daily 10 a.m.-10 p.m.	Mailing address	P. O. Box 490, Cochrane, ON P0L 1C0
Admission	Adults $1, children 16 and under $1, age 60 and over $1, families $3	Phone	(705) 272-3327, 272-4361 year-round

P&A🎁

COCHRANE RAILWAY AND PIONEER MUSEUM

Cochrane, Ontario, was incorporated in 1910 at the junction of two railways, the Temiskaming & Northern Ontario (now Ontario Northland) and the National Transcontinental (now a secondary line of the Canadian National). When a museum of Cochrane's pioneer days was established in 1970 it was appropriate that the railroads be included. Among the museum's displays are T&NO 2-8-0 No. 137, a CN caboose, a CN baggage car housing displays of pioneer life, and a CN coach that contains a model railroad and numerous railroad artifacts.

The museum is at the Ontario Northland-VIA station at Railway Street and Seventh Avenue in Cochrane. Food and lodging are available across the street.

Displays	2 stations, 2 steam locomotives, caboose, artifacts
Dates open	May 1-June 15, weekends; June 15-Labor Day, daily; Labor Day-Thanksgiving (October 8, 1990), weekends: 11 a.m.-5 p.m.
Admission	Adults $2; children under 13, 50 cents. Checks accepted. Group discounts available.
Memberships	Write for information.
Nearby attractions	Niagara Falls, Willowby Museum, Battlefield Museum
Mailing address	P. O. Box 339, Ridgeway, ON L0S 1N0
Phone	(416) 871-1412; (416) 894-5322 year-round

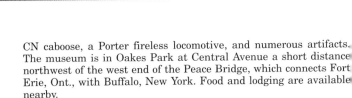

FORT ERIE RAILROAD MUSEUM

The Fort Erie Railroad Museum has two station buildings originally belonging to the Grand Trunk Railway: One is GT's first station in Fort Erie, built in 1873; the other (built in 1891) is from Ridgeway, Ontario, 8 miles away.

On display at the museum are Canadian National 4-8-4 6218, a CN caboose, a Porter fireless locomotive, and numerous artifacts. The museum is in Oakes Park at Central Avenue a short distance northwest of the west end of the Peace Bridge, which connects Fort Erie, Ont., with Buffalo, New York. Food and lodging are available nearby.

Dates open	May 1-Labor Day, daily 10 a.m.-8 p.m.; remainder of the year open 9-5, closed Mondays, but open on Mondays that are holidays
Admission	Adults $4, seniors and students $3, children $1, family $8. Group rates available.
Schedule	Steam trains operate to Hull May 12, 13, 14, 20, and 21, June 24, July 8 and 22, and August 12 and 26, 1990; to Brockville September 16, to Pembroke October 7, and to Hawksbury October 14, 1990.
Fares	Hull: Adults $16, children 3-12 $10; Brockville, Pembroke, and Hawksbury: $60 per person
Nearby attractions	Parliament buildings, National Aviation Museum
Mailing address	1867 St. Laurent Boulevard, Ottawa, ON K1G 5A3
Phone	(613) 991-3044

STEAM LOCOMOTIVES ON DISPLAY

Railroad	Number	Type	Builder	Date
Grand Trunk	40	4-4-0	Portland	1873
Grand Trunk	247	0-6-0T	GTR	1895
Canadian Pacific	926	4-6-0	CPR	1912
Canadian Pacific	2858	4-6-4	Montreal	1938
Canadian Pacific	3100	4-8-4	CPR	1928
Canadian National	6200	4-8-4	Montreal	1942
Canadian National	6400	4-8-4	Montreal	1936

NATIONAL MUSEUM OF SCIENCE AND TECHNOLOGY

Among the displays in Ottawa's National Museum of Science and Technology are seven steam locomotives and several passenger cars.

Another locomotive, CPR 4-6-2 No. 1201, built by Canadian Pacific's Angus Shops in 1944, operates occasionally under the sponsorship of the Bytown Railway Society, usually to Hull, Quebec, across the Ottawa River from Ottawa, but occasionally to more distant points. Train tickets are available from the museum or Bytown

Railway Society, P. O. Box 141, Station A, Ottawa, ON K1N 8V1.

The museum is southeast of downtown Ottawa on St. Laurent Boulevard south of Queensway East (Route 417). City buses can take you there from downtown or the VIA station — the museum is about 2 miles from the VIA station. The museum has a cafeteria, and there are several fast-food restaurants within walking distance. Lodging is available in Ottawa.

Ottawa

Cars	2 open cars, 2 cabooses
Displays	Business car, cabooses, Burro crane, work equipment
Schedule	May and June, Saturdays on the hour 1-3 p.m., Sundays 1-4; July and August, Tuesday-Friday, 1-3, Saturdays 1-5, Sundays 12-5; September, Saturdays and Sundays 1-4; October, Saturdays and Sundays 1-3; November, Sundays 1-3. Charter trips available.
Fares	Adults $5, children under 13 $2.50, age 65 and over $4.50. Checks and credit cards accepted. Group discounts available.
Memberships	Write for information.
Special events	Santa Claus trains: December 2, 9, 15, 16, 22, and 23, 1990, 1, 2, and 3 p.m.
Nearby attractions	Pinafore Park Railroad, Village of Sparta, monument to Jumbo the elephant
Mailing address	Box 549, Port Stanley, ON N0L 2A0
Phone	(519) 782-9993; (519) 681-1643 or (519) 672-7953 year-round

DIESEL LOCOMOTIVES

No.	Type	Former owner	Builder	Date
L1	25 ton	Consolidated Sand & Gravel	GE	1952
L2	50 ton	Consolidated Sand & Gravel	CLC/Whitcomb	1950
L3	SW9	Chesapeake & Ohio	GMD	1951

PORT STANLEY TERMINAL RAIL

The London & Port Stanley, an electric railway connecting London, Ontario, with Lake Erie at Port Stanley, became part of Canadian National in 1966. The portion of the line between St. Thomas and Port Stanley was abandoned, but in 1983 a 3-mile segment from Port Stanley to Union was returned to excursion service as Port Stanley Terminal Rail. Trains run from a station next to Kettle Creek and make a 50-minute round trip.

Food and lodging are available in Port Stanley, about 9 mile south of St. Thomas on Route 4.

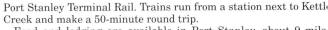

Cars	Streetcars and interurbans
Displays	Cars under restoration
Dates open	May 6-October 28, 1990, weekends and holidays 10 a.m.-5 p.m.; June, Wednesday-Sunday 10-5; July and August, daily 11-5. Charters available.
Admission	Adults $4, students $2.50, children 3-12 $2, age 65 and over $2.50. Higher prices apply for special events; lower when cars are not operating. Admission includes unlimited rides. Credit cards accepted. Group discounts available.
Memberships	Write for information.
Special events	Extravaganzas (June 24 and September 23, 1990), Summer Night Shows (July 21 and August 18, 1990), Silver Anniversary (October 7, 1990), Christmas Fiesta (December 2, 1990), Christmas Night Shows (December 8 and 15, 1990)
Nearby attractions	Ontario Agriculture Museum, Rockwood Conservation Area
Mailing address	R. R. 2, Rockwood, ON N0B 2K0
Phone	(519) 856-9802

HALTON COUNTY RADIAL RAILWAY MUSEUM

The Halton County Radial Railway Museum (in Ontario interurbans were called "radial railways") was begun in 1953 when several enthusiasts saved a historic Toronto streetcar from being scrapped. The group acquired a section of the roadbed of a defunct Toronto-Guelph interurban line, and track construction began in 1961, about the time the group organized as the Ontario Electric Railway Historical Association.

The track is the same gauge as the Toronto streetcar system, 10⅞" — just about 1.5 meters. The collection includes more than a dozen operating streetcars and interurbans and numerous pieces of freight and work equipment. The museum offers a 20-minute round-trip ride over 1¼ miles of track; admission to the museum includes unlimited rides. To reach the museum from Toronto and Hamilton, take Queen Elizabeth Way to the Guelph Line exit in Burlington, then follow Guelph Line northwest 22 miles to the museum. From London, take Exit 312 (Guelph Line) from Highway 401, then go 9 miles northwest to the museum. Food can be found in Rockwood; lodging in Guelph.

Locomotives	Diesels
Cars	Air-conditioned coaches, dining car. Private cars available for charter.
Schedule	Agawa Canyon: early June to mid-October, leave Sault Ste. Marie 8 a.m. daily , at Agawa Canyon 11:30-1:30, arrive Sault Ste. Marie 5 p.m. Hearst: late May to mid-October, leave Sault Ste. Marie 9:30 a.m. daily except Monday, arrive Hearst 7:15 p.m.; leave Hearst 8:15 a.m. daily except Tuesday, arrive Sault Ste. Marie 6:10 p.m.; remainder of the year, leave Sault Ste. Marie 8:30 a.m. Friday-Sunday, arrive Hearst 5:50 p.m., leave Hearst 7:15 a.m. Saturday-Monday, arrive Sault Ste. Marie 4:30 p.m.
Fares	Agawa Canyon: adults $37; children through high school $14 June-August, $18.50 during September and October; children under 5 $6.50; babies in arms free; age 60 and over $26 only during June. Hearst: adults $88, children 5-18 $44. Credit cards accepted.
Nearby attractions	Soo Locks tours
Mailing address	129 Bay Street, Sault Ste. Marie, ON P6A 1W7
Phone	(705) 254-4331

ALGOMA CENTRAL RAILWAY

The Algoma Central Railway is a common carrier extending 297 miles north from Sault Ste. Marie, Ontario, to Hearst. Its principal business is carrying iron ore and forest products, but it operates excursion trains over its entire main line.

The most popular trip is a one-day ride from Sault Ste. Marie 114 miles north through forests and along lakes and rivers to spectacular Agawa Canyon and return. A tour of the entire line requires two days and an overnight stay in Hearst.

The Agawa Canyon train carries a dining car offering hot meals, sandwiches, snacks, and box lunches. During summer the Hearst train offers take-out food service except Monday and Tuesday between Sault Ste. Marie and Eton, 120 miles. During the remainder of the year the Hearst train carries a dining car Saturdays and Sundays between Sault Ste. Marie and Eton.

Tickets may be purchased between 7 a.m. and 7 p.m. the day before departure at the station in Sault Ste. Marie or by telephone using a credit card. The remaining tickets are sold the next morning from 7 to 8. Advance purchase is advised during the fall foliage season. Handicapped persons can be accommodated with advance notice. Food and lodging are available within walking distance of the stations at Sault Ste. Marie and Hearst.

Locomotive	1 diesel	**Nearby attractions**	Storybook Gardens, Port Stanley Terminal
Car	1 coach converted from an open streetcar		Rail, monument to Jumbo the elephant
Schedule	May 15-October 15, weekends 1 p.m. to sunset	**Mailing address**	477 Charlotte Street, London, ON N5W 4A5
Fares	Adults $1; children 2-11, 50 cents. Checks	**Phone**	(519) 455-2852
	accepted. Group discounts available.		

P 𝝿 🎁 ☕

PINAFORE PARK RAILROAD

Pinafore Park is a 90-acre attraction in St. Thomas, Ontario, which includes picnic tables, gardens, woods, tame deer — and a 1-mile loop of narrow gauge track, the Pinafore Park Railroad. The train consists of a 25-ton 4-wheel diesel that originally worked in Newfoundland and an excursion coach that was rebuilt from an open streetcar. The ride takes about 10 minutes. Pinafore Park is southeast of the intersection of Highways 3 and 4, near the crossing of the CSX (ex-Chesapeake & Ohio) and Canadian National's ex-London & Port Stanley line. Food and lodging are available in St. Thomas.

Displays	Diesel switcher, freight cars, artifacts	**Special events**	Annual open house (September 15,
Dates open	May-August, daily 9 a.m.-5 p.m.; September,		1990) — train rides offered
	weekends 10-4; October, Sundays 10-4	**Nearby attractions**	Rideau Canal, Hershey Chocolate plant
Admission	Free, donations welcome	**Mailing address**	P. O. Box 962, Smiths Falls, ON K7A 5A5
Memberships	Individual, $10 per year; family, $15	**Phone**	(613) 283-5696

P ♿ 𝝿 🎁 ☕

SMITHS FALLS RAILWAY MUSEUM

The Rideau Valley Division of the Canadian Railroad Historical Association maintains a museum in the former Canadian National (earlier, Canadian Northern) station at Smiths Falls, Ontario. The building was constructed in 1914; it was designated a National Historic Site in 1985.

On display are several freight cars and ex-Canadian Pacific diesel switcher No. 6591, an S3 built by Montreal Locomotive Works in 1957. Inside the station are artifacts and memorabilia. The museum is at William and Church Streets on the west side of Smiths Falls, about six blocks from the Canadian Pacific station used by VIA's Ottawa-Toronto trains.

There are restaurants within a few blocks of the museum, and lodging is available in Smiths Falls. Smiths Falls is about 40 miles south of Ottawa and 30 miles northwest of Brockville.

Displays	Station, photos, artifacts
Dates open	Mid-June to Labor Day, daily 9 a.m.-5 p.m.
Admission	Individuals free, donations welcome; $1 per person for bus tours
Memberships	Write for information.
Nearby attractions	East Point Lighthouse, Basin Head Fisheries Museum, beaches, deep-sea fishing
Mailing address	Elmira, PE C0A 1K0
Phone	(902) 357-2481

P &. 🎁

ELMIRA RAILWAY MUSEUM

The Prince Edward Island Railway was built in the early 1870s with a track gauge of 42 inches. It was taken over by the Canadian government soon after Prince Edward Island became part of Canada in 1873, and it eventually became part of Canadian National Railways. It was standard-gauged in the 1920s and given a mainland connection by means of ferries between Borden and Cape Tormentine, New Brunswick.

Passenger service was discontinued about 1970, and CNR shut down all rail operations on the island on December 31, 1989. The station at Elmira, easternmost point of the railroad, has become a museum illustrating the development and operation of railroads on Prince Edward Island.

Elmira is on Route 16A at the eastern tip of Prince Edward Island. Restaurants and motels are about 5 miles away.

Locomotives	1 steam, 3 diesel, 1 diesel motor car
Cars	Steel combination and commuter cars
Displays	More than 100 locomotives, cars, and streetcars
Dates open	May 6-September 8, 1990, daily 9 a.m.-5 p.m.; September 9-October 31, 1990, Saturdays and Sundays, 9-5
Schedule	Streetcars operate daily; trains run Sundays and holidays.
Admission	Sundays and holidays, adults $4.25, children 13-17 $3.50, children 5-12 $2.25 (under 5 free), age 65 and over $3.50; other days 50 cents less. Credit cards accepted. Group discounts available.
Nearby attractions	Montreal, St. Lawrence Seaway Locks
Mailing address	P. O. Box 148, St. Constant, PQ J0L 1X0
Phone	(514) 632-2410, (514) 638-1522 year-round

CANADIAN RAILWAY MUSEUM

The Canadian Railway Museum, operated by the Canadian Railroad Historical Association, is the largest collection of railroad and street railway equipment in Canada. Included are 4-6-4s from Canadian National and Canadian Pacific, a CN 2-10-2 and a CP 2-10-4, several historic diesels, CP 4-4-0 No. 144, the oldest Canadian-built locomotive in existence (built in 1886 by the CP), and an operating replica of the John Molson, a locomotive built in 1849 for the Champlain & St. Lawrence Rail Road.

The museum offers streetcar and train rides on a 1-mile loop of track around the property. Other museum activities include a series of art exhibitions and a puppet theater.

The museum is about 30 minutes from downtown Montreal. From the Champlain Bridge follow Route 15 south to exit 42, then Route 132 west to its junction with Route 209, then 209 a mile south to the museum. From the Mercier Bridge follow Route 132 east to Route 209. Restaurants and lodging are nearby.

Displays	Caboose, motor car, station, tool shed
Dates open	June 5-Labor Day, Monday-Saturday 10 a.m.-5 p.m.
Admission	Adults 50 cents; families $2. Checks accepted.
Memberships	Write for information.
Nearby attractions	Moose Mountain Provincial Park, Cannington Manor Historic Park
Mailing address	Box 840, Carlyle, SK S0C 0R0
Phone	(306) 453-2266

P & A 🎁

RUSTY RELIC MUSEUM

The Rusty Relic Museum is primarily a museum of pioneer days in Saskatchewan, but it is housed in a former Canadian National station. A Canadian Pacific caboose and a CN motor car are on display outside; a tool shed complete with railroad tools is in the yard.

The museum is near the Canadian Pacific tracks at Third Street West and Railway Avenue in Carlyle. Food and lodging are available in Carlyle, which is in southeast Saskatchewan about 60 miles north of the U. S. border and 40 miles west of the Manitoba border.

Displays	Steam locomotive, caboose, station, artifacts
Dates open	June-August, daily 11 a.m.-4 p.m.
Admission	Free; donations appreciated
Nearby attractions	Melville Regional Park, Melville Golf Course, Motherwell Site, Ochapowace Ski Resort, Qu'Appelle Valley Beach Resort
Mailing address	Box 2863, Melville, SK S0A 2P0
Phone	(306) 728-4205

MELVILLE RAILWAY MUSEUM

Melville is the junction of Canadian National Railways' transcontinental main line and CNR's line from Regina north to Churchill, Manitoba. The town was named for Charles Melville Hays, president of the Grand Trunk Railway. The Melville Tourism & Convention Bureau operates the Melville Railway Museum in the Melville Regional Park. On exhibit there are a station building from Duff, Saskatchewan; Canadian National 4-6-2 No. 5114, built by Montreal Locomotive Works in 1919; a flatcar; and a caboose. The museum displays include station furniture and hardware, mannequins, photos, and other artifacts.

Melville is in eastern Saskatchewan, on Route 10 northeast of Regina. There are motels and restaurants in Melville.

Dates open	April-October, daily 10 a.m.-6 p.m.	**Fares**	$1 per person
Schedule	Steam locomotive operates Sundays and holiday Mondays in summer.	**Memberships**	Write for information.
		Special events	Wings and Wheels (August 18-19, 1990)
Admission	Adults $3, children under 12 $1 (preschoolers free), age 65 and over $2.50. Credit cards accepted. Group discounts available.	**Nearby attractions**	Wild Animal Park, Pioneer Village Museum
		Mailing address	Box 185, Moose Jaw, SK S6H 4N8
		Phone	(306) 693-6556

WESTERN DEVELOPMENT MUSEUM

The Moose Jaw branch of the Saskatchewan Western Development Museums specializes in transportation of all types, from birchbark canoes to airplanes, with emphasis on the role of railroads in opening western Canada. On the museum grounds is a short railroad with a Vulcan-built steam locomotive that operates on summer Sundays. The museum is at 50 Diefenbaker Drive, southeast of the intersection of the Trans Canada Highway Bypass and Main Street (Route 2). Food and lodging are available nearby.

Melville   Moose Jaw   SASKATCHEWAN-299

TOURIST RAILROADS AND RAILROAD MUSEUMS IN MEXICO

It is difficult to obtain information on Mexican railroads and Mexican railroad museums. Only one tourist railroad has come to light: The Club Amigos del Ferrocarril (Friends of the Railroad) and the state of Morelos jointly operate several miles of 3'-gauge track between Yecapixtla and Cuautla, about 50 miles south of Mexico City. Motive power is 2-8-0 No. 279, built by Baldwin in 1921; passengers ride in wood coaches. At press time, operation had been suspended for some time.

The best-known and most scenic train ride in Mexico is over the Chihuahua Pacific Railway (now the Region Norte of the National Railways of Mexico, but the Chihuahua Pacific name is still in use). The route connects the city of Chihuahua, south of El Paso, Texas, and Los Mochis, on the shore of the Gulf of California. West of Chihuahua the line traverses high plains and then forested country before reaching the Continental Divide. Trains pause for sightseeing at the rim of Copper Canyon. The western slope of the Sierra Madre is some of the wildest topography in North America, and the scenery is worth riding through twice. The 405-mile ride takes 14 hours; departure from both ends is at 7 a.m. At press time, the one-way fare between Chihuahua and Los Mochis was 55,000 pesos, about $20.

It's easiest to ride the line as a round trip from Chihuahua. It takes most of a week: a day from the border at El Paso or Presido, Tex., to Chihuahua; an entire day to Los Mochis; a day there out of deference to the late-evening arrival and the early-morning departure; a day back to Chihuahua; and a day from there to the border. You might enjoy a 24-hour stopover at a lodge or hotel near Copper Canyon.

Chihuahua has air service from El Paso, Ciudad Juarez, and Tijuana. National Railways of Mexico operates three trains a day between Ciudad Juarez and Chihuahua — 221 miles, 4 hours. Starting and ending your trip at Los Mochis is preferable only if you are already on the west coast of Mexico. Highway mileages from Tucson, Arizona, to Los Mochis and Chihuahua are virtually the same.

Several U. S. tour operators offer escorted tours over the route. For individual bookings, write or call Columbus Travel (an official representative of the railroad), 6017 Callaghan Road, San Antonio, TX 78228; phone (800) 225-2829; or write or telephone the railroad directly: Ferrocarril de Chihuahua al Pacifico, P. O. Box 46, Chihuahua, Chih., Mexico; phone 011-52-141-22284 or 141-57756. The best time to call is between 8 a.m. and 1 p.m. Central Time.

PHOTO CREDITS

Many photos in the book were provided by the railroads and the museums. Others came from individual photographers, as noted below:

Page 2, Scott Hartley; 3, Bud Rothaar; 4, Harre W. Demoro; 5, John P. Killoran; 6, Fred H. Matthews Jr.; 15, Barry Robinson; 16, William J. Husa, Jr.; 18, Bob Hayden; 20, Larry Rose; 27, Brad Horn/Joseph Bispo; 31, Victor D. Ryerson; 36, Harre W. Demoro; 40, Fred Bennett; 46, Sandy Worthen; 50, Darrell T. Arndt; 58, Ann Flesor; 60, Howard Pincus; 63, Brian R. Woodcock; 70, James C. Bogle; 84, Robert Sorg; 87, Edward Rysz; 90, TRAINS: J. David Ingles; 91, K. W. Breher; 93, Dick Webb; 96, Paul Swanson; 97, Wayne Kuchinsky; 101, Daryl Grannis; 107, Bob Hayden; 113, Lance Bell; 114, Nancy Kavanagh O'Neill; 116, Mark Yalon; 117, Jay Chatterton; 120, John Staber; 121, James Higgins; 124, Tom Nelligan; 162, Ronald N. Johnson; 164, Bob Hayden; 165, D. T. Walker; 167, William J. Husa, Jr.; 168, Bruce Russell; 169, Bob Pennisi; 180, Christoper Hauf; 181, William Fries; 185, David Younts; 188, Jim Wrinn; 192, Robert L. McFaddin; 193, Paul W. Prescott; 194, Paul R. Lasky; 198, John B. Corns; 202, Doyle Yoder; 206, Bob Moore; 213, Ed Wojtas; 214, Scott Johnson; 215, Peter Tadsen; 218, Bob Tomaine; 220, Michael Hartman; 226, Kalmbach Publishing Co.: George Drury; 229, Richard C. Roden; 232, Herbert H. Harwood, Jr.; 242, John W. Coniglio; 252, Charlie Maple; 255, William J. Husa, Jr.; 256, Donald Sims; 257, National Park Service: Thomas Curran III; 258, Scott Hartley; 259, James R. Dufour; 266, Dan Olah; 267, Dale G. Kraus; 270, Kris Coleman; 271, Elmer E. Burruss, Jr.; 277, Gary E. Children; 286, Joe McMillan; 287, William J. Husa, Jr.; 289, Brian C. Nickle; 294, George Drury.

INDEX

UPDATE

Listed here are a few railroads and museums which had not responded to mail and telephone inquiries by press time. This is not to be taken as an indication that they are out of business — if you are in the neighborhood, on-the-spot research might reveal they are alive and well.

Arizona Central Railroad, Clarkdale, Arizona
Auburn Valley Railroad, Yorklyn, Delaware
Duncans Mills Depot Museum, Duncans Mills, California
Beaver-Hawk Express, Brazil, Indiana
Edmonton Radial Railway Society, Edmonton, Alberta
Florida Gulf Coast Railroad Museum, Tampa, Florida
Galloping Goose Historical Society, Dolores, Colorado
Great Miniature Railroad, Allegheny Square, Pittsburgh, Pa.
Indiana Erie Railroad, Monterey, Indiana
Kansas City Railroad Museum, Kansas City, Missouri
L'Univers du Rail, Cap a l'Aigle, Quebec
Purple Martin Train, Atlantic, Iowa
Salem & Hillsborough Railroad, Hillsborough, New Brunswick
Yuma Valley Railroad, Yuma, Arizona

Two companies offer train rides that extend the dinner-train concept. Princess Rail Tours operates the California Sun Express, which offers top-bracket daytime accommodations and service in a former Milwaukee Road Super Dome car carried on the rear of Amtrak's *Coast Starlight* between Oakland, San Luis Obispo, and Los Angeles. For information, call (800) 835-8907. The American-European Express, which is affiliated with the *Nostalgie Istanbul Orient Express*, offers luxury service between Chicago and Washington in cars attached to Amtrak's *Capitol Limited*. The company plans to add a Chicago-New York route in mid-1990. Telephone (800) 677-4233 for information. Bookings for both can also be arranged by travel agents.

ABOUT THE COUPONS

Throughout the book you have seen the discount coupon symbol with many of the railroad and museum listings. In the 14 pages that follow you'll find coupons good for discounts of one kind or another — totaling far more in value than the price of this book.

The coupons are arranged alphabetically by museum and rail road name. Although this book was published in 1990, many of the coupons are valid through 1991, and many others have no expira tion date. Happy clipping!

SAVINGS COUPON

10% off admission
Valid through May 1991

A&D TOY TRAIN VILLAGE
Middleboro, Massachusetts

SAVINGS COUPON

50¢ off adult fare
25¢ off child's fare

ARDEN TROLLEY MUSEUM
Washington, Pennsylvania

SAVINGS COUPON

50¢ off fares or admission
Valid during 1990

BLUEGRASS RAILROAD MUSEUM
Versailles, Kentucky

SAVINGS COUPON

50¢ off admission
0% off bookstore or gift shop purchase
Valid until September 3, 1990

ALBERTA RAILROAD MUSEUM
Edmonton, Alberta

SAVINGS COUPON

50¢ off fare
Valid until September 3, 1990

BELLEFONTE HISTORICAL RR SOCIETY
Bellefonte, Pennsylvania

SAVINGS COUPON

50¢ off admission
Valid until October 31, 1990

CANADIAN RAILWAY MUSEUM
St. Constant, Quebec

SAVINGS COUPON

One free ride
Valid during 1990

ANACORTES RAILWAY
Anacortes, Washington

SAVINGS COUPON

50% off adult admission

BIG SHANTY MUSEUM
Kennesaw, Georgia

SAVINGS COUPON

$1 off fare
Valid through October 20, 1990

CAPE COD SCENIC RAILROAD
Hyannis, Massachusetts

SAVINGS COUPON

Adults: 75¢ off fare
Children: 50¢ off fare
Seniors: 75¢ off fare with AARP card
Valid through October 1990

ARCADE & ATTICA RAILROAD
Arcade, New York

SAVINGS COUPON

Adult fare: $6
Limit: 2 adults per coupon
Valid May-October 1990

BLUE MOUNTAIN & READING RAILROAD
Hamburg, Pennsylvania

SAVINGS COUPON

Adults: $1 off fare
Senior citizens: $1 off fare
Children: 50¢ off fare
Valid during 1990

CASS SCENIC RAILROAD
Cass, West Virginia

GUIDE TO TOURIST RAILROADS

KALMBACH BOOKS

Not valid with other coupons or discounts

GUIDE TO TOURIST RAILROADS

KALMBACH BOOKS

Not valid with other coupons or discounts

GUIDE TO TOURIST RAILROADS

KALMBACH BOOKS

Not valid with other coupons or discounts

GUIDE TO TOURIST RAILROADS

KALMBACH BOOKS

Not valid with other coupons or discounts

GUIDE TO TOURIST RAILROADS

KALMBACH BOOKS

Not valid with other coupons or discounts

GUIDE TO TOURIST RAILROADS

KALMBACH BOOKS

Not valid with other coupons or discounts

GUIDE TO TOURIST RAILROADS

KALMBACH BOOKS

Not valid with other coupons or discounts

GUIDE TO TOURIST RAILROADS

KALMBACH BOOKS

Not valid with other coupons or discounts

GUIDE TO TOURIST RAILROADS

KALMBACH BOOKS

Not valid with other coupons or discounts

GUIDE TO TOURIST RAILROADS

KALMBACH BOOKS

Not valid with other coupons or discounts

GUIDE TO TOURIST RAILROADS

KALMBACH BOOKS

Not valid with other coupons or discounts

GUIDE TO TOURIST RAILROADS

KALMBACH BOOKS

Not valid with other coupons or discounts

SAVINGS COUPON

50¢ off admission

CHILDREN'S MUSEUM
Utica, New York

SAVINGS COUPON

75¢ off fare
Valid during 1990 season

CUYAHOGA VALLEY LINE RAILROAD
Independence, Ohio

SAVINGS COUPON

$1 off adult fare
50¢ off child's fare
Valid June through August 1990
Not valid with any other coupon

EAST TROY ELECTRIC RAILROAD
East Troy, Wisconsin

SAVINGS COUPON

50¢ off fare
Valid until January 1, 1991

CONNECTICUT TROLLEY MUSEUM
Warehouse Point

SAVINGS COUPON

10% off fare

DEADWOOD CENTRAL RAILROAD
Deadwood, South Dakota

SAVINGS COUPON

$1 off fare
Valid through 1991

EDAVILLE RAILROAD
South Carver, Massachusetts

SAVINGS COUPON

50¢ off fare

CONWAY SCENIC RAILROAD
North Conway, New Hampshire

SAVINGS COUPON

50% off fare
Valid until October 28, 1990

DELAWARE & ULSTER RAIL RIDE
Arkville, New York

SAVINGS COUPON

10% off coach fare
Not valid during October

ENTERTRAINMENT LINE
Union Bridge, Maryland

SAVINGS COUPON

$1 off adult fare
Valid until November 4, 1990

CORYDON SCENIC RAILROAD
Corydon, Indiana

SAVINGS COUPON

50¢ off admission
Valid until May 1, 1991

DENNISON RAILROAD DEPOT MUSEUM
Dennison, Ohio

SAVINGS COUPON

50¢ off adult admission
50¢ off teen admission
25¢ off child admission
Valid during 1990

FORNEY TRANSPORTATION MUSEUM
Denver, Colorado

GUIDE TO TOURIST RAILROADS

KALMBACH BOOKS

Not valid with other coupons or discounts

GUIDE TO TOURIST RAILROADS

KALMBACH BOOKS

Not valid with other coupons or discounts

GUIDE TO TOURIST RAILROA

KALMBACH BOOK

Not valid with other coupons or discour

GUIDE TO TOURIST RAILROADS

KALMBACH BOOKS

Not valid with other coupons or discounts

GUIDE TO TOURIST RAILROADS

KALMBACH BOOKS

Not valid with other coupons or discounts

GUIDE TO TOURIST RAILROA

KALMBACH BOOKS

Not valid with other coupons or discour

GUIDE TO TOURIST RAILROADS

KALMBACH BOOKS

Not valid with other coupons or discounts

GUIDE TO TOURIST RAILROADS

KALMBACH BOOKS

Not valid with other coupons or discounts

GUIDE TO TOURIST RAILROA

KALMBACH BOOKS

Not valid with other coupons or discour

GUIDE TO TOURIST RAILROADS

KALMBACH BOOKS

Not valid with other coupons or discounts

GUIDE TO TOURIST RAILROADS

KALMBACH BOOKS

Not valid with other coupons or discounts

GUIDE TO TOURIST RAILROA

KALMBACH BOOKS

Not valid with other coupons or discour

SAVINGS COUPON

50% off admission
Valid until Thanksgiving (Canadian) 1990

FORT ERIE RAILROAD MUSEUM

Fort Erie, Ontario

SAVINGS COUPON

Free ride on miniature train
Valid during 1990

GOLETA DEPOT RAILROAD MUSEUM

Goleta, California

SAVINGS COUPON

One free admission with paid admission of equal or greater value
Valid during 1990

THE HUNTSVILLE DEPOT

Huntsville, Alabama

SAVINGS COUPON

50¢ off admission

GALVESTON RAILROAD MUSEUM

Galveston, Texas

SAVINGS COUPON

$1 off adult fare
75¢ off child's fare
Not valid on any holiday
Valid until October 10, 1990

HEBER CREEPER

Heber City, Utah

SAVINGS COUPON

$2 off adult fare
50¢ off child's fare
Regular weekend and holiday trips only
Valid until November 18, 1990

INDIANA & OHIO SCENIC RAILWAY

Mason, Ohio

SAVINGS COUPON

50¢ off fare

GETTYSBURG RAILROAD

Gettysburg, Pennsylvania

SAVINGS COUPON

$1 off fare
Limit: 4 persons
Valid during 1990 season

HOBO RAILROAD

Lincoln, New Hampshire

SAVINGS COUPON

20% off gift shop purchase

INDIANA DINNER TRAIN

Indianapolis, Indiana

SAVINGS COUPON

20% off fare
Valid through June 1991

GOLD COAST RAILROAD MUSEUM

Miami, Florida

SAVINGS COUPON

$1 off combination railroad-village ticket
Valid until December 30, 1990

HUCKLEBERRY RAILROAD

Flint, Michigan

SAVINGS COUPON

Free guided tour at your convenience for group of 10 or more. Call (216) 293-5532 for an appointment.

JEFFERSON DEPOT

Jefferson, Ohio

SAVINGS COUPON

10% off fare
Not valid for Halloween and
Christmas special trains
Valid until January 1, 1992

JUNCTION VALLEY RAILROAD

Bridgeport, Michigan

SAVINGS COUPON

25¢ off admission

LOMITA RAILROAD MUSEUM

Lomita, California

SAVINGS COUPON

One free fare with one paid fare
Valid during 1990

NATIONAL CAPITAL TROLLEY MUSEUM

Wheaton, Maryland

SAVINGS COUPON

10% off fare
Not valid during October

KETTLE MORAINE RAILWAY

North Lake, Wisconsin

SAVINGS COUPON

50¢ off adult fare
50¢ off child's fare
Valid during 1990 season

MICHIGAN TRANSIT MUSEUM

Mt. Clemens, Michigan

SAVINGS COUPON

10% off bookstore purchase
Valid through April 1991

NATIONAL RAILROAD MUSEUM

Hamlet, North Carolina

SAVINGS COUPON

2 adult fares for $15
oupon may be used only once, but it can
be applied to several pairs of adults.
Valid only for summer 1990 trains

LAKE WHATCOM RAILWAY

Wickersham, Washington

SAVINGS COUPON

$1 off fare
Valid during 1990 season

MOUNT HOOD RAILROAD

Hood River, Oregon

SAVINGS COUPON

$1 off adult admission
50¢ off child's admission
50¢ off senior admission
Valid until October 1, 1990

NATIONAL RAILROAD MUSEUM

Green Bay, Wisconsin

SAVINGS COUPON

$1 off adult fare
50¢ off child's fare

ITTLE TRAVERSE SCENIC RAILWAY

Alanson, Michigan

SAVINGS COUPON

$1 off adult admission
50¢ off child's admission

**MUSEUM OF
ALASKA TRANSPORTATION & INDUSTRY**

Palmer, Alaska

SAVINGS COUPON

50¢ off fare
Good for South Dayton Flyer only
Valid until October 28, 1990

NEW YORK & LAKE ERIE RAILROAD

Gowanda, New York

GUIDE TO TOURIST RAILROADS

KALMBACH BOOKS

Not valid with other coupons or discounts

GUIDE TO TOURIST RAILROADS

KALMBACH BOOKS

Not valid with other coupons or discounts

GUIDE TO TOURIST RAILROAD

KALMBACH BOOKS

Not valid with other coupons or discount

GUIDE TO TOURIST RAILROADS

KALMBACH BOOKS

Not valid with other coupons or discounts

GUIDE TO TOURIST RAILROADS

KALMBACH BOOKS

Not valid with other coupons or discounts

GUIDE TO TOURIST RAILROAD

KALMBACH BOOKS

Not valid with other coupons or discount

GUIDE TO TOURIST RAILROADS

KALMBACH BOOKS

Not valid with other coupons or discounts

GUIDE TO TOURIST RAILROADS

KALMBACH BOOKS

Not valid with other coupons or discounts

GUIDE TO TOURIST RAILROAD

KALMBACH BOOKS

Not valid with other coupons or discount

GUIDE TO TOURIST RAILROADS

KALMBACH BOOKS

Not valid with other coupons or discounts

GUIDE TO TOURIST RAILROADS

KALMBACH BOOKS

Not valid with other coupons or discounts

GUIDE TO TOURIST RAILROAI

KALMBACH BOOKS

Not valid with other coupons or discount

SAVINGS COUPON

50¢ off admission
Valid during 1990 season
**NORTH CAROLINA
TRANSPORTATION MUSEUM**
Spencer, North Carolina

SAVINGS COUPON

Two admissions for the price of one
OGDEN UNION STATION
Ogden, Utah

SAVINGS COUPON

50% off fare
10% off gift shop purchase
Valid through April 1992
OLD COLONY & NEWPORT RAILWAY
Newport, Rhode Island

SAVINGS COUPON

$10 off adult and senior coach fare
$5 off child's coach fare
Not good in first class or parlor car
Valid during 1990 season
NORTH COAST DAYLIGHT
Willits, California

SAVINGS COUPON

Purchase one admission or ride
get one of equal value free
OGLEBAY'S GOOD CHILDREN'S ZOO
Wheeling, West Virginia

SAVINGS COUPON

$1 off fare,
except for special events
Valid through 1991
ORANGE EMPIRE RAILWAY MUSEUM
Perris, California

SAVINGS COUPON

25¢ off admission

ORTHERN PACIFIC DEPOT RR MUSEUM
Wallace, Idaho

SAVINGS COUPON

25% off admission
Valid through June 1991
OKEFENOKEE HERITAGE CENTER
Waycross, Georgia

SAVINGS COUPON

25¢ off fare
Valid until November 25, 1990
PENN'S LANDING TROLLEY
Philadelphia, Pennsylvania

SAVINGS COUPON

50¢ off admission

NOSTALGIA STATION
Versailles, Kentucky

SAVINGS COUPON

25¢ off admission
Limit: 4 person per coupon
Valid until December 2, 1990
OLD COLONY & FALL RIVER RR MUSEUM
Fall River, Massachusetts

SAVINGS COUPON

50% off admission

RAILROAD & PIONEER MUSEUM
Temple, Texas

GUIDE TO TOURIST RAILROADS

KALMBACH BOOKS

Not valid with other coupons or discounts

GUIDE TO TOURIST RAILROADS

KALMBACH BOOKS

Not valid with other coupons or discounts

GUIDE TO TOURIST RAILROAD

KALMBACH BOOKS

Not valid with other coupons or discount

GUIDE TO TOURIST RAILROADS

KALMBACH BOOKS

Not valid with other coupons or discounts

GUIDE TO TOURIST RAILROADS

KALMBACH BOOKS

Not valid with other coupons or discounts

GUIDE TO TOURIST RAILROAD

KALMBACH BOOKS

Not valid with other coupons or discount

GUIDE TO TOURIST RAILROADS

KALMBACH BOOKS

Not valid with other coupons or discounts

GUIDE TO TOURIST RAILROADS

KALMBACH BOOKS

Not valid with other coupons or discounts

GUIDE TO TOURIST RAILROAD

KALMBACH BOOKS

Not valid with other coupons or discount

GUIDE TO TOURIST RAILROADS

KALMBACH BOOKS

Not valid with other coupons or discounts

GUIDE TO TOURIST RAILROADS

KALMBACH BOOKS

Not valid with other coupons or discounts

GUIDE TO TOURIST RAILROAD

KALMBACH BOOKS

Not valid with other coupons or discount

GUIDE TO TOURIST RAILROADS

KALMBACH BOOKS

Not valid with other coupons or discounts

GUIDE TO TOURIST RAILROADS

KALMBACH BOOKS

Not valid with other coupons or discounts

GUIDE TO TOURIST RAILROAD

KALMBACH BOOKS

Not valid with other coupons or discounts

GUIDE TO TOURIST RAILROADS

KALMBACH BOOKS

Not valid with other coupons or discounts

GUIDE TO TOURIST RAILROADS

KALMBACH BOOKS

Not valid with other coupons or discounts

GUIDE TO TOURIST RAILROAD

KALMBACH BOOKS

Not valid with other coupons or discounts

GUIDE TO TOURIST RAILROADS

KALMBACH BOOKS.

Not valid with other coupons or discounts

GUIDE TO TOURIST RAILROADS

KALMBACH BOOKS

Not valid with other coupons or discounts

GUIDE TO TOURIST RAILROAD

KALMBACH BOOKS

Not valid with other coupons or discount

GUIDE TO TOURIST RAILROADS

KALMBACH BOOKS

Not valid with other coupons or discounts

GUIDE TO TOURIST RAILROADS

KALMBACH BOOKS

Not valid with other coupons or discounts

GUIDE TO TOURIST RAILROAD

KALMBACH BOOKS

Not valid with other coupons or discount

GUIDE TO TOURIST RAILROADS

KALMBACH BOOKS

Not valid with other coupons or discounts

GUIDE TO TOURIST RAILROADS

KALMBACH BOOKS

Not valid with other coupons or discounts

GUIDE TO TOURIST RAILROA

KALMBACH BOOKS

Not valid with other coupons or discour

GUIDE TO TOURIST RAILROADS

KALMBACH BOOKS

Not valid with other coupons or discounts

GUIDE TO TOURIST RAILROADS

KALMBACH BOOKS

Not valid with other coupons or discounts

GUIDE TO TOURIST RAILROA

KALMBACH BOOKS

Not valid with other coupons or discoun

GUIDE TO TOURIST RAILROADS

KALMBACH BOOKS

Not valid with other coupons or discounts

GUIDE TO TOURIST RAILROADS

KALMBACH BOOKS

Not valid with other coupons or discounts

GUIDE TO TOURIST RAILROA

KALMBACH BOOKS

Not valid with other coupons or discour

GUIDE TO TOURIST RAILROADS

KALMBACH BOOKS

4895

Not valid with other coupons or discounts

GUIDE TO TOURIST RAILROADS

KALMBACH BOOKS

Not valid with other coupons or discounts

GUIDE TO TOURIST RAILROA

KALMBACH BOOKS

Not valid with other coupons or discour